DEATH, SIN AND THE MORAL LIFE
Contemporary Cultural
Interpretations of Death

American Academy of Religion
Academy Series

edited by
Susan Thistlethwaite

Number 59
DEATH, SIN AND THE MORAL LIFE
Contemporary Cultural
Interpretations of Death
by
Bonnie J. Miller-McLemore

Bonnie J. Miller-McLemore

DEATH, SIN AND THE MORAL LIFE
Contemporary Cultural
Interpretations of Death

Scholars Press
Atlanta, Georgia

DEATH, SIN AND THE MORAL LIFE
Contemporary Cultural
Interpretations of Death

by
Bonnie J. Miller-McLemore

© 1988
American Academy of Religion

Library of Congress Cataloging-in-Publication Data

Miller-McLemore, Bonnie J.
  Death, Sin and the Moral Life

  (American Academy of Religion academy series ;
no. 59)
  Bibliography: p.
  1. Death—Moral and ethical aspects.   I. Title.
II. Series.
BJ1409.5.M55   1988   179'.7   87-28872
ISBN 1-55540-202-X (alk. paper)
ISBN 1-55540-203-8 (pbk. : alk. paper)

Printed in the United States of America
on acid-free paper

To my grandmothers,
Lois McAdow Miller
and
Mildred Fürst Cobb,
for their gracious generativity

TABLE OF CONTENTS

ACKNOWLEDGEMENT

Over the several years that I have worked on this book, the reasons behind my interest have changed. I recognized at the beginning that I could apply the kind of moral critique that I applied to death to a vast variety of topics. On one level the subject itself seemed to hold only minor, secondary importance. Yet, on a deeper level, in retrospect death symbolized one of the many life events that hold tragic, guilt-ridden implications and evoke deep thoughts and feelings. In some cases, it becomes the supreme instance. Both professionally and personally, I sought entrance into such moments in life simply to find what they hold and to gain thereby more abundant life.

I could not have accomplished this or the task of research, writing, and publication without the support and encouragement of several people. For his extensive advice and knowledgable counsel over more than eight years of conversation, I thank Don S. Browning of The University of Chicago Divinity School. His ideas about the dialogue between the personality sciences and theology and his ability to guide the projects of others have provided an example for which I will always remain grateful. I have also benefited from the insights of Langdon Gilkey and James M. Gustafson and thank them for their careful reading and shaping of the ideas behind this book in its earliest thesis stage.

Besides theoretical clarification, I am indebted to several persons at three clinical settings: to James Gibbons, Mary Wilkins, and several other colleagues at The University of Chicago Hospitals and Clinics for providing me space to grow while the ideas first germinated; to James P. Wind and staff of The Park Ridge Center: An Institute for the Study of Faith, Health, and Ethics for allowing me time to polish what I had produced; and to Terry Lyon, supervisor and friend at The Center for Religion and Psychotherapy, who has heard me into speech all along the way and in many different ways.

Most recently, I thank Susan B. Thistlethwaite of Chicago Theological Seminary for assuming that I should publish this and for making the path clear. I do not doubt that I will acknowledge gratitude for her clarity and collegiality many more times before my career is exhausted.

I almost omitted this acknowledgement entirely because words cannot fully express my gratitude to my husband, Mark Miller-McLemore. I thank him for his patience over the long haul but more importantly, for his friendship, companionship, conversation, love and encouragement. At various crucial points these gifts made and continue to make all the difference. Last, never least, I am grateful for the new life and love who arrived as a blessing on the end of this project, Christopher, our now almost two-year-old son.

INTRODUCTION

The Fork in the Road: A "Second Phase" in Death Research

Death is the "one great certainty,"[1] the one event in life on which everyone can absolutely count. Yet we remain largely unaware of the degree to which captivating trends of popular cultural images determine our attitudes toward death. Nearly everyone who heard that I was writing on the subject of death immediately connected it with the research of Elisabeth Kübler-Ross. This gradually became a poignant, confirming example of this phenomenon. And Kübler-Ross is just one among the many shaping modern consciousness. Recent articles and books on the subject comment almost without fail on the abundant proliferation of death-related literature: the "flood of popular attention," the "commercialization," the "growth industry of serious publishing," the "remarkable crescendo," the "exponential growth of interest," the "fad and fetish of our time," a "bandwagon" phenomenon of "terminal chic" that has deluged the troubled public with all manner of advice on the problem of death in Western culture.[2]

I hope, however, to "do more than contribute still another series of assorted essays on death," as Renée Fox puts it, "to what may already be an overabundant literature."[3] Contrary to the swift equation of this thesis with Kübler-Ross, my argument and analysis aim instead at what William F. May calls a "second phase" of research:

> Quite recently in American life certain changes have occurred that open up the *possibility of movement beyond the twin responses of concealment and obsession.* Measured against the total organization of the culture, these changes in attitudes toward death may seem quite modest, but they should not go unnoticed. . . .
> Once a society develops a certain measure of self-consciousness about a problem, the problem is no longer quite the

same. This measure of transcendence through awareness does not in itself dissolve the problem, but it does open up the *possibility of moving beyond certain institutional reflexes and responses*. Diagnosis itself generates the possibility of certain prescriptive moves.[4]

In other words, we have reached a fork in the road where a different level of analysis becomes necessary, one, in short, with a more critical ethical and philosophical bent. Although the task of moral discourse is certainly not new, it takes on a qualitatively new significance at this particular point in the history of Western attitudes. We have reached what Robert Blauner has characterized as a "crisis in our sense of what is an appropriate death."[5] Whereas most societies have traditionally formulated a set of ideal conditions under which persons learn to tolerate and understand death, in line with value orientations and mores, modern society stands largely without such a notion. "Today nothing remains," historian Philippe Ariès comments, "of the sense that everyone has or should have of his impending death."[6] Research in psychology often appears to be in search of a solution to this impasse. The popular literature tells us repeatedly that there is something wrong with us moderns and how we approach death, that we either deny or are obsessively preoccupied with it, but most importantly, that there are *better* ways to approach it. An unspoken question looms behind these studies: How *should* persons morally "cope" with death? How should I regard my own death as future event? What values are to be derived from considering it at all as opposed to ignoring it? How should any human being approach the fact that we must each and all die? It is not enough merely to urge the public to recognize death as a "fact of life" or to challenge the unnecessary indignities placed upon dying. We are ready to move beyond these initial consciousness raising responses of psychologists and social critics to critical reflection upon the norms and visions behind these responses.

What Do We Mean by "Moral"?

While the word "moral" is used to mean many things, I use it here to refer to human responsibility in interpersonal relationship. In H. Richard Niebuhr's classic definition of responsibility, the human moral life signifies a clearly chosen *response* by the moral agent to actions upon her based on her *reading* of the full meaning of

those actions and her sense that she is *accountable* to future responses within the larger *interaction and solidarity* of the human
community.[7] The term moral includes concern for building and
fostering human community, equality, and justice. For James M.
Gustafson, the moral life includes consideration of "our basic pos-
tures toward the world of which we are a part, our dispositions
toward the others with whom we interact, as well as our reflections
on what we should do and our actions that seek to fulfill purposes."[8]
Hence to say that death has a moral dimension is to affirm that the
problem of death is not merely one of finitude and extinction of the
individual alone but involves questions of human freedom and obligation in relation to others and to one's world. In this sense, death
just as birth has never been and can never become a purely natural
event, but is "one of the most highly charged events of our lives."[9]

To qualify this further, I remain deeply interested in theological and philosophical perspectives on death, as these relate to the
moral component. In theology the moral component is integrally
related to the religious, to concern for an ultimate relationship and,
as Paul Tillich states, to "a solution in relation to the eternal." My
focus, however, remains primarily the impact of the religious on the
range of obligations in everyday life. How have prevalent cultural
images shaped the moral component in our attitudes toward death?
What are the implications for the moral life of the decreasing prominence of traditional ideas concerning death, sin, judgment and
eternal life, and the increasing prominence of death as a natural
event? One such implication is that modern interpretations of death
have tended to neglect the moral component, focusing instead almost entirely on technical, physical, and psychological aspects. The
implicit value is often to satisfy individual desires and to maximize
personal happiness. We lose sight of the idea that death entails a
web of moral obligations and responsibilities for all parties involved
and raises issues of ultimate judgment about the moral and religious
significance of our lives.

As this illustrates, we can evaluate cultural images of death
from a critical ethical and philosophical perspective in terms of what
they offer moral praxis. This assumes that the psychologist as well as
the medical doctor act as practical moral thinkers. That is, they
shape the practical norms and images that govern modern understandings of death and dying.[10] Modern psychology and medicine
have tuaght us how we ought to go to our deaths—that we should
"fight" cancer or that we should reach a stage of acceptance and so

forth. No longer purely psychologists and physicians, they become practical moralists and we should examine them as such.

Hence a hermeneutical concern and a broader concern for cultural praxis govern my definition of the moral component. I intend to adjudicate between different levels of interpretation with an eye toward cultural praxis. Psychology interprets death from the perspective of its empirical study of diffuse personal and cultural attitudes. Medicine gives death many meanings in its attempt to foster health and cure disease. Theology understands death in terms of questions of the meaning and value of life. An adequate moral model for death would need to encompass issues on these many different but interrelated levels.

I add one final qualification. I focus not upon the truth or falsity of the religious or quasi-religious horizons of a particular vision of death but upon critical examination of exactly what visions and norms are promoted and comparative evaluation of their practical moral implications. I bracket the truth question—whether, for instance, a particular view persuasively and credibly dispels the premonition of those who think of death with fear and trembling. The inquiry is restricted to the moral significance of the emerging psychologies of death, the culture of medicine, and current theology. I consider matters of belief insofar as they make a fundamental difference or become a determining factor in many so-called ethical debates and insofar as they form an ultimate backdrop for ethical reasoning and action.

The Slow Demise of Death's Moral Significance

In various cultural interpretations of death, particularly in certain psychologies and in medicine, the moral significance of death has been overlooked. Both Eric J. Cassell and Larry R. Churchill have described one particular dimension of this problem. In Churchill's opinion, death has been moved "as a human experience from the moral to the technical order."[11]

> Death is a technical matter, a failure of technology in rescuing the body from a threat to its functioning and integrity. For the moment it does not matter that death of a person cannot be removed from the moral order by the very nature of personhood; what matters is the mythology of the society. The widespread mythology that things essentially moral can be made

technical is reinforced by the effect of technology in altering
other events besides death.[12]

In Churchill's words, "Our current attitudes about death and those
who are dying are amoral, that is, largely outside the realm of our
moral sensibilities and ethical thinking."[13] We encounter a vacuum
of normative models, a sterility in the content of moral matters.
Cassell asks, "How can it be that questions of morality and human
values, [once] so basic to the care of the dying seem remote,
'strange,' or tangential in the actual setting of care?"[14]

   In contrast to Cassell and Churchill, however, I believe that
we can address this question adequately only through more comprehensive analysis. The assessments of Cassell and Churchill need
to be broadened to include not only the demise of the moral in the
realm of technology but also comparable trends in the cultural
domains of psychology and theology. We need fuller understanding
of the historical development of this problem in terms of the important shifts in the moral meaning of death in religion, theology, and
psychology, as well as in medicine.

   Moreover, I would argue, there are defensible ways to restate
the moral issue and meanings of death. Death has become morally
problematic, not so much because there are *no* norms presently
controlling it, but more because the moral norms available are
impoverished, unclear, and inadequate. We employ inherited but
outdated principles, insofar as they fail to respond to the modern
shape of death. Or we are too little concerned or conscious of the
incongruities between our inherited principles and those norms we
absorb unawares from popular culture—that is, from domains ill-
equipped and limited by their very definitions as disciplines, such as
psychology and medicine, to domineer in value assessment and
determination. It is my conviction that without a more direct attempt to state properly the moral dimension of death, various
destructive moralisms may rise up to fill the vacuum left by the
demise of former religious and moral points of view.

The Appearance of Troubling Moralism

   Let us look at a few concrete examples of such moralisms. By
moralisms I mean legalistic, reductionistic, or negative atrophy of
what may originally have been positive moral principles or values.

Theologian Langdon Gilkey cites one such instance in more conservative branches of American Protestantism. "Insofar as death
remained an important issue, it was understood and comprehended
within [narrow] moral categories: a 'bad' life resulted in eternal
death after death, a 'good' life in salvation from death."[15] "Religious"
persons are regarded "as 'saints' bound for a very happy eternity."[16]
This orientation promotes the stereotype that Christianity has little
moral guidance to offer other than the bribe of heavenly bliss for
good behaviour and the threat of condemnation for bad. It loses the
richness of the tradition and ignores the complexity of modern moral
questions.

A more striking instance appears in the supposedly value-free
sphere of psychology. Theology itself has been less concerned than
perhaps it ought over the new psychologies of death and what has
been a usurping of its normative role. Psychology has begun to
define death's meaning for the general public, including its moral
meaning. This transformation illustrates what Don S. Browning
describes as psychology "becoming culture." Scientific psychology,
interested in charting material causes and consequences of human
actions and feelings, seldom abides by these strict definitions of its
boundaries. Psychology, narrowly conceived, easily becomes a
broadly conceived project which shapes culture and projects an
ideology based upon its own metaphors, myths, and norms.[17] This
is particularly true when psychologists take up existential questions
of death as the subject of their investigation.

The acclaim of Kübler-Ross herself is a good example of this
phenomenon. She is portrayed as an "advertent . . . charismatic
leader,"[18] and "accepted authority."[19] Her name is a "household
word" among lay persons and professionals alike, "better known
than that of anyone else's working on the concerns of death and
dying." Her stages are considered "the single best-known piece of
information extant."[20] Not only have they permeated the profes-
sional world of the hospital, they have also shaped attitudes and
oriented the thinking of the general public:

> Kübler-Ross' portrayal of the dying person as passing through
> stages has become, if not an official doctrine, *the dominant,*
> *exemplary paradigm for understanding dying*—one without
> significant rival either in the health sciences or the general
> culture.[21]

More often than not, however, the moral presuppositions of Kübler-Ross and other psychologists go unnoticed. Without critical examination, these assumptions have tended to degenerate into unquestioned moralisms, such as the glamorization of death. By this I mean what some describe as the "new orthodoxy of the 'good death' "[22] or the "Myth of a Meaningful Death."[23] We can see this in book titles such as *To Die With Style, Death: The Final Stage of Growth*, or *Death is All Right*.[24] We ought to experience dying as a beautiful event, another satisfying experience in life, a blissful, meaningful, pleasurable, or "happy ending." Individuals and social institutions should assist the dying in getting what they want to satisfy themselves, whether it be a new heart or the right to end life.

However, these psychological moralisms did not arise without provocation. They appeared, at least in part, as a warranted response to moralistic tendencies in yet a third area, that of modern medicine. One of the more blatant moralisms to which the Kübler-Ross discussion reacted was the technological imperative, the assumption that the medical technology that we invent must be used. If we can, we must. The tool, made as a means to an end, becomes an end in itself.[25] Cardiovascular machinery, invented to support traditional indicators of life, has become the locus of life itself until life's only purpose seems to be, ironically enough, the further support of medical devices. The machine "becomes *the patient* in stating that he has died."[26] Death is simply that "point at which the human organism refuses any further input."[27]

Psychologists protested another related moralism: that life, regardless of quality or circumstances, should be prolonged. Death becomes an enemy to be conquered and vanquished. At one extreme, physicians see death as an inconvenience. At the other, physicians experience it as a sign of failure. In both cases, it is an evil to be eradicated through the use of technology.[28]

Ethicist Kenneth Vaux, among others, has named other moralisms plaguing the medical world more recently. He complains about the "superficial casuistry, econometrics, or facile cost-benefit analysis" and about the "sterile morality of secular humanism and cultural syncretism [which] most often deteriorates into utilitarianism, expediency, econometrics rights theory, and eventually adversarial or Machiavellian power play."[29]

A final instance of the deterioration of the religious and moral perspective is a matter not of twisted moralisms so much as a case of growing indifference to theology as a field. According to theologians James M. Gustafson and Stanley M. Hauerwas, until recently theology made primary contributions to the domain of medical ethics.[30] Now, however, even those with theological training and religious affiliation see religious traditions, symbols, and communities as divisive. What was once "lively, interdisciplinary enterprise" has become a "separate profession" and one that theologians enter only by disguising their natural colors.

Another Factor Behind Our Moral Confusion: Demographic and Structural Changes

This book attends to other factors behind contemporary moral dilemmas besides the radical changes in how, when, and where people die. But because circumstances of death and dying have altered so drastically in the last century and do play a role, a quick summary of the more obvious changes is merited.

This slight digression from the main focus also alludes to the different definitions of death and highlights the definition operating in all other sections of this thesis. Charles Hartshorne states, "The abstract principle of eventual death is one thing, quite another is the specific times, still more the concrete places, circumstances, and manners of dying."[31] For the most part, I am interested in the generic, the abstract, what Leon R. Kass demarcates as "the fact of human mortality."[32] This concern with the universal fact that we die and the implications for each of us that this is a necessary, inescapable condition of life differs from a concern with the specifics of when and how we die and with the actual dying process itself. It is helpful to keep this distinction in mind as we look briefly at the specifics before turning back to the general.

Philosophical ethicist Robert M. Veatch aptly depicts the dramatic modifications in medicine and our manner of dying as a "biological revolution": "People have radically changed their style of dying. Scientific advance has meant that more die in institutions, die older, take longer to die, and spend more money doing it."[33] Let me document each of these four changes more fully.

An increasing percentage of the population die in institutional settings. "Seventy-three percent of adult Americans dying in 1965 had hospital or other institutional care during the last year of their lives. If you are average in your dying you will spend eighty days during your last year in a hospital or institution."[34] Care of the sick and the dying at home has rapidly become a forgotten art. The site of death has shifted from family and community to a setting monitored by medical specialists.[35] This change results primarily from the invention of elaborate mechanical apparatus that sustain respiration, circulation, nutrition, and elimination, and from the concentration of this apparatus in major medical centers. Nonmedical personnel do not know how to regulate such machinery. On the one hand, death is said to be more public.[36] It is overseen by more people. But on the other, it is more privatized insofar as these persons are employed strangers.[37] Aside from intimates, support from the community at large has been more and more an anomaly. Kass believes that "At a time of life when there is perhaps the greatest need for human warmth and comfort, the dying patient is kept company by cardiac-pacemakers and defribillators, respirators, aspirators, oxygenators, catheters, and his intravenous drip."[38]

In the last century, human life expectancy has increased 76 percent for women, 70 percent for men.[39] In 1983 life expectancy at birth reached a new high of 74.6 years. The startling nature of this increase is more apparent when seen in contrast with other averages over history: 20 years in ancient Greece, 22 in ancient Rome, 33 in England during the Middle Ages, 41 in England and Wales during the nineteenth century, and even 47.3 in the United States at the turn of this century.[40] Historian William H. McNeill describes this change as "one of the most massive and extraordinary ecological upheavals the planet has ever known."[41] Today Americans live almost twice as long as a century ago and experience more deaths of significant others throughout life, especially of persons older than them.[42]

Lingering deaths, anticipated over months, sometimes years, predominate. Due to improved sanitation, immunization, and antibiotics, the major causes of death have changed from acute infectious diseases (smallpox, the plague, cholera) to chronic degenerative diseases (heart disease, cancers). The latter often progress in an orderly, though poorly understood, fashion for some years. Potentially therapeutic interventions exist, but no absolute cures. Although in one sense our destiny appears to lie more and more in human hands and death seems almost "a matter of deliberate decision,"[43] the hands which intervene in new ways belong to the medical expert who often cannot predict the outcome of treatment. The dying themselves feel less and less able to direct the course of either their treatment or their living whilst dying.

Last, the sheer cost of dying has become a constant source of anxiety and a potential threat to the relationships of persons involved. "The chances are thirty-eight in a hundred that your medical bills will be over $1,000; over 50 percent if death is from cancer."[44] Next to defense spending, health care has become the largest expenditure in many nations, and our own nation's "largest industry." The percent of the nation's gross national product spent on health care has nearly doubled in the last twenty years, from 5.9 percent in 1965 to 10.6 percent in 1984.[45] Hospitals have become corporate structures. Administrators must engage in aggressive activities centered on capital development, merger, investment, and profit simply to remain solvent.[46]

Nonetheless, these various developments alone do not explain why old moral problems have acquired new force. If we want to avoid either a flippant disregard for the moral or a tragic return to oppression by new moralisms, we need better ways to discern and evaluate the values that govern prevalent cultural images and attitudes toward death. We must renew rational "public discourse," as theologian David Tracy suggests, in the "realm of culture," through art, religion, theology, and philosophy, rather than simply in the realm of technology, economics, or polity.[47] In other words, if modern society wants to benefit from medical procedures to postpone death or from psychological techniques to enhance life before death, we must cultivate society's moral disciplines as well.

The Road Ahead

One way to restore a "more systematic understanding of the moral order"[48] is to initiate a revised correlational conversation.[49] We can bring the religious heritage on death in the Christian tradition and in selected contemporary reinterpretations of it into critical dialogue with historical and contemporary cultural understandings in psychology and medicine. (Other religious traditions and cultural understandings could be studied equally. I have chosen these as my foci.)

The endeavor of correlational discourse is distinct from, but propaedeutic to, a critical practical theology. Browning highlights four comprehensive steps necessary to practical theology.[50] Of these four, I am interested in certain dimensions of the first three: (1) the "step of experiencing and initially defining the problem" (this chapter and Part I as a whole); (2) the "step of attention, listening, and understanding" (primarily Part II); and (3) the "step of critical analysis and comparison" (through cumulative effect, largely in the later chapters of Part II and in my concluding remarks). Step (4) "decision and strategy," receives only rudimentary exploration in the concluding chapter.

Distinct from a full-fledged practical theology of death and dying that would explore each step completely and construct a new approach to death, I concentrate on the first two steps and certain aspects of the third. In Part I, I intend to "tell the story" of the development of a problem in modernity's approach to the moral significance of death. Ariès observes that most scholars studying contemporary attitudes toward death remain unable to detach their investigations "from their modernity and situate them within a broader historical perspective."[51] Part I counters this parochial concern for the present by attending to certain significant historical and cultural shifts in normative attitudes toward death.

However, Part I is preliminary and subordinate to Part II. It merely provides contextual background for the more in-depth critical evaluation of contemporary responses in Part II. While we have much to learn from the voices of history, I find these voices most intriguing as they shape the contours of the twentieth-century discussion. It is on the contemporary front that I wish to encourage creative dialogue. I believe that we can greatly enhance the overall quality of the conversation by including theological reflection, specifically that of Paul Tillich and Paul Ramsey. We can, under the guidance of their insights, retrieve a more adequate moral order of death.

Footnotes to Introduction

/1/   Morris B. Abram, *Defining Death: A Report on the Medical, Legal and Ethical Issues in the Determination of Death* (Washington, D. C.: Government Printing Office, 1981), p. 3.
/2/   Ibid., p. 4; Barbara A. Backer, Natalie Hannon, and Noreen A. Russell, *Death and Dying: Individuals and Institutions* (New York: Wiley and Sons, 1982), p. 299; David L. Gutmann, "Dying to Power: Death and the Search for Self-Esteem," in *New Meanings of Death*, ed. Herman Feifel (New York: McGraw-Hill, 1977), p. 336; Renée C. Fox, special ed., Preface

to "The Social Meaning of Death," *The Annals of the American Academy of Political and Social Science* 446 (July 1980), vii; Kenneth Vaux, *Will to Live/ Will to Die* (Minneapolis: Augsburg, 1979), p. 13, cited by Moses C. Crouse, "Reflections on Our Fascination with Death," *Religion in Life* 49 (Summer 1980), 135; David E. Standard, ed., with an Introduction, *Death in America* (Philadelphia: University of Pennsylvania Press, 1975), p. vii.

/3/ Fox, Preface to "Social Meaning of Death," p. vii.

/4/ William F. May, "The Sacral Power of Death in Contemporary Experience," in *Death in American Experience*, ed. Arien Mack (New York: Schocken Books, 1973), p. 108. Emphasis added.

/5/ Robert Blauner, "Death and Social Structure," *Psychiatry* 29 (1966), 392.

/6/ Philippe Ariès, "The Reversal of Death: Changes in Attitudes Toward Death in Western Societies," in Stannard, *Death in America*, p. 138.

/7/ H. Richard Niebuhr, *The Responsible Self: An Essay in Christian Moral Philosophy* (New York: Harper and Row, 1953), pp. 45, 61–65, 87–88.

/8/ James M. Gustafson, *Ethics From a Theocentric Perspective*, vol. 2: *Ethics and Theology* (Chicago: University of Chicago Press, 1984), p. 3.

/9/ See Stanley Hauerwas, "Having and Learning How to Care for Retarded Children: Some Reflections," in *Ethics in Medicine: Historical Perspectives and Contemporary Concerns*, ed. Stanley Joel Reiser, Arthur J. Dyck, and William J. Curran (Cambridge, Mass.: The MIT Press, 1977), p. 631.

/10/ See Don S. Browning, "Psychology as Religioethical Thinking," *The Journal of Religion* 64, no. 2 (April 1984), 139–141, 149–157.

/11/ Larry R. Churchill, "The Amoral Character of Our Attitudes About Death: Some Implications," *Journal of Religion and Health* 17, no. 3 (1978), 169.

/12/ Eric J. Cassell, "Dying in a Technological Society," *Hastings Center Studies* 2, no. 2 (May 1974), 31. See also idem., *The Healer's Art* (Philadelphia: J. B. Lippincott, 1976), p. 113.

/13/ Churchill, "Attitudes About Death," p. 169.

/14/ Eric J. Cassell, "Being and Becoming Dead," in *Death in American Experience*, p. 163.

/15/ Langdon Gilkey, "The Role of the Theologian in Contemporary Society," in *The Thought of Paul Tillich*, ed. James Luther Adams, Wilhelm Pauch, and Roger Shinn (San Francisco: Harper and Row, 1985).

/16/ Talcott Parsons and Victor M. Lidz, "Death in American Society," in *Essays in Self-Destruction*, ed. Edwin S. Shneidman (New York: Science House, 1967), pp. 149–150.

/17/ Don S. Browning, *Pluralism and Personality: William James and Some Contemporary Cultures of Psychology* (Lewisburg, Pa.: Bucknell University Press, 1980), pp. 20–22. See also *Religious Thought and the Modern Psychologies* (Philadelphia: Fortress, 1987).

/18/ Fox, Preface to "Social Meaning of Death," p. ix.

/19/ Carol P. Germain, "Nursing the Dying: Implications of Kübler-Ross' Staging Theory," *The Annual of the American Academy of Political and Social Science* 447 (January 1980), 47.

/20/ Richard A. Kalish, "Attitudes Toward Death," in *Encyclopedia of*

Bioethics, ed. Warren Reich, 4 vols. (New York: Free Press, 1978), vol. 1, p. 287.

/21/ Larry R. Churchill, "The Human Experience of Dying: The Moral Primacy of Stories over Stages," *Soundings* 62 (Spring 1979), 24. Emphasis added.

/22/ Peter Steinfels, Introduction to *Death Inside Out*, ed. Peter Steinfels and Robert M. Veatch (New York: Harper and Row, 1974), p. 4.

/23/ Martin E. Marty, *Context: A Commentary on the Interaction of Religion and Culture*, May 15, 1982, p. 6.

/24/ Marjorie Casebier McCoy, *To Die With Style* (New York: Abingdon, 1974), cited by Steinfels, Introduction to *Death Inside Out*, p. 3; Elisabeth Kübler-Ross, *Death: The Final Stage of Growth* (Englewood Cliffs, N. J.: Prentice Hall, 1975); Glenn H. Asquith, *Death is All Right* (Nashville, Tenn.: Abingdon, 1970).

/25/ Hans Jonas, "The Philosophy of Technology," *Hastings Center Studies* 9 (February 1979), 35, 38.

/26/ Paul Ramsey, *The Patient as Person* (New Haven: Yale University Press, 1970), p. 87.

/27/ Ivan Illich, *Medical Nemesis: The Expropriation of Health* (New York: Bantam, 1977), p. 206.

/28/ Leon R. Kass, "Biology and Human Affairs: Whether to Wither and Why?" presented at a Woodward Court Lecture, The University of Chicago, October 1979, pp. 2–3; idem., "Regarding the End of Medicine and the Pursuit of Health," *The Public Interest* 40 (Summer 1975), 16–18. Both articles have since been revised and published in a collection, *Toward a More Natural Science: Biology and Human Affairs* (New York: Free Press, 1985).

/29/ Kenneth L. Vaux, "Topics at the Interface of Medicine and Theology," in *Health/Medicine and the Faith Traditions: An Inquiry into Religion and Medicine*, ed. Martin E. Marty and Kenneth Vaux (Philadelphia: Fortress, 1982), p. 189; idem., "Theological Foundations of Medical Ethics," in *Health/Medicine and the Faith Traditions*, p. 220.

/30/ James M. Gustafson and Stanley M. Hauerwas, "Editorial," *Journal of Medicine and Philosophy* 4 (1979), 345; James M. Gustafson, "Theology Confronts Technology and the Life Sciences," *Commonweal* 105 (June 1978), 386–387, 391.

/31/ Charles Hartshorne, "The Acceptance of Death," in *Philosophical Aspects of Thanatology*, ed. Florence M. Hetzler and Austin H. Kutscher, 2 vols. (New York: Arno Press, 1978), vol. 1, p. 86. For a similar analysis, see H. Tristram Engelhardt, Jr., "The Counsels of Finitude," in *Death Inside Out*, p. 188.

/32/ Leon R. Kass, "Averting One's Eyes or Facing the Music?—On Dignity in Death," *Hastings Center Studies* 2, no. 2 (May 1974), 70.

/33/ Robert M. Veatch, *Death, Dying, and the Biological Revolution: Our Last Quest for Responsibility* (New Haven: Yale University Press, 1976), p. 4.

/34/ Ibid., pp. 3–4.

/35/ Philippe Ariès, *Western Attitudes Toward Death: From the Middle Ages to the Present*, trans. Patricia M. Ranum (Baltimore: Johns Hopkins

14   Death, Sin and the Moral Life

University Press, 1974), pp. 87–90; Monroe Lerner, "When, Why, and Where People Die," in *Death: Current Perspectives*, ed. Edwin S. Shneidman (Palo Alto, Calif.: Mayfield, 1976), pp. 153–159.

/36/   Morris B. Abram, *Deciding to Forego Life-Sustaining Treatment: A Report on Ethical, Moral and Legal Issues in Treatment Decisions* (Washington, D. C.: Government Printing Office, 1983), p. 1.

/37/   John Hick, *Death and Eternal Life* (San Francisco: Harper and Row, 1976), pp. 83–85; Ariès, *Western Attitudes*, p. 87; Parsons and Lidz, "Death in American Society," p. 145.

/38/   Leon R. Kass, "Man's Right to Die," *The Pharos of Alpha Omega Alpha* 35 (April 1972), 74.

/39/   Calvin Goldscheider, "The Mortality Revolution," in Shneidman, *Death: Current Perspectives*, p. 172.

/40/   Lerner, "When, Why, and Where People Die," pp. 141–142.

/41/   William H. McNeill, *Plagues and Peoples* (Garden City, N. Y. : Anchor Books, 1977), p. 106.

/42/   Veatch, *Biological Revolution*, p. 4; Talcott Parsons, "Death in the Western World," in *Encyclopedia of Bioethics*, vol. 1, p. 259.

/43/   Abram, *Deciding to Forego Treatment*, pp. 1, 16.

/44/   Veatch, *Biological Revolution*, p. 4.

/45/   Hastings Center Research Group, "Values and Life-Extending Technologies," in *Life Span: Values and Life-Extending Technologies*, ed. Robert M. Veatch (New York: Harper and Row, 1980), p. 36.

/46/   Alvin R. Tarlov, "Shattuck Lecture—The Increasing Supply of Physicians, the Changing Structure of the Health Services System, and the Future Practice of Medicine," *New England Journal of Medicine* 308, no. 20 (May 19, 1983), 1238. For a more popular treatment of this issue, see "The Big Business of Medicine," *Newsweek*, October 31, 1983, pp. 62–74.

/47/   David Tracy, *Analogical Imagination: Christian Theology and the Culture of Pluralism* (New York: Crossroad, 1981), pp. 3–14.

/48/   Cassel, "Dying in a Technological Society," p. 36.

/49/   David Tracy, *Blessed Rage for Order: The New Pluralism in Theology* (New York: Seabury, 1975), pp. 32–63.

/50/   Don S. Browning, *Religious Ethics and Pastoral Care: Protestant and Catholic Ethics and the Cure of Souls* (Philadelphia: Fortress, 1983), pp. 51–52, 99.

/51/   Philippe Ariès, "Death Inside Out," *Hastings Center Studies* 2, no. 2 (May 1974), 3.

PART I

HISTORICAL ILLUSTRATIONS: MAJOR SHIFTS IN THE MORAL IMPORT OF DEATH

CHAPTER I

ILLUSTRATIONS IN THEOLOGY: THE SHIFT
FROM RELIGIOUS AND MORAL
TO NATURAL VIEWS OF DEATH

Historian Jacques Choron argues that prior to the Enlightenment, the Christian approach to death "supplanted all others in the western world and enjoyed a virtual monopoly for a period of almost a thousand years."[1] Talcott Parsons describes this period as one of "relative closure" on the problem of death's meaning.[2] Rigid institutional practices and social rituals neatly prescribed the proper attitude toward death. Little or no room remained for individualized reactions. Much of our current moral confusion about death results from the collapse of this monolithic worldview in the seventeenth and eighteenth centuries.

In this chapter we will trace this historical shift in emphasis from a religious and moral view of death to a natural approach and even at times, to a naturalistic approach. I use these three categories as heuristic tools for discerning central historical trends. They are by no means a rigid typology of mutually exclusive thought constructs or historical phases. I contend, in fact, that there is an important place for both moral and natural views. In a narrow sense, I use the religious and moral view to refer to an understanding of death as the "wages of sin" and of sin as the "sting of death." But more generally and more centrally, it refers to the connection between death and principles of human worth, freedom, and responsibility in relationship. By "natural" I mean the emphasis on death as an inherent part of created nature. Significantly, a natural approach need not exclude the moral component. This is a danger unique to what I call a "naturalistic" approach. The latter sees death as simply a mechanical, biological phenomenon, no more, no less.

An historical survey of death in theology has yet to be written.

I suggest instead a look at primary resources. Listening firsthand to the words of St. Augustine's *City of God*, John Calvin's *Institutes* and selections from the *Commentaries*, and Frederick Schleiermacher's *The Christian Faith*[3] vividly illustrates the tenor of the changes that have occurred. I choose these authors not because they represent the final and only word on theological interpretation nor in order to examine their entire theologies of death, but because they provide examples of the changes. Augustine (350–430) and Calvin (1509–1564) lift up the Pauline view of death as consequential punishment of Adam's sin and as leading to judgment and eternal life. Calvin connects these premises to the medieval view of individual judgment at the moment of death. And Schleiermacher (1768–1834) adopts the more natural view of death as a necessary, essential part of our finitude and not as the direct result of "original sin."[4]

Today persons seldom link death, sin or alienation from God, and grace. The belief that because Adam sins, we die, sounds nonsensical, antiquated, irrelevant, and logically inconsistent. Why return to the dated sources of these ideas? Foremost, fuller understanding of our history allows for fuller understanding of today's problems.[5] Moreover, assuming that "tradition contains within itself permanent human possibilities," retrieval and reinterpretation offers a rich "repository of options" that can supplement resources for reflection and resolution.[6] Indeed, we stand in need of relearning how death might involve spiritual and moral components. Finally, we must resist the temptation to oversimplify and stereotype the richness of religious traditions, saying, for instance, as Veatch does, that the "Judeo-Christian notion" is simply "that death is an evil, a punishment for sinfulness which cost man immortality."[7]

Based on Tracy's normative paradigm of disciplined, responsive conversation, I hope to move past self-consciousness of our own framework of thought in order to fully enter the "world" of the text of each writer.[8] For instance, while Augustine's use of terms such as "heaven," "hell," or "immortal soul" assumes a frame of reference foreign to our own, we may still get caught up in the truth and meaning disclosed once inside the world of the text. Tracy likens this experience to that of playing a game. When immersed in the created world of a game and its rules, one loses consciousness of oneself and transcends one's world. "The game becomes not an object over against a self-conscious subject but an experienced-relational and releasing mode of being in the world distinct from the ordinary, non-playful one."[9] And, in the end, the game "plays me."

If we choose to "play the game" or allow ourselves to be played by the game of death in the fourth, sixteenth, and nineteenth centuries, we can hardly help but be impressed by the richness of an untapped part of the *traditum*. All three scholars might agree that contemporary understandings of human mortality neglect basic moral and spiritual considerations. They might be troubled by our narrow definitions of such considerations or by our acceptance of psychological or medical platitudes in the place of serious moral reflection.

After briefly situating each scholar within the overarching flow of history in the first section, I ask each scholar in turn how they might answer first, the more theological question of the relation between death, sin, and grace, and second, the normative question of how one should regard human mortality. With the first question, I want to illustrate the distinct differences between their views on this issue and modern revisions since Schleiermacher. With the second, I lift up a possible consequence of these differences by studying the normative counsel offered by each respective theologian. Where Augustine and Calvin richly depict the many significant moral and religious concerns that a person ought to have in regards to his or her own death, Schleiermacher has much less to say. His advice is more ambiguous and tentative. For him, living a fuller life in the present world takes precedence over any lengthy didactics, much less polemic, on death and dying. Later chapters attend to further consequences of this shift in modern society as a whole.

Western Attitudes: From "Tamed" to "Forbidden" Death

AUGUSTINE AND "TAMED DEATH"
Historian Philippe Ariès provides a good characterization of the overall pattern of Western attitudes toward death. Each of our thinkers can be positioned within this broad framework. Augustine lived in the period of "tamed death," as Ariès calls the first phase. Until the twelfth century, there existed a calm "familiarity" with death rather than "fear or awe." The spectacle of death made little impression on the living. Persons were resigned to it as part of the collective destiny of the whole species. "They were as familar with the dead as they were familiarized with the idea of their own death."[10] This did not mean persons ignored death. Rather, they anticipated it, often far in advance, either through natural signs or

through intuited conviction. Thus persons prepared for its coming "without haste or delay but with a sense of proper timing."[11] When a death occurred, the death chamber became a place to be entered freely and death, a public, communal event. Dying entailed a clearly defined, calmly enacted ritual attended by the whole community, children and adults alike. The ritual included expression of sorrow, pardon, absolution, a turning from the world to God, and then, silence until death came, whether immediately or not.[12]

Shaped by the attitude of "tamed death," Augustine observes, "From the moment a man begins to exist in this body which is destined to die, he is involved in a process whose end is death."[13] In his testimony of his mother's death in *The Confessions*, she foresees her end far in advance. She prepares herself and the community of her son and friends accordingly. "My son," she declares, "as to me, I no longer find any pleasure in this life. What more I have to do here and why I am still here I do not know since I have no longer anything to hope for in this world."[14] He has fulfilled her hopes that he become a Christian. She simply awaits the fever that comes five days later and the death which follows shortly. Although Augustine feels tears and sorrow, he does not experience the kind of fear or denial typical of later centuries. Death is "tamed," "simple," always "near."

The early Jewish and Christian traditions agree with Ariès's portrayal. Neither the Jews in the Hebrew Bible nor Paul in the New Testament seem inordinately preoccupied with anxiety or fear of death or personal survival after death. Of greater consequence is the destiny of the whole community of chosen people and the "moral drama enacted in historical time."[15] The earliest ideas of resurrection emphasize the corporate, rather than individual, nature of judgment and restoration.[16] The writing of *City of God* itself is motivated, not so much by concern for the individual destiny of immortal souls in isolated progression toward a final goal of perfection, as by concern for the destiny of embodied souls as fellow pilgrims and citizens in the eternal history of God's entire city.

CALVIN AND "ONE'S OWN DEATH"

A heightened, and at time, haunting, obsession with "one's own death" characterized the late Middle Ages. Death of the individual soul acquires a "dramatic and personal meaning" unknown to Augustine.[17] In place of the communal vision of an "entire quasi-biological population" or of "heavenly Jerusalem" bodily resurrected at the end of all time, we find the bed of the dying individual.[18]

Here each person faces the final reckoning of her good and bad deeds to decide her fate for all eternity. Hence the very hour of death assumes a dramatic significance. The deathbed becomes "the battleground of the last and desperate fight which the Devil and his cohorts waged for the soul," the ultimate "contest between the forces of Good and Evil," or the final temptation luring a person one last time into the hands of Satan.[19]

In this way, the "final test has replaced the Last Judgment." "Concern for the individuality of each person" has supplanted the idea of the "collective destiny of the species."[20] Death, individual biography, and the "moral importance of the way the person behaved and the circumstances surrounding" death become intertwined in a new and often terrifying way.[21] Like a Bosch painting, each person envisions a particular torture based upon individual temptations, fears, and weaknesses. The hereafter becomes less a source of consolation than terror. "The idea of unnaturalness—the abnormality—of death begins to appear."[22]

Theological reflection contributed to this change. Thomas Aquinas gave the images of individual judgment and the afterlife force and cogency within the metaphysical framework of Aristotelian philosophy. He considered systematically such questions as the relation of specific individual sins to punishment and the relation of an individual's body and soul after death.[23] Reform theology challenged a number of these doctrines. But Luther's and Calvin's criticism of such beliefs as the doctrine of purgatory was more an attack on the sacramental system of penance than any real qualification of the medieval understanding of death.[24]

In Calvin's theology, the last moment becomes even more central. He refutes the possibility of working for salvation after death in an intermediary state of purgatory. Nor can a person's destiny be modified through intercessory prayers and propitiatory offerings of the still living.[25] Thus sudden death is dreaded because it robs a person of a last chance for repentance, confession, and reconciliation.[26] The act of dying becomes a high point in the Christian's career. It is a crucial time for witness, admonition, exhortation, and prayer for the dying and for the dying person's friends and family.[27]

SCHLEIERMACHER AND "FORBIDDEN DEATH"

Beginning in the nineteenth century, death, once so familiar and omnipresent, is effaced. It becomes "shameful and forbidden."[28] Ariès believes that this change relates to a deeper metamorphosis in moral values. People "cast off" the deeply rooted belief in the moral import of death and personal biography. Instead, society forbids even thinking about death because the new moral obligation is to "contribute to collective happiness."

> The cause of the interdiction [or denial of death] is at once apparent: the need for happiness—the moral duty and the social obligation to contribute to collective happiness by avoiding any cause for sadness or boredom, by appearing to be always happy, even if in the depths of despair. By showing the least sign of sadness, one sins against happiness, threatens it, and society then risks losing its *raison d'etre*.[29]

Because death poisons enjoyment of life, persons consider it a "transgression" or a rude "rupture." It unfairly tears them from daily life and rational society. If persons can hush up the disturbance of death, they spare society its ugliness.

> The accent was on life, and death was merely the unavoidable and unpleasant "natural accident," the thought of which had better be kept in the background. And in keeping with the spirit of Enlightenment, with its extravagant and fervent belief in the powers of reason, life could be improved and happiness attained in this life, the only one there can be and therefore the only one that matters. . . . To achieve a better life in freedom and happiness for all here and now, or at least for future generations, this and not salvation of the soul, was the paramount goal.[30]

Persons took Bentham's transposition of Hamlet—"to be *happy* or not at all"—seriously.[31] They forgot about death and began to place confidence in progress and fulfillment in this life. Those who did contemplate death considered it a "disease" from which humankind might one day be cured. The campaign to prolong life indefinitely through ingenious techniques, appearing then for the first time, remains with us today.[32]

We can understand Schleiermacher's commentary on death within this context. Proclamation of the ideal of progress does color his thought. Karl Barth's accusation that Schleiermacher identifies the Kingdom of God with the advance of civilization has some validity.[33]

Even his chief twentieth-century opponent, however, must admit the deep "earnestness" and "personal sincerity" with which

Schleiermacher seeks to be a Christian theologian.[34] He is truly "an ambassador and interpreter of one world to another."[35] But now the other world has new moral ideas about death. Instead of moral and religious concern about communal or individual judgment and salvation, persons had begun to think about fulfillment in the here and now, almost to the exclusion of meditation on death's moral and spiritual dimensions. In the Middle Ages and the Reformation, persons lived with a strong sense of stewardship of life. They faced death in the midst of a moral ethos of regimentation and self-abnegation. This often meant willing renunciation of temporal happiness and life itself. In the Enlightenment, persons lived instead with an optimistic sense of the folly of asceticism. They faced death as an unfortunate but, as of yet, unavoidable obstacle to further progress.

The Relation between Death and Sin

AUGUSTINE AND CALVIN: DEATH AS A CURSE

For Augustine and Calvin, human mortality is not a necessary or inevitable part of creation. Humans are made with the potential for immortality. Death is a curse condemning Adam and altering human nature for the worse. Death can only become a blessing for believers.

Paul, the earliest spokesperson on death in the Christian tradition, first articulates the idea that death is a punishment for sin (Rom. 5:12) and that it is overcome on our behalf by Christ (Rom. 6:23). Still "it was above all Augustine, in the fifth century, who first wove the dark themes of guilt, remorse and punishment into the tremendous drama of creation, fall, incarnation, heaven and hell which has dominated the Christian imagination in the West until within the last hundred years or so."[36] He plays so crucial a role in Western thought on death that no brief overview can do justice.

In spite of the centuries separating Calvin and Augustine, Calvin does not so much alter these ideas as systematically purify and extend them. At certain points, he follows Augustine's exegesis nearly word for word, although he adds some worthy distinctions and omits others. Above all else, his reflection on death is notable by its sheer quantity. He has "a good deal to say," more than Augustine and much more than Schleiermacher, "about the way in which a Christian should face and overcome not only suffering but death itself."[37] In part, this is because he addresses an era uniquely preoccupied with death.

All three of our theologians agree that the whole of creation is dependent upon God. If God takes our breath away, we vanish into dust. Life is a gift we neither create nor sustain. Schleiermacher talks about the "*Whence*," [38] Augustine, about the God who abides "forever, without becoming old" in whom we are "established firm" and without whom we "would pass away and be no more,"[39] and Calvin, about God's sovereignty without which "our very being is nothing."[40] Despite the different language, the understanding of God's omnipotence in creation is the same.

Augustine believes that the decay and dissolution of those beings not created for eternal life is "progress toward something they were designed to become" and not "a process of annihilation." Schleiermacher makes a similar argument. Change, growth, and death of the transient world contributes to the "good and improvement" of the "total pattern" in a "harmonious and beautiful way."[41]

Augustine, however, makes an important distinction. In sharp contrast to Schleiermacher, the natural process of decay does not include human nature. Humans are created for eternal life. Their development and dissolution has an entirely different meaning. He enters into strident controversy with the Pelagians over just this point. They hold that physical death belongs to the very nature of human beings. Adam would have died, they contend, even had he not sinned. Against this idea Augustine argues, among other things, that "there was no necessity" for human death.[42] The soul "was created immortal [and] does not cease to live with a kind of life of its own, however wretched."[43] Souls never "desist from that flicker of life which they call their own, that is, the life which makes them immortal."[44]

Both Calvin and Augustine assert that God created for Adam and Eve an immortal destiny. The death of the body is not a necessary law of nature. Augustine distinguishes between *mortale*, being "mortal," and *moriturus*, being "subject to death." Adam's body, although created *mortale* or capable of dying, was not thereby *moriturus* or destined to die. He would have grown "full of years without decrepitude, and when God pleased, passed from mortality to immortality without the medium of death." We should not worry that if Adam "had happened to live on here longer in his natural body, he would have been oppressed with old age, and gradually, by increasing age, arrived at death." While still in a "natural and mortal body," these first human beings were not "reduced to the decrepitude of old age by their long life."[45] They were "supplied with sustenance" from the fruit of the trees of the garden. This fruit would have protected them "against decay" and "against old age" until they attained an eternity of bliss without the interposition of death.

Calvin's assertions parallel Augustine's. Adam "had the power, if he so willed, to attain eternal life."[46] Like the distinction between *mortale* and *moriturus*, he talks of "life which was only earthly" yet bound to mount up to God and "eternal bliss." Although Adam had "an earthly and perishable life," a life which "would have been temporal," and although his state was not yet perfected, from the start he was made with the potential for heavenly life. He "would have passed into heaven without death and without injury."[47]

Rather, Adam was subject to death "as just punishment for sin." With this idea Schleiermacher will take issue. "Dust thou art, and unto dust thou shalt return" refers to God's penal sentence divinely pronounced on the transgressor, Augustine asserts.[48] In Calvin's words, because Adam had forsaken God, God saw fit to forsake Adam, thereby allowing the "capacity" to die to become "destiny." In short, sin produces death.[49]

Moreover, no one else "would ever have died had not the first two . . . merited this death by disobedience."[50] By their act, our natural condition was vitiated and altered, making all human nature susceptible to the corruption of decay and death. The damage, Augustine reasons, is congenitally transmitted from generation to generation, entangling the whole race in the curse of degeneration. "What first happened as . . . punishment . . . continued in their posterity as something natural and congenital."[51] For Calvin, the taint spreads in an even more insidious way:

> Adam was not only the progenitor but, as it were, *the root of human nature* . . . Hence Adam, *when he lost the gifts received, lost them not only for himself but for us all.* . . . For the contagion does not take its origin from the substance of the flesh or soul, but because it had been so ordained by God that the first man should at one and the same time have and lose, both for himself and for his descendants, the gifts that God had bestowed upon him.[52]

SCHLEIERMACHER: DEATH AS A NATURAL IMPERFECTION

Schleiermacher shows less concern than either Augustine or Calvin in the relation between death, sin, and grace. In discussing the Genesis story, at a point where Augustine and Calvin find it natural to discuss death and sin at length, Schleiermacher simply notes, "The connexion of sin and evil, sin and death on which [Gen. 2:8 f.] evidently proceeds, does not in and of itself, need to be discussed here."[53] He almost dismisses the subject as immaterial.

Instead Schleiermacher attempts to rethink the categories of faith in a meaningful way for a scientific and empirical age. In certain cases, and such is the case with the church's view of death, he considers "traditional terminology . . . in every aspect unsatisfactory."[54] We must move beyond authorized ecclesiastical dogmas, considered supernaturally and infallibly transmitted, to the primary religious affections behind their inspiration. By appealing to "inward" and "immediate" experience of universal religious "consciousness," we can discern and extract the essence of the traditional terms.

Guided by this new interpretative principle, he challenges the traditional doctrines of death. If "we can have no experience in common with our first parents" as to how sin originates, is passed on, and alters our nature so as to bring death as punishment, we are under no obligation to honor such a doctrine. "We can thus readily dispense with all these artificial theories which . . . lay stress upon the divine justice in imputing Adam's sin to, and exacting its penalty from, his posterity."[55]

In so arguing, Schleiermacher influences one of the most important changes in theological understandings:

> One of the most significant changes modern experience and reflection have effected in the classical tradition of theology is with regard to the status of death. More specifically, almost universally since Schleiermacher death has been interpreted as an aspect, a necessary and essential aspect, of our finitude rather than as the result of an "original sin" by the two progenitors of the race.[56]

He thoroughly dispels the traditional view of the Mosaic narrative as an historical account. It represents, he argues, neither a factual chronicle of a definitive event in the past nor an action causative of our having to die. It is contrary to "our religious consciousness" to presuppose a "paradisical" condition at the beginning of time and lasting a certain limited period in which the first couple lived in perfect and eternal sinlessness. This "fable of a Golden Age" assumes that the entrance of sin changed the nature of the physical world and human nature itself. It would have us believe that if this "life of

Paradise" had only endured, no one would have died. In essence, "apart from sin there would have been neither evil or death."[57]

By contrast, "our religious consciousness makes no claim to substantiate the theory of some sort of magical effect which sin at its first appearance must have produced upon the world as a whole."[58] It is ridiculous to even suppose that God should leave the ultimate decision between death and immortality to "two such inexperienced individuals, who, moreover, never dreamt" that a simple moment of temptation would have such consequence.[59] This is simply a "fantastic notion," a "wholly untenable idea deduced from certain Mosaic passages [Gen. 3:14, 16] on quite insufficient grounds."[60]

> Neither the Old Testament story [Gen. 2:17] nor the relevant indications in the writings of the New Testament [Rom. 4:12] compel us to hold that man was created immortal, or that, with alteration in his nature, the whole arrangement of the earth relative to him was altered as well.

In an adjoining footnote, he emphasizes:

> Rom. 5:12, based on Gen. 2:17, just as little excludes the possibility that Adam may have been created mortal; and 1 Cor. 15:56 actually indicates death as existing before the advent of sin.[61]

Thus *objectively considered*, death and decay do not arise from sin. They are "natural maladjustments of the individual life to its environment . . . found where no sin exists." God ordained "natural death and the bodily afflictions that precede it in the shape of disease and debility" as part of the creation and preservation of the world.[62] "Real history could only begin" with their presence. Without them, the conditions for life's progress would also disappear.[63] In fact, death numbers among the most powerful motives for human development. It actually enhances life's possibilities.

Only *subjectively considered* does death *appear* a penalty of sin. Because persons no longer live every moment determined by God-consciousness—that is, in wholehearted dependence on and fellowship with God—they misconstrue the "relative opposition" of death as an obstruction. Only from this perspective is death "reckoned as an evil."[64] Given sin, the world appears different, its original harmony disturbed and death experienced as evil—a "semblance arising from our way of isolating things."[65]

> Without sin there would be nothing in the world that could
> properly be considered an evil but . . . whatever is bound up
> with the transitoriness of human life would be apprehended as
> at most an unavoidable imperfection, and the operations of
> natural forces which impede the efforts of men as but incen-
> tives to bring these forces more fully under human control.[66]

In this way, Schleiermacher revises the "misleading assumption"
that God arbitrarily conjoined sin with death as an "eternal penal
suffering." The "true significance" of the symbolic Mosaic narrative
is simply "that it is through sin alone that natural imperfections
come to be incorporated with social evils"—that is, with evils which
arise from human activity.[67] Death is not in itself a social evil due to
sin. It is a natural shortcoming which impedes human efforts and
growth.

Counsel on the Moral Life

AUGUSTINE: ACCEPT THE "FIRST DEATH" AND FEAR THE "SECOND"

Albeit outmoded, Augustine's and Calvin's ideas enable them
to explore a dimension of human dying that often eludes modern
reflection and in a sense, Schleiermacher as well. We may find the
idea of death as "curse" due to God's "judgment" confusing and
alien. Yet when comprehended within the world internal to the
text, these terms reveal the attempts of both Augustine and Calvin
to elucidate a moral and spiritual side of death.

Augustine talks about "first" and "second death." The first
death is the double death of the body and the soul to which Adam
condemns us and into which we enter the minute we are born. This
death occurs when the soul forsaken by God in turn forsakes the
body. The first death may lead to the second death. The second
death occurs when the soul, after an interim following the first
death,[68] is reunited with the resurrected body but confers a "life" of
"torment" and "everlasting punishment" upon the body. This second death is an "eternal death without any possibility of dying."
Death itself become deathless.[69] The person is eternally alienated
from God.

Calvin drops the typology of first and second death. But he
offers in its place a description of the fear of death more appealing to
modern ears. We fear death because it threatens annihilation of

bodily existence *and also* because it involves chastisement in which the soul feels the curse of God.[70] All persons naturally experience both these fears, not just believers. All fear extinction, "for the wish to be dissolved is revolting to nature."[71] But, second, and equally as important, all fear death because, through their "consciences," however imperfectly formed, they experience death not only as annihilation, but as God's judgment.

> Calvin asserts that even pagans and unbelievers are constrained to recognize that death is a curse of God pronounced on Adam and all his seed, not only because everyone wishes to live, and in death we are, as it were, annihilated, but also because God has left some kind of mark so that men understand this without knowing hardly a word of Christian teaching. Death, then, has a twofold purpose. It is ordained "not only for the dissolution of man, but also to make him feel the curse of God."[72]

Hence for both Augustine and Calvin it is not physical but moral and spiritual death which is rightly to be feared or mourned, whether they talk about this in terms of first and second deaths or in terms of fear of annihilation and judgment. Both typologies address the question of "moral rather than physical corruption" and the problem of "loss of life with God."[73] It is "the terror of this spiritual and eternal death," the "alienation of the soul from God,"[74] Calvin observes, "which makes bodily death—in itself already an evil—still more terrible."[75] Likewise, Augustine argues that persons ought not fear the first death but the second. The first happens to everyone; the second only to the godless. Above all else, we ought to fear eternal alienation from God which follows inevitably upon the first death unless we are saved by God.

> Careful consideration shows that the very act of dying faithfully and laudably is a precaution against death. A partial death is certainly accepted, but that is so that total death may not come, so that second death may not supervene, that death which has no end. . . . The separation of soul from body is accepted, so that the soul may not be separated from God.[76]

In other words, persons would accept the first death in order to avoid the second. The second inevitably follows the first unless a person is "set free by grace." Only Christ's intercessions, through the application of his single earthly death to our double death, cures us like a "healing remedy" or "medicine" of both deaths.[77]

> For Augustine death is principally an eschatological concept
> with a spiritual rather than physical significance. Physical
> death is neither a part of life nor that which confers an authen-
> tic existence upon the individual as some contemporary exis-
> tentialists hold. The source of meaning . . . lies not in the fear
> or dread of a physical death but in the relationship the individ-
> ual established with the living God. . . . Augustine shows a
> lack of concern or anxiety with physical death. . . . He has an
> "infinite concern" for spiritual death, for such a death means
> the total death of the person. It is this death which deprives us
> eternally of God. . . . It is this second death that we should
> regard with anxiety and dread.[78]

We foolishly "seek with all our power not to die even though this is
unattainable," inanely attempting to avoid "the punishment more
than the cause of the punishment." Rather, say Augustine and
Calvin, be concerned "about not sinning" and about the death that
you can avoid, that of "godlessness."[79] Only in this way is life truly
received.

Thus persons should endure death not as a good in itself but
"for the attainment and possession of a good." We should accept it so
that we avoid that total death separating us from God's love. By
"acceptance" of death Augustine has something very specific in
mind. He does not refer to something we might envision today
under the shadow of Kübler-Ross. Acceptance means three things—
we ought to accept death only "when that acceptance means the
avoidance of sin and the cancellation of sins committed, and the
award of the palm of victory as the just reward of righteousness."[80] A
"good death" demands a "penalty . . . paid [by Christ] in the name
of justice and piety." It includes the "sorrows of repentance," a
"certain salutary agony of self-denial," endurance in "devout faith,"
and pious reconciliation with others and God. The act of a good
death is not simply a human act existentially lived out but an act of
faith and reconciliation. The possibility of acceptance resides in
Christ's death.

In reality death itself is ambiguous. On the one hand, the
severing of soul and body of the first death is

> not good for anyone, as it is experienced by those who are . . .
> dying. This violent sundering of the two elements, which are
> conjoined and interwoven in a living being is bound to be a
> harsh and unnatural experience as long as it lasts, until the
> departure of all feeling.[81]

This death is wholly "contrary to life."

Nonetheless death also has the potential for good. The "good die a good death although death itself is an evil."[82] In choosing God and love of others, the good person turns death, by no virtue of its own, to "great advantage" or to "good employment." Death becomes a way to true life.

> Undoubtedly death is the penalty of all who come to birth on earth as descendants of the first man; nevertheless, if the penalty is paid in the name of justice and piety, it becomes a new birth in heaven. Although death is the punishment of sin, sometimes it secures for the soul a grace.[83]

Why then has God not simply abolished death, along with sin and guilt, for the faithful? If absolution of sins included immediate deliverance from death, "faith itself would be weakened." Everyone "would rush . . . to Christ" for all the wrong reasons. Instead, faith is "tested by the fact that its reward" remains unseen.[84] Death is "an exercise of discipline in order that our great fear . . . may be overcome by us as we advance in holiness." Indeed, those who conquer their excessive concern about death procure "a great glory and just recompense" for their faith.[85] The best examples are those martyrs and saints who have died promoting the righteousness of God rather than forsaking their faith. They transform death, an evil, into a good.

CALVIN: DESPISE LIFE AND LOOK FORWARD TO DEATH

What is measured in Augustine becomes more stern and unyielding in Calvin. Upon his mother's death Augustine chastizes himelf for his "tears and groans and lamentations," but allows that his grief belongs to the "proper order and lot of the human condition."[86] Calvin casts fear and grief in more negative terms as signs of unbelief.

> Monstrous it is that many who boast themselves Christians are gripped by such a great fear of death, rather than a desire for it, that they tremble at the least mention of it, as of something utterly dire and disastrous. Surely, it is no wonder if the natural awareness in us bristles with dread at the mention of our dissolution. But it is wholly unbearable that there is not in Christian hearts any light of piety to overcome and suppress that fear, whatever it is, by a greater consolation.[87]

Granted Christian consolation does not mean Stoic calm, indifference, or denial of passion. In fact, Calvin decries these as unrealistic. No one, even Christ, has the ability to achieve such forbearance. Moreover, it brings no relief from despair since persons must still face God's judgment.

Nevertheless, among the faithful these emotions are inappropriate when excessive and uncontrolled. We must tame, subjugate, and bear "willingly and even cheerfully" any contrary affections. Mourning must be moderated, fear kept within proper bounds, care expressed within ordered limits.[88] We may feel anxious or upset, but

> the conclusion will always be: the Lord so willed, therefore let us follow his will. Indeed, amid the pricks of pain, amid groaning and tears, this thought must intervene: to incline our heart to bear cheerfully those things which have so moved it.[89]

Calvin adds to Augustine's imperative of acceptance the virtues of patience, cheerfulness, forbearance, self-denial, and bearing the cross or suffering for righteousness' sake. The true mark of faith is ultimately joy, cheerfulness, and bold confidence. We are called "not only to live blessedly but also to die happily."[90] For Augustine, death, an unnatural rupture of body and soul, is far from a happy occasion. For Calvin, while death may certainly seem a "calamity," when transformed, it can become "happiness for us."[91] It does not spell the abrupt end of all life, but merely the temporary separation of body and soul, a transition to the blessed life to come which in some ways is not quite death at all: "We do not perish utterly in death, since the soul merely departs from the body. Hence . . . death is *nothing but* an exodus of the soul from the body.[92]

Not surprisingly, death itself becomes a provisional goal. It ends the present disgrace of a sinful, imperfect life, relieves us from confinement on earth, and leads us heavenwards.[93]

> No one rejoices in death or the cutting off of his lifetime in and for itself; but when we think of the heavenly glory and bliss which beckon to us on the other side then not only do we go obediently to death but hasten gladly towards it as a goal to which we are summoned by faith and love.[94]

By faith we must "ardently seek what nature dreads":

> Let us . . . consider this settled: that no one has made progress in the school of Christ who does not joyfully await the day of

death and final resurrection . . . not only with longing but also
with groaning and sighs, as the happiest thing of all.[95]

At the same time Calvin also urges contempt for death. Taken
all together, these comments on despising life and death *and* rejoic-
ing in life and in death reveal that for him, faith relativizes both.
Persons ought not feel ungrateful for life in their desire for death nor
ought they ignore death in pursuit of the pleasures of life. Rather,
the person of faith ought to use both life and death to the glory of
God. In living and in dying believers must neither desire to depart
before their time nor resist when called. They must patiently retain
life or obediently yield it up as it best serves God's will and glory in
accord with one's calling and one's duties.[96] A good life and a good
death happen when a person applies herself to her calling and that
up until death.

SCHLEIERMACHER: DEATH AS A STIMULUS FOR DEVELOPMENT

Both Augustine and Calvin offer more specific normative advice than Schleiermacher. Along with the dissolution of the "historical Adam" vanishes not only the explanation of death as
consequence of sin but also the articulation of moral, religious, and
spiritual direction. Although Schleiermacher intones some of the
same themes, he greatly simplifies his advice. The *Soliloquies* of the
early Schleiermacher reflect an optimistic confidence in human
growth and a romantic glorification of death. He himself admits in a
letter to his sister that his thoughts on death in this work seem at
times a "trifle obscure," although once understood, "right
enough."[97] In contrast to Augustine and Calvin, we can draw only
modest conclusions as to Schleiermacher's position from a few select
passages, some of which are indeed a bit "obscure." He leaves many
genuine moral and religious issues largely unaddressed.

In a view of death as the natural progression of life, death itself
does not command as much concern. It is mostly an impediment to
life or an unpleasant "imperfection." In a more positive vein, it is a
necessary part of human evolution that persons can use creatively to
further growth. Death can provide incentive to human development. Lest this merely confirm Karl Barth's criticism that Schleiermacher compromises the Christian gospel to proclaim the advancement of humankind, we should note that he means specifically a
spiritual development of God-consciousness. Indeed, if each moment occurred without sin, death would not present the "obstruction" to growth that it does.

Sin and death function less as a radical "no" to human life and more as a "not yet." This idea reflects what John Hick calls a "pilgrim attitude toward death":

> On this view man was not created in a finitely perfect state from which he then fell, but was initially brought into being as an immature creature who was only at the beginning of a long process of growth and development. Man did not fall disastrously from a better state into one of sin and guilt, with death as its punishment, but rather he is still in process of being created. . . .
>
> The ideal . . . is not a lost reality, forfeited long ago . . . but something lying before us as a state to be attained in the distant future. . . . This theology prompts an understanding of the meaning of life as a divinely intended opportunity . . . to grow towards the realization of the potentialities of our own nature.[98]

Development occurs through growth to full creation rather than by radical conversion to Christ on one's deathbed.

In *The Christian Faith* he comes to describe the "casual fluctuation" of birth and death as "progressive development up to a certain climax, from thence, gradually decreasing until death." In *On Religion* he talks about the potential this ebb and flow has to awaken "a general susceptibility to religion."[99]

> For humanity in all its present environment there are certain windows open to the infinite, . . . past which every man is led in order that his sensibility may find a way to the great All. . . . These outlets are also prudently stopped up by the worldly-wise. . . . Birth and death are such outlets. In their presence it is impossible to forget that our own selves are completely surrounded by the infinite. . . . They always cause an inner pang and a holy reverence.[100]

This passage touches a number of themes. Like Calvin, Schleiermacher disparages the "worldly-wise" for seeking security in the "external" trappings of worldly improvements. He criticizes an era in which the latest trapping is the "noble art of lengthening life." The full measure of human worth and destiny does not rest on externals, like length of life.[101]

Moreover, as Brian Gerrish points out, we should greet death "as an opportunity to transcend the individual personality." It is a chance to surrender to the One and the All in which "all that is individual and fleeting disappears."[102] "Only the man who denying himself sinks himself in as much of the whole Universe as he can attain, and in whose soul a greater and holier longing has arisen, has a right to the hopes that death gives."[103]

In contrast to Augustine and Calvin, death does not promise eternal life as a superadded "reward" or "prize" after death. Instead, eternal life is an extension of religious consciousness experienced on some deeper level of present existence. It is "folly" to make a distinction between this world and the next and to take refuge in the next. "In the religious life then we may well say we have already offered up and disposed of all that is moral, and that we actually are enjoying immortality."[104] If we hope to conquer death, we must do so in "the midst of finitude" and not "outside of time."

In the fourth meditation he gets slightly carried away. Nothing, not even death, can "hinder the progress of my self-development." By "sheer force of will" one can actively "fight off the death" of the spirit: "I shall never consider myself old until I am perfect, and I shall never be perfect, because I know and desire what I should. . . . Nought can happen to affright my heart, and the pulse of my inner life will beat with vigor until death."[105]

For Schleiermacher, fear of death is simply immature. He does not connect the fear directly to the curse and fear of condemnation, as does Calvin, nor to God's abandonment of the soul and the unnatural separation of two elements meant to be joined, as does Augustine. Yet he does connect fear of death to sinfulness, even if in a more tenuous way. Fear, he argues, results from a consciousness dominated by "the flesh apart from the higher consciousness" whereby "every obstruction of our bodily and temporal life must be reckoned as an evil." Rooted in the disharmony between human endeavors to advance and the world's "relative opposition" to this, fear is due to a distorted perception of the world, given sin. Hence he agrees with Calvin and Augustine, "it is not by death but as Scripture says, by the fear of death that we are subject to bondage."[106]

Where from Here?

The dated nature of traditional terminology aside, all three theologians attempt to achieve some sort of comprehensive treatment of death's moral dimension. They make an effort to hold together the physical and the moral as well as the individual and communal aspects of death and dying. Death is far more than biological cessation of human activity. It involves questions of moral and spiritual commitment to life in community, to values that make life meaningful, and to the source of all life.

We have observed a pattern of change in the three authors, from an emphasis on death as a specifically moral and religious problem to a greater emphasis on death's inevitability as a part of life. For Schleiermacher, death is less a moral event and more a natural one. Certainly his natural view of death does not exclude the moral. Indeed, he has a profound understanding of the moral nature of human life in general.

But Schleiermacher hesitates to give normative counsel on death. His approach opens the door, not only to natural approaches, but *naturalistic* views that overtly dismiss the moral component. We will examine several instances in later chapters. It is a short step from Schleiermacher to a worldview in which faith in the future of material progress dominates. He participated in the beginnings of society's disenchantment with moral reflection on death.

However, when the moral tradition is reduced to the truism that a "bad" life results in eternal death and a "good" life in salvational reward, perhaps it is not a bad idea to throw it all out. Earnest skepticism about death's relation to sin and grace makes sense. But as a result, we lack language to articulate moral or religious meaning, implications, and imperatives. If we throw it all out, we stand to lose much more within the tradition than the oversimplified truism above. The attempt to retrieve religious traditions, moving beyond outdated terminology to the essence of traditional language, gives us a clearer sense of today's problems as well as three more "options" to consider.

Footnotes to Chapter I

/1/   Jacque Choron, *Death and Western Thought* (New York: Macmillan, 1963), p. 79.
/2/   Parsons, "Death in the Western World," p. 259.
/3/   Augustine, *City of God*, trans. Henry Bettenson (London: Penguin, 1972); John Calvin, *Institutes of the Christian Faith*, ed. John T. McNeill (Philadelphia: Westminster Press, 1977); idem., *Commentaries* (Edinburgh: Edinburgh Printing, 1845); Frederick Schleiermacher, *The Christian Faith*, ed. H. R. Mackintosh and J. S. Steward with an introduction by Richard R. Niebuhr, 2 vols. (New York: Harper and Row, 1963).
/4/   More tangentially, these figures are chosen as examples because of their influence on history and on each other. Augustine's thought on death

has had major impact on the Western worldview. His life spanned a decisive period in the history of the Roman state and in the move from Roman paganism to Christianity and more generally, from classical antiquity into the Middle Ages. In such a context he was concerned with the problem of his own destiny as well as human destiny in general. Calvin found Augustine his most compatible theological colleague next to Paul and Luther. By comparison Calvin did not originate new doctrines on death so much as purify and reform aspects of traditional ones. But he wrote extensively about death. His thought is an excellent representation of the movement of theology through the scholasticism of the medieval period into the Reformation. Finally, Scheiermacher has been depicted by Richard R. Niebuhr as the "most influential thinker since Calvin:"

> His critical reflection on theological issues . . . sets the basic problems for the succeeding nineteenth century and the greater part of the twentieth . . . so firmly entrenched . . . in the spirit of the times we call modern . . . that very little published today of a theological nature does not borrow consciously or otherwise from some facet of his thinking. (*Schleiermacher on Christ and Religion: A New Introduction* [New York: Charles Scriber's Sons, 1964], pp. 6, 192, and "Introduction" in Schleiermacher, *The Christian Faith*, pp. ix, x.)

Based on an empirical approach to Christianity and in response to the growing authority and challenge of science, he rethinks traditional categories of faith, including ideas about death.

/5/   See Talcott Parsons, Renée C. Fox, and Victor M. Lidz, "The 'Gift of Life' and Its Reciprocation," *Social Research* 34 (Autumn 1972), p. 414.

/6/   Eugene Goodheart, *Culture and Radical Conscience* (Cambridge, Mass.: Harvard University Press, 1973), pp. 9, 15, cited by Martin E. Marty, "Tradition and the Traditions in Health/Medicine and Religion," in *Health/Medicine and the Faith Traditions p. 23*.

/7/   Veatch, *Biological Revolution*, pp. 277–278.

/8/   Tracy, *Analogical Imagination*, pp. 100, 101–102.

/9/   Ibid., pp. 113–114.

/10/   Ariès, *Western Attitudes*, pp. 13, 25. See also idem., "Reversal of Death," pp. 134–158, and "Death Inside Out," pp. 3–18.

/11/   Ariès, *Western Attitudes*, p. 7.

/12/   Ibid., pp. 7–12.

/13/   Augustine, *City of God*, p. 518 (XIII.10).

/14/   Augustine, *The Confessions of St. Augustine*, trans. Rex Warner with an Introduction by Vernon J. Bourke (New York: The New American Library, 1963), p. 202 (IX.10).

/15/   Choron, *Death and Western Thought*, p. 14, See also Hick, *Death and Eternal Life*, pp. 57, 70; Lloyd Bailey, "Death in Biblical Thought," in *Encyclopedia of Bioethics*, vol 1, p. 244; Gerald J. Gruman, "Ethics of Death and Dying: Historical Perspective," *Omega: Journal of Death and Dying* 9, no. 3 (1979), 207; Milton McC. Gatch, *Death: Meaning and Mortality in Christian Thought and Contemporary Culture* (New York:

Seabury, 1969), pp. 35–49; and Ninian Smart, "Death in the Judaeo-Christian Tradition," in *Man's Concern with Death*, ed. Arnold Toynbee (London: Hodder and Stoughton, 1968), p. 117.

/16/   Thomas F. Torrance, *Space, Time and Resurrection* (Grand Rapids: Eerdmans, 1976), pp. 28–29, cited by Crouse, "Fascination with Death," p. 143.

/17/   Ariès, *Western Attitudes*, p. 27.

/18/   Ibid., pp. 29–33; Gatch, *Meaning and Mortality*, p. 95.

/19/   Choron, *Death and Western Thought*, pp. 92, 289, n. 5. See also Ariès, *Western Attitudes*, p. 38, and Hick, *Death and Eternal Life*, pp. 194–196.

/20/   Ariès, *Western Attitudes*, pp. 28, 37.

/21/   Ibid., pp. 37–39.

/22/   H. F. Lovell Cocks, "Death," in *A Handbook of Christian Theology: Definition Essays on Concepts and Movements in Contemporary Protestantism*, ed. Marvin Halverson and Arthur A. Cohen (New York: Meridian Books, 1958), p. 72.

/23/   Gatch, *Meaning and Mortality*, pp. 96–102; Hick, *Death and Eternal Life*, pp. 205–206.

/24/   Gatch, *Meaning and Mortality*, pp. 112–113, 115–120.

/25/   Heinrich Quistorp, *Calvin's Doctrine of the Last Things*, trans. Harold Knight (London: Lutterworth Press, 1955), pp. 102–107.

/26/   Calvin, *Institutes*, p. 223 (1.17.10).

/27/   John Calvin, *Letters of John Calvin Compiled from the Original Manuscript and Edited with Historical Notes by Jules Bonnet*, trans. David Constable, et al., 3 vols. (Philadelphia: Presbyterian Board of Publication, 1958); letters numbered LXXXXVI, CCXXXXIX, CCXL; I, 331–335; II, 217–223, cited by William A. Clebsch and Charles R. Jackle, *Pastoral Care in Historical Perspective* (Englewood Cliffs, N. J.: Prentice-Hall, 1975), pp. 224–232.

/28/   Ariès, *Western Attitudes*, p. 85.

/29/   Ibid., pp. 39–94.

/30/   Choron, *Death and Western Thought*, pp. 134–135.

/31/   Gruman, "Ethics of Death," pp. 214–215. See also idem., "Historical Introduction," pp. 98–99, and "Euthanasia and Sustaining Life: Historical Perspectives," in *Encyclopedia of Bioethics*, vol. 1, p. 264.

/32/   Ibid.

/33/   Karl Barth, *Protestant Theology in the Nineteenth Century: Its Background and History* (Valley Forge: Judson Press, 1973), pp. 435, 437.

/34/   Ibid., pp. 429–434.

/35/   R. R. Niebuhr, Introduction to *Christian Faith*, pp. ix–xx.

/36/   Hick, *Death and Eternal Life*, p. 207.

/37/   Ronald S. Wallace, *Calvin's Doctrine of the Christian Life* (Grand Rapids: Eerdmans, 1959), p. 266.

/38/   Schleiermacher, *Christian Faith*, p. 16.

/39/   Augustine, *Confessions*, pp. 81 (IV.12), 210 (IX.10).

/40/   Calvin, *Institutes*, p. 35 (1.1.1).

/41/   Augustine, *City of God*, an abridged version, trans. Gerald G. Walsh, et al., with a condensation of the original Foreword by Etienne

Gilson, ed. Vernon J. Bourke (Garden City, N. Y.: Doubleday, 1958), pp. 248–150 (XII.4–5).

/42/   Augustine, *A Treatise on the Merits and Forgiveness of Sins and on Baptism of Infants in Three Books*, addressed to Marcellinus, A. D. 412, in *The Nicene and Post-Nicene Fathers*, vol. 5, ed. Philip Schaff (Grand Rapids: Eerdmans, 1971), p. 16 (1.3).

/43/   Augustine, *City of God*, trans. Bettenson, p. 545 (XIII.24).

/44/   Augustine, *City of God*, trans. Walsh, p. 270 (XIII.2). Augustine sees the immortal soul as an intermediary between the mortal body it animates and God. At first glance, this rationale appears to be an introjection of Neoplatonic terminology into Christian theology. The soul receives life from God and in turn, confers life and movement to the body. The body was not made as was the soul "so as to be incapable of dying" and "can be completely bereft of life." On further investigation, however, we discover that he interweaves Neoplatonic and specifically scriptural and Pauline understandings. He aligns himself more and more completely with the latter, especially in his later years. On no uncertain terms he rejects the simplistic view of the body as grossly inferior or of the human as less than a whole being, a "composite of body and soul." Indeed, in resurrection the body has a certain priority over the soul: it must be recreated before the soul can attain eternal life. (Henri Irénée Marrou, *The Resurrection and St. Augustine's Theology of Values*, trans. Mother Maria Consolata [Villanova, Pa.: Villanova University Press. 1966], pp. 12–16; and John Arthur Mourant, *Augustine on Immortality* [Villanova, Pa.: Villanova University Press, 1969], pp. 16–17, 34).

Calvin differs somewhat from Augustine in terms of what Heinrich Quistorp calls his "spiritualizing tendency" (*Calvin's Doctrine*, p. 62). The difference, however, remains more one of emphasis than of content. He gives enormous preeminence to the individual soul and the immortality granted at the moment of death. At times he devalues the body. He equates the soul with spirit or immortality and the body with sinful flesh and mortality. The "soul is the really good, better and nobler part," notes Quistorp. The body is "only its despicable abode, a rotten vessel" (Ibid., p. 63; see also Torrance, *Calvin's Doctrine*, pp. 26–27). Calvin himself describes the body as an "unstable, defective, corruptible, fleeting, wasting, rotting tabernacle" (*Institutes*, p. 717 [3.9.5]). "Almost no word is strong enough for Calvin in order to express this his disesteem, indeed contempt of the body. . . . He often calls it 'charongue'—a rotting carcase . . . 'but dung'" (Quistorp, *Calvin's Doctrine*, p. 60). The body comes from below, formed from the loam of the earth and returns thence. The soul comes from above, from the living breath of God and must return hence. The soul truly lives only when divested of the fetters of the body and when "freed from the prisonhouses . . . of clay . . . the tabernacle of the flesh" (Calvin, *Institutes*, pp. 184–186 [1.15.2]). Instead of a cohesion of body and soul, the soul stands in dualistic tension with the body. Immortality is more an escape of the individual soul from imprisonment in the body than it is a communal resurrection and reunion of bodies and souls at the end of time. He emphasizes the imperishability of the soul and deemphasizes the necessary resurrection of the body (Quistorp, *Calvin's Doctrine*, p. 73).

/45/   Augustine, *Treatise on Forgiveness and Baptism*, p. 16 (1.3, 5).

/46/   Calvin, *Institutes*, 195 (1.15.8).

/47/   John Calvin, *Commentaries on the Book of Genesis* 2:7, vol. 1, trans. John King (Grand Rapids: Eerdman's, 1948), pp. 112–113.

/48/   Augustine, *City of God*, trans. Bettenson, p. 524 (XIII.15).

/49/   John Calvin, *Commentaries on the Epistles of Paul the Apostle to the Romans and to the Thessalonians* 6:22, 23; 7:13, trans. Ross MacKenzie, eds. David W. Torrance and Thomas F. Torrance (Grand Rapids: Eerdman's, 1960), pp. 135–136, 146.

/50/   Augustine, *City of God*, trans. Walsh, p. 295 (XIV.1).

/51/   Augustine, *City of God*, trans. Bettenson, pp. 537 (XIII.23), 512–513 (XIII.3).

/52/   Calvin, *Institutes*, pp. 248–150 (2.1.6–7). Emphasis added.

/53/   Schleiermacher, *Christian Faith*, p. 243 (59.3).

/54/   Ibid., p. 281 (69, postscript).

/55/   Schleiermacher, *Christian Faith*, pp. 291–292 (72.1), 300 (72.4).

/56/   Langdon Gilkey, "Meditation on Death and Its Relation to Life," in *Instituto Di Studi Filosofici* (Roma: N. p., 1981), pp. 20–21.

/57/   Schleiermacher, *Christian Faith*, pp. 241–243 (59, postscript).

/58/   Ibid., p. 317 (75.3).

/59/   Ibid., p. 301 (72.4).

/60/   Ibid., p. 315 (75.1).

/61/   Ibid., p. 244 (59.3).

/62/   Ibid., pp. 319 (76.2), 315 (75.1).

/63/   Ibid., p. 243 (59, postscript). See also p. 187 (48.2).

/64/   Ibid., pp. 315–316 (75.1), 319 (76.2).

/65/   Ibid., p. 340 (82.2).

/66/   Ibid., p. 317 (75.2, 3). Emphasis added.

/67/   Ibid., p. 320 (76.3).

/68/   Augustine, *Enchiridian, Or Manual to Laurentius Concerning Faith, Hope, and Charity*, trans. Ernest Evans (London: Richard Clay, 1953), p. 95 (109); Mourant, *Augustine on Immortality*, p. 26.

/69/   Augustine, *City of God*, trans. Walsh, p. 270 (XIII.2); idem., *Enchiridion*, pp. 79 (.92), and 98 (.122). The minute life begins we can see evidence of the first death in the soul's inability to rule over the body. Because the soul willingly rebels against God, God abandons it. Yet when God deserts it, it must, against its will, abandon the body. In other words, apart from God the soul no longer rules over the body as God had ordained. The body is then subject to corruptibility until it dies completely, "wasted and worn out with old age." Then the second part of the first death is complete. In the first part the soul "becomes foolish" in its disobedience. In the second part the body becomes progressively more "lifeless," "corrupted, either by age or by disease, or by various afflictions, until it comes to the last affliction which all call death." (Augustine, *The Trinity*, trans, Stephen McKenna, in *The Fathers of the Church*, vol. 45 [Washington, D. C.: Catholic University of America Press, 1963], p. 135 [IV.3.5]). This physical dissolution throughout life is the soul's burden. "For in spite of his will, his spirit is . . . troubled and his body feels pain, grows old, and dies. Now, if only our nature, wholly and in all its parts would obey our will, we would not have to suffer this and all our other ills so unwillingly." (Augustine, *City of God*, trans. Bettenson, pp. 510–511. See also idem., *The Trinity*, p. 150 [IV.13.16] and XIII.2]).

/70/   Calvin, *Commentary on Genesis* 2:16, pp. 127–128.

/71/   John Calvin, *Commentary on John* 21:18, Joannis Calvini Opera, in Corpus Reformatorum (Brunswich, 1969–96) 74:455, cited by Wallace, *Calvin's Doctrine*, p. 266, n. 6. Augustine has also spoken about this, less in terms of fear of extinction and more in terms of the desire to exist. "Merely to exist," he says, "is, by the very nature of things, so pleasant that in itself it is enough to make even the wretched unwilling to die." Even lifeless bodies, plants, and animals "shrink from annihilation." They show "in every movement . . . that they long to live and escape destruction" (*City of God*, trans. Walsh, pp. 236–237 [XI.27]). The struggle to put death off runs deep: "I know you want to keep living," he tells his congregation. "You do not want to die. And you want to pass from this life to another in such a way that you will not rise again, as a dead man, but fully alive and transformed. This is what you desire. This is the deepest human feeling: mysteriously, the soul itself wishes and instinctively desires it" (*Sermon*, 344, 4, cited by Peter Brown, *Augustine of Hippo: A Biography* [Berkeley: University of California Press, 1969], p. 431, n. 6).

/72/   Wallace, *Calvin's Doctrine*, p. 267.

/73/   Mourant, *Augustine on Immortality*, p. 19.

/74/   Calvin, *Commentary on Ephesians* 2:1, *Institutes, Commentaries, and Tracts* (Edinburgh: Calvin Translation Society, 1843–55), cited by Torrance, *Calvin's Doctrine*, p. 108, n. 3.

/75/   Calvin, *Commentary on Romans* 5:21, cited by Quistorp, *Calvin's Doctrine*, p. 76.

/76/   Augustine, *City of God*, trans. Bettenson, p. 517 (XIII.8).

/77/   Augustine, *The Trinity*, pp. 133–136 (IV.2.4; IV.3.5, 6).

/78/   Mourant, *Augustine on Immorality*, p. 21.

/79/   Augustine, *The Trinity*, p. 150 (IV.12.15).

/80/   Augustine, *City of God*, trans. Bettenson, pp. 516–517 (XIII.7).

/81/   Augustine, *City of God*, p. 515 (XIII.6).

/82/   Ibid., pp. 517 (XIII.8), and 515 (XIII.5).

/83/   Augustine, *City of God*, trans. Walsh, p. 275 (XIII.6).

/84/   Augustine, *City of God*, trans. Bettenson, p. 513 (XIII.4).

/85/   Augustine, *Treatise on Forgiveness and Baptism*, p. 66 (II.54).

/86/   Augustine, *Confessions*, pp. 204–205 (IX.12).

/87/   Calvin, *Institutes*, p. 717 (3.9.5).

/88/   He is pleased that upon his wife's death, he did what he could to keep himself from being "overwhelmed with grief." He controls his sorrow so that his duties are not "interfered with." Through Christ's strength, "this heavy affliction" did not overcome him (Calvin, *Letters*, in Clebsch, *Pastoral Care*, pp. 228–229).

/89/   Calvin, *Institutes*, pp. 710–711 (3.8.10).

/90/   Ibid., p. 523 (2.16.14). See also Quistorp, *Calvin's Doctrine*, p. 50; and Wallace, *Calvin's Doctrine*, p. 270.

/91/   Calvin, *Institutes*, p. 707 (3.8.7).

/92/   Calvin, *Commentary on 2 Timothy* 4:6, *Corpus Reformatorum*

(Calvin's Works, ed. Baum and others, Brunswick, 1863–1900), 80, 389, cited by Quistorp, *Calvin's Doctrine*, p. 59, n. 3. Emphasis added. To postulate the total death of believers, Quistorp observes, would threaten Calvin's idea of God. The soul is the seat of God's image. Total death would call into question the progress of regeneration (Quistorp, *Calvin's Doctrine*, pp. 56, 74, 78–81).

/93/　　Calvin, *Institutes*, p. 717 (3.9.5).

/94/　　Calvin, *Commentary on Luke* 12:50; C. R. 73, 682, cited by Quistorp, *Calvin's Doctrine*, pp. 56–57, n. 1.

/95/　　Calvin, *Institutes*, 718 (3.9.5).

/96/　　Calvin, *Institutes*, pp. 716 (3.9.4), 724–725 (3.10.6). See also Quistorp, *Calvin's Doctrine*, pp. 46–47; and Wallace, *Calvin's Doctrine*, p. 32.

/97/　　See Horace Leland Friess's editorial note, trans., *Soliloquies by Friedrich Schleiermacher* (Chicago: Open Court Publishing Co., 1957), p. 86, n., cited by Brian Gerrish, *Tradition and the Modern World: Reformed Theology in the Nineteenth Century* (Chicago: University of Chicago Press, 1978), p. 155, n. 9.

/98/　　Hick, *Death and Eternal Life*, pp. 209–210.

/99/　　Schleiermacher, *Christian Faith*, p. 186 (48.2).

/100/　　Friedrich Schleiermacher, *On Religion: Speeches to its Cultured Despisers*, trans. John Oman, with an Introduction by Rudolf Otto (New York: Harper and Row, 1958), pp. 130–131.

/101/　　Schleiermacher, *Soliloquies*, p. 91.

/102/　　Gerrish, *Tradition and the Modern World*, p. 154; Schleiermacher, *On Religion*, p. 100.

/103/　　Ibid., p. 101.

/104/　　Ibid., pp. 20, 101 (see n. 21, pp. 117–118).

/105/　　Schleiermacher, *Soliloquies*, pp. 97, 103.

/106/　　Schleiermacher, *Christian Faith*, pp. 315–316 (75.1).

CHAPTER II

ILLUSTRATIONS IN PSYCHOLOGY: THE SHIFT
FROM EMPIRICAL TO QUASI-RELIGIOUS
AND MORAL VIEWS

Philip Rieff makes a forceful argument in *The Triumph of the Therapeutic* that the "battle between Freud and Calvin" is the "major cultural conflict" of contemporary society. He contends that Freud's "psychological man" competes with Calvin's "religious man" as the dominant symbolic of modern character. Don S. Browning captures the essence of Rieff's thesis:

> The symbolics that surrounded these men, their thought, and the social movements that followed them have constituted, during the first half of the twentieth century, the major cultural options contending for supremacy in organizing those "smaller units of the social self," i.e., the character and self-definition of modern Western man.[1]

In Rieff's eyes "the battle is largely over" and "Freud has clearly emerged the victor."[2] Today persons construct their worlds with psychological imagery by second nature. They talk more easily about unconscious wishes and sexual drives than about bending desires in faithful obedience to a higher power. This phenomenon has definite implications for modern views of death and its moral import.

Whether or not Freud has truly triumphed, few experiences of life, including its termination, escape his influence. Not only do we possess new vocabulary but we make decisions according to new psychological ideals. In other words, Freud initiated a "moral value revolution."[3] This revolution plays a crucial role in the moral confusion surrounding death. For a manifestation of our tendency to "psychologize" death, we need only survey the bookstore's stack of

self-help and popular, religious literature. Advice for the terminally
ill and the grieving comes primarily from psychology and, digging
slightly deeper, from Freud.

Many commentators fail to notice that Freud's moral imagination has insidiously imposed order and form on the disorderly
experience of dying. His psychological propositions, and behind
them, his philosophical assumptions, are assumed as givens.[4] Yet do
we dare ignore the meanings, ethical and otherwise, embedded in
these ideas? Do we not need to slow down and ask, as Tracy does,
whether this way of being in the world is a valuable one for the
ethical person?[5]

Paul Ricoeur and Philip Rieff suggest answers to these questions. Both view Freud's psychological infrastructure as "a monu-
ment of our culture." His work interprets culture for us and introduces a "new understanding of man."[6] In Book II of *Freud and
Philosophy,* Ricoeur momentarily suspends his philosophical investigation to give Freud's writings a detailed analytical reading. He
demonstrates that the entrance of the idea of the death instinct later
in Freud's life marks a decisive transition. The concept of a death
instinct turns "psychoanalysis . . . from science to philosophy, perhaps even to mythology," or from a scientific, quantitative "physico-
physiological theory" of human behavior to a "sort of mythical
philosophy."[7] The original theory becomes a "dramaturgy, all the
'personages' of which are mythical: Eros, Thanatos, and Ananke."[8]

Ricoeur's analysis helps us uncover implicit normative horizons of Freud's observations on death. Rieff takes us one step
further. His study of the impact of psychoanalysis on moral character
confirms what Ricoeur suggests: in Freud we discover the "mind of
the moralist" and, in Freud's followers, the reappearance of faith and
new moralisms.[9] Research on death in psychology is a prime example.

The necessary restrictions of this chapter are apparent. I cannot begin to exhaust Fraud's thought on death or clarify the many,
sometimes contradictory, ways in which he employs the concept of
death instinct. This is not my main intent. Rather, I want to demonstrate the "psychologizing" of death in psychology and culture at
large, first, by documenting pivotal modifications in Freud's writings
that appear with the introduction of the death instinct, and second,
by documenting a shift from an empirical to a quasi-religious, moralistic approach to death in Freud and in his followers.

Freud's Theory: From "Scientism" to "Romanticism"

Freud began his career in the last two decades of the nineteenth century, first as lab assistant to the toughminded physiologist Ernst Brücke and then as a physician and neurologist. It comes as no surprise, therefore, that when his interests narrowed to the treatment of hysterics and other emotional disorders, he developed a theory of psychopathology modeled after natural science and medicine. His early "Project for a Scientific Psychology," an ambitious, but largely unsuccessful, attempt in 1895 to formulate a physiologically oriented psychology, is a good example. He views the psyche as a "machine" governed by measurable units of exchangeable energy and the laws of physics. He intends, he says, "to furnish us with a psychology which shall be a natural science."[10]

Although Freud is literally "plagued" by the drive to formulate a theory of mental functions based upon "quantitative considerations,"[11] a second urge afflicts him. He reveals in his 1927 postscript to *The Question of Lay Analysis* that

> After forty-one years of medical activity, my self-knowledge tells me that I have never really been a doctor in the proper sense. I became a doctor through being compelled to deviate from my original purpose; and the triumph of my life lies in my having, after a long and roundabout journey, found my way back to my earliest path.[12]

What is this "earliest path"? He has had "an overpowering need to understand something of the riddles of the world in which we live and perhaps even contribute something to their solution." In 1896 he defines this as a deep longing "for nothing else than philosophical knowledge." Philosophy has been and remains his "original ambition, before I knew what I was intended to do in the world." He believes he has attained his goal "by passing over from medicine to psychology," or, as Ricoeur adds, by returning "to philosophy by way of medicine and psychology."[13]

Yet Freud holds a distinct distaste for abstract philosophy. He disclaims any desire to read Nietzsche and argues against contrary evidence that he has not based his ideas on Schopenhauer.[14] He remains, Gregory Zilbourg contends, "an *organicist*" to the end. Freud never lost his nineteenth-century mechanistic bias that some-

day the whole complexity of human behavior would be reduced to a
still undiscovered physical or chemical reaction.[15]

Not until *Beyond the Pleasure Principle* in 1920 does death
take center stage and the death instinct a leading part.[16] Certainly
this new focus grew out of a reaction to World War I, the departure
of two of his sons for the front, his own cancer, and the unexpected
death of his daughter. Yet Freud actively tries to dispel any connection between the latter, the resulting depression, and the origin of
his theory of the death instinct in *Beyond the Pleasure Principle*.[17]

In either case, Freud's deflection to the question of the origin
and demise of life accentuates the tension between scientific mate-
rialism and philosophical speculation. On the one hand, he literally
transforms death from a moral, religious, and philosophical matter
to a subject for scientific scrutiny. He thereby sanctions and be-
queaths to posterity a positivistic model for the study of death. This
model pictures death in all its facticity as ultimately a biological and
at most, a psychological reality. Even in contemplating the nature of
human morality, he felt he was investigating purely scientific data,
distinct from any similar enterprise in moral philosophy and theology.

On the other hand, Freud's growing intrigue with death, what
some call his obsessive "preoccupation," bears witness to a change of
heart and mind.[18] He himself senses this change. In the 1935
postscript to *An Autobiographical Study* he observed:

> Shortly before I wrote this study it seemed as though my life
> would soon be brought to an end by the recurrence of a
> malignant disease; but surgical skill [the first of thirty-three
> operations for cancer of the jaw and the beginning of sixteen
> years of discomfort and pain] saved me in 1923. . . . In the
> period of more than ten years since then . . . I myself find that
> a significant change has come about . . . an alteration in my-
> self.[19]

He began to consider the hypothesis of two primary instincts, Eros
and the death instinct, one of his most "decisive contributions"
alongside the division of the personality into id, ego, and superego.
Almost despite himself, these theories became a tool for cultural
analysis and his interests "returned to the cultural problems which
had fascinated me long before."[20]

With the introduction of speculation on death, Freud's language undergoes significant revision. Quite simply, death alters Freud's scientific language of cause and effect and involves him more deeply in the "language of meaning" or "hermeneutics."[21] His work progresses, Ricoeur's asserts, from "a mechanistic representation of the psychic mechanism to a romantic dramaturgy of life and death."[22] He reworks the entire theory of instincts. Libido becomes the mythological figure of Eros over against Thanatos. Under the sign of death, we have in Ricoeur's words, "Truly a recasting from the top to bottom." The death instinct imposes an alteration on the preceding edifice that "reaches the very foundations of existence."[23]

What exactly is involved in this recasting? Freud creates the theory of the death instinct as part of a renewed outburst of productivity after what had appeared to be a final period of theoretical summation in 1915. He aims to "go beneath" his first two concepts of libido to "the very substrate of existence."[24] He claims in *Beyond the Pleasure Principle* that he has solved "the riddle of life" by supposing two instincts "struggling with each other from the first." These two instincts are universal characteristics of *all* living matter, "every vital process," even that of protoplasm itself.[25]

In the earlier chapters of *Beyond the Pleasure Principle* Freud attempts to whet our appetite. He sorts through elucidating, but inconclusive, data in a feigned effort to solve the odd observation that we repeat unpleasurable experiences. This contradicts his premise that all human motivation rests upon the pursuit of pleasure. There must be some other life force at work, he hints. Drawing out the drama by suspending solution, he hopes to convince, by the end of the book, "that *inanimate things existed before living ones*." Presupposing this, the other operational life force apparent in such inexplicable repetition-compulsion is the urge to restore this inanimate state, "*an earlier state of things* which the living entity has been obliged to abandon under the pressure"[26] of Eros, the "mischiefmaker," who has eternally disturbed the peace.[27]

The rest of the essay, Ricoeur notes, "consists . . . in pushing the hypothesis" that the aim of all life is death "to an extreme."[28] Life is merely a long complicated detour, with many circuitous paths, to death.[29]

That organisms bring their own destruction upon themselves, that "everything dies for *internal* reasons" is an idea that will capture the moral imagination of later psychology.[30] He maintains that there is no impulse to develop, progress, perfect. For Freud, Ricoeur reiterates,

> Life itself is not the will to change, to develop, but the will to
> conserve itself. . . . Change is imposed by external factors. . . ;
> progress is disturbance and divergence, to which life adapts in
> order to pursue its conservative aim at this new level.[31]

Freud's speculative, even apologetic, comments, adopted originally on a trial basis in *Beyond the Pleasure Principle*, become
dogmatic certainty three years later in *The Ego and the Id*. By
Civilization and Its Discontents in 1930, they gain such a hold on
him that he "can no longer think in any other way."[32] He confesses
to his student Ernest Jones that these tentative ideas that once only
privately amused him have now "become indispensable to him."[33]

Seeming to possess a life of their own, the ideas appear and
reappear throughout his later writings: the "phenomenon of life," or
"life itself," or "all life," "essentially consists" or "arises from" or can
be "explained" by the "concurrent or mutually opposing action of
these two instincts."[34] He thinks that he has arrived at the scientific
"simplification" that could account in toto for the kind of world in
which we live. The death instinct is "active in every particle" from
the "single cell" to the "most general characteristic of life." *Civilization and Its Discontents* carries the latter idea to its final global
application. The meaning of civilization's evolution itself lies in the
conflict and compromise between these two "'Heavenly Powers,'
eternal Eros . . . [and] his equally immortal adversary. . . . Death,"
as this "works itself out in the human species."[35] Culture represents, Ricoeur asserts, "the great theater of the 'battle of the gi-
ants.'"[36]

Freud does not deny the abstruse character of these speculations. He concedes that his instinctual theory as a whole has an
undeniable mythic character. We know about instincts only through
representatives once removed from the reality of "seeing" them
"clearly."[37] And in *Beyond the Pleasure Principle* he admits that his
latest theory cannot even lay claim to this. He bases his two earlier
theories on direct clinical observation of psychical representatives of
the instincts. We hear the "clamor" of the "mute" death instinct only
in the hostility discussed in "The Economic Problem in Masochism"
in 1924 and in *Civilization and Its Discontents* in 1930, long after he
has postulated the original theory.[38] Clinical confirmation does not
appear until "Analysis Terminable and Interminable" in 1937. He
admits that undoubtedly he leaves the reader with a "positively
mystical impression" of "sham profundity."[39] Unlike anything written prior, excessive hypothesis outweighs empirical verification.

Despite these concessions, however, Freud still feels that he has not departed from science. He does not lose hope of tying these speculations to more fundamental biological structures of life. In this effort, *Beyond the Pleasure Principle* resembles the materialistic psychology of the "Project." He compares the life and death drives to the processes of anabolism and catabolism and to the scientific distinction between the soma and germplasm.[40] In later writings he refers to examples in nature—"the whole of embryology," the "power of regenerating lost organs," the "spawning of migrations of fishes, the migratory flights of birds" or in physics, the magnetic forces of "attraction and repulsion"[41]—to bolster his argument.

By applying psychoanalysis beyond its original locus of dreams and neuroses to the subject of death, Freud elevates his narrowly circumscribed study of psychopathology to "its initial philosophical horizon."[42] Eros and Thanatos become symbolic, orienting images that operate like religious postulates. They constitute metaphors, Browning argues,

> for the ultimate or more determinative context of human expe-
> rience. . . . He [Freud] takes a positivist stand that these and
> only these two forces are the relevant effective forces influenc-
> ing human action. At this level, his thinking is not unlike
> religious thinking in that he takes two metaphors from common
> experience and uses them to give exhaustive account of the
> effective forces determinative of human destiny. His positivism
> ends in a fideism—a belief that these and only these forces
> constitute the ultimate context of experience.[43]

Ricoeur suspects Freud of emulating the philosophy of Goethe and romantic thought:

> [Freud] sets free the romantic demands of his thought which
> the mechanistic scientism of his first hypotheses had only
> masked over.
>   Thus what is suspect in this essay *[Beyond the Pleasure
> Principle]* is also the most revealing: under a scientific surface,
> or rather under the coating of a scientific mythology, there
> arises the Naturphilosophie which the young Freud admired in
> Goethe.[44]

The theory is recast. Freud moves from "scientism" to "romantism." A conceptual revolution occurs, a revolution symbolized by "the great emblematic roles of Eros, Thanatos, and Ananke."[45]

Freud: The Mind of the Moralist

Eros and Thanatos partially describe the nature of reality, but they are by no means exhaustive. Moreover, if Freud intended these as exhaustive, they deserve critical comparison with equally valid metaphors in religion and philosophy.

Furthermore, these metaphors belong to a moral as well as a conceptual revolution and merit critical reflection on this level also. Freud's extremely negative view of moral authority evolves hand in hand with his theory of the death instinct. Ethics itself is a function of the latter. For in the "harshly restraining, cruelly prohibiting quality" of "even ordinary normal morality," the mute instinct begins to cry out. [46] The mute instinct cries out mainly through the superego, the enforcing agency of the psyche that results from internalization of parental authority. The superego becomes harsh when the death instinct is turned in on the self rather than projected outwardly in war and hatred. The superego, like

> a pure culture of death instinct, . . . manifests itself essentially
> as a sense of guilt . . . and . . . develops such extraordinary
> harshness and severity towards the ego . . . [that] it often
> enough succeeds in driving the ego into death, if the latter
> does not fend off its tyrant in time. [47]

Freud sees this harassment of a guilty conscience as a major source of neurotic suffering: "in fact it may be precisely this element that determines the severity of a neurotic illness." [48]

In *Civilization and Its Discontents* morality and guilt embody more than personal conflict between ego and superego. Guilt expresses the conflict between Eros and the instinct of death or destruction, or between love and death on yet a broader cultural scale. Guilt is "now seen as the instrument which culture uses . . . against aggressiveness." [49] Culture pits internalized violence against externalized violence, inner death against outer death so that civilization can survive and develop. The death instinct, the severity of the superego, even moral precepts are irreplaceable elements in maintaining social stability. [50]

If Freud sees the death instinct as integral to morality and civilization, what does he have to say about death as "my own destiny," rather than as death instinct? He advocates an ideal of resignation to and acceptance of death with a lucidity free of illusion. The world remains basically an inhospitable environment, not a context in which aspirations or values have much, if any, voice. Rather "dark, unfeeling and unloving powers determine human destiny" in a way that is "incompatible with a universal principle of benevolence or . . . of justice."[51] Death is simply one of the remorseless, immutable laws of blind nature. To face harsh necessity, Ananke, or in Ricoeur's words, "the world shorn of God . . . an order that is anonymous and impersonal," we must have "a wisdom that dares to face the harshness of life. Such wisdom is an art of 'bearing the burden of existence.'"[52]

Persons resist "bearing the burden" on a number of fronts. As later psychologists frequently quote, "at bottom no one believes in his own death, or to put the same thing in another way, in the unconscious every one of us is convinced of his own immortality."[53] He likens people to the dreamer who, when "seized with a presentiment of death," knows all too well how to "turn even that dreaded event into wish-fulfillment," or to a character in Shakespeare's *The Merchant of Venice* or *King Lear* who believes he can ward off the last of the Fates, the "Goddess of Death," by choosing beauty and the "Goddess of Love." Persons pretend that

> Choice stands in the place of necessity, of destiny. In this way man overcomes death, which he has recognized intellectually. No greater triumph of wish-fulfillment is conceivable. A choice is made where in reality there is [only] obedience to compulsion.[54]

We also resist acquiescence to fate through misplaced fear. Freud derides the reality of fear of death by declaring it simply a secondary derivation of the fear of castration. "Fear of death should be regarded as analogous to the fear of castration." Since all anxiety is at heart a reaction to this *real* situation of danger, and since death is neither experienced nor unconsciously accepted, fright at death can never be real. It is only the final developmental "transformation which the fear of the superego undergoes . . . fear projected on to the powers of destiny."[55]

A final obstacle to acceptance of death is religious hope. In modernity, as morality became the only domain that religion could continue to claim as its own, it began to construe death not as "the extinction" and "return to inorganic lifelessness" that it is, but as a new kind of existence in which "all good is rewarded and all evil punished."[56] But the illusion of the reward of heavenly life after death, Freud complains, is better left "to the angels and the sparrows."

For Freud "hushing up," "shelving," "eliminating" death in these varying ways exact too much from earthly life and its enhancement. Like King Lear, persons must learn the message of "Eternal wisdom" which bids us to "renounce love, choose death and make friends with the necessity of dying."[57] He offers even more explicit counsel in "Reflections on War and Death": "*Si vis vitam, para mortem*. If you would endure life, be prepared for death." For "To endure life remains, when all is said, the first duty of all living beings. Illusion can have no value if it makes this more difficult for us."[58] In *The Future of an Illusion* Freud writes, "As for the great necessities of Fate, against which there is no help . . . endure them with resignation."[59] To do otherwise is to live "psychologically beyond our means."

Embedded in this advice about death is what Rieff calls Freud's "penultimate ethic," a negative ethic of pleasurable release from all community loyalties and renunciatory moral systems. Rather than renunciation, Freud encourages pursuit of individual "fulfillment based on an appetitive mode." "Private wants of private man," each cultivating his "own plot," define the appetitive mode. Where "religious man was born to be saved; psychological man is born to be pleased."[60] Through cultivated detachment and analytic toleration of ambiguity, persons should achieve a durable and prudent sense of personal well-being and cautious amplitude in living.

Browning translates these observations into the language of moral philosophy:

> In terms of moral philosophy, Freud's image of human fulfillment was a trait-ethical egoism of a hedonistic kind, even though his hedonism was restrained, skeptical, and cautious. . . . Behind Freud's trait-ethical egoism is an implicit ethical egoist theory of obligation, which suggests that our only objective moral requirement is to live in such a way as cautiously or prudently to enhance our own sense of well-being.[61]

Freud's "culture of detachment," as Browning calls it, advocates a "retreat into self-conscious and prudential husbandry of one's pleasures in a basically inhospitable world."[62]

Ricoeur adds a final comment. He notes that full acceptance of death cannot rest on mere intellectual knowledge of Ananke. Knowledge of necessity alone, apart from Eros and its vital energy, is "lost

in an impasse." Besides the "path of disillusion," genuine acceptance must contain an affective component and a principle which
Ricoeur characterizes as the "love of life." To accept death one must
"overcome a final counterfeit which would be precisely the death
instinct, the wish to die."[63] Against this only Eros can struggle. The
moral ideal in this case is "to struggle against the human instinct of
aggression and self-destruction, hence never to love death, to love
life, in spite of my death."[64] There is nothing explicit along these
lines in Freud, but Ricoeur believes that the idea appears implicitly
in various allusions and occasional remarks.

We glimpse this attitude in the drama of Freud's own bout
with cancer and with death, whether true or only a romantic legend.
In a visit to an ailing Freud in London in 1938, Stefan Zweig gave
birth to the story of Freud's "Olympian resignation" and "'mature'
acceptance" of death:

> It was my first experience of a true sage, exalted beyond
> himself, to whom neither pain nor death longer counted as a
> personal experience but as a supra-personal matter of observa-
> tion and contemplation; his dying was no less a moral fact than
> his life.[65]

Marthe Robert verifies that Freud strove, at times with boundless
energy, to remain "master of his fate" despite his debilitating illness.[66] Theoretically, as well as personally, he appreciated the value
of life and sought in his writing not only to accustom us to death's
necessity but to embolden us "above all . . . to sing the paean of life,
of libido, of Eros!"[67]

Nevertheless, the dissonance between Freud's negative ethic
of detached resignation and the implicit commitment to the enrich-
ment of life remains. The principle of cold consideration of reality
and the principle of lyrical love of life are never fully harmonized,
connected, or unified. Only in a limited way does Freud answer the
problems posed by the question of death.

Freud's Followers: The Return of "Faith" and New Moralisms

Contemporary psychologies of death are still attempting to
resolve the ambiguities, moral and otherwise, in Freud's thought on
death. Critic Lee Yearley asserts,

> Freud never gives us even the beginnings of an adequate
> account of what morality would be if it were not the patholog-
> ical phenomenon born of the death instinct that he has de-
> scribed. . . . [This] striking absence . . . of any developed view
> of nonpathological morality left those who accepted some sig-
> nificant part of the Freudian vision with the job of "complet-
> ing" Freud's work either by extrapolating hints in it or by
> developing it in directions that it "should" have gone.[68]

Rieff notes a similar development. In Weberian style, he assumes
that "culture is made from the top down."[69] A small number of
captivating, colorful personalities establish and maintain civilized
values. Freud numbered among this elite. We live, Rieff contends,
in an age of "psychological man" which Freud created as the only
viable replacement for three other seemingly antiquated Western
ideals, "religious," "political," and "economic man."[70] The psychoanalytic model gathered cultural momentum when psychoanalysis
became a "transferable art." Eventually it became an organized
movement with an official cadre of teachers who pass on the tradition and the canon or the authoritative body of knowledge.[71]

Although Freud intended to usher in a new "unfaith" or
"unreligion" and thereby dislodge the prevailing but disintegrating
authority of the Christian symbol system, his followers "refused to
approach reality in his neutralist terms." Instead, "faith reappeared,
understood [now] in terms of therapy."[72] Rieff laments the adultera-
tion of the tradition in his Preface to *Freud: The Mind of the
Moralist:* "Vulgar Freudianism has buried Freud."[73] Adler, Jung,
Reich, among others, have reinstated a "theology at the end" of their
therapies in place of Freud's strict "anti-doctrine." Instead of the
negative community of the therapeutic in which one learns the
power to choose without needing to pledge loyalty to any one
choice, these psychologists created "commitment therapies," "psychotherapeutic faiths," and "fresh sacramental language."[74]

Similar "religious aspirations" lie behind the fascination with
the subject of death in psychology. Controversy over the idea of a
death instinct was only the starting point. From there psychoanalysis and psychologists began to argue that models of personality
and pathology needed, alongside an understanding of life's early
phases, amplified representation of death.

More specifically, the development from Freud's death instinct
to the mass production of death literature began slowly at first with
Eric Lindemann's research on the symptomatology of acute grief in
1944.[75] This was succeeded about a decade later by Geoffrey Gorer's

article and oft-quoted title, "The Pornography of Death."[76] In the following year, Herman Feifel battled with the American Psychological Association over the appropriateness of death as a subject of psychological study at the annual meeting. He earns recognition for forcing the discussion of death into academic circles, publishing one of the first collections of essays in psychology on death in 1959.[77]

Others are acclaimed for moving the discussion into popular press in the years since: Jessica Mitford and her social criticism in *The American Way of Death* in 1963; Kübler-Ross and her "landmark" or "path-breaking" *On Death and Dying* in 1969; and Ernest Becker and the cultic following created by his *Denial of Death* in 1973.[78] On one level, the general aim was to examine the relationship between death and neurosis. On another level, however, the intent was to promote psychology as a new source of guidance and as a new model replacing seemingly antiquated religious counsel.

Becker's book is an excellent specimen of this conjecture. He all but confirms Rieff's worst premonitions. He asserts that belief in the providential and the sacred has collapsed. Psychology, a "new belief system," must come to the rescue.[79] He proposes a "closure of psychoanalysis on religion" or a "merger" between psychology and what he calls "mythico-religious perspectives" as the only way to deal with denial of death. Psychology offers a salvation of sorts when it "gives way to 'theology,'"—a unique "theology" that he sets off by punctuation marks to indicate his peculiar psychological definition.[80]

Likewise, Norman Brown agrees in *Life Against Death*, "construction of a human consciousness strong enough to accept death is a task in which philosophy and psychoanalysis can join hands."[81] Carl Jung, whom Rieff finds particularly culpable of perverting the original doctrine, cannot resist delving into the deeper meanings of human mortality. He moves quickly past Freud's analysis to what Rieff describes as "religious aspirations to reinterpret man as a whole and thus cure him in his entirety," including that part that faces death.[82] His essay, "The Soul and Death," is the first chapter in Feifel's pace-setting collection. The desire to return to a "state of rest" is not, as Freud would have us believe, purely a biological drive, he argues. Rather, persons should "grant goal and purpose" to the descent of life:

> We are so convinced that death is simply the end of a process that it does not occur to us to conceive of death as a goal and a

fulfillment . . . of life's meaning . . . in the truest sense, instead of mere meaningless cessation.[83]

Life resembles the rising and setting of the sun, a clock wound up
and running down, or a "parabola of a projectile which, disturbed
from its initial state of rest, rises and then returns to a state of
repose." He refers to Christianity and Buddhism for additional
evidence that death is life's consummation, rather than simply its
end. Only when he suggests that life's trajectory continues as a
dotted line "in a form of existence beyond space and time . . .
inadequately . . . described as 'eternity'" does he finally admit that
he has moved beyond the "competence of empirical science," but
not until then.[84]

Jung has definite moral obligations in mind here that he does
not fully articulate, but urges upon his readers nonetheless. Persons, he says, ought to attune themselves to this natural rise and fall
of life's "foundations." Either learn to live according to the "law of
nature" and "nature's timing," or be subject to "soul-sickness,"
"neurotic restlessness," and "meaninglessness."[85]

> As a physician, I am convinced that it is hygenic to discover in
> death a goal toward which one can strive and that shrinking
> away from it is something unhealthy and abnormal which robs
> the second half of life of its purpose. I therefore consider
> religious teaching of life hereafter as consonant with psychic
> hygiene.[86]

He talks about the "urge to set to rights whatever is still wrong"
prior to death, but calls this a "psychological," not a moral, "preparatory act."[87]

These reflections demonstrate, as Ariès notes, "not only the
beginning of a scientific bibliography on death, but . . . a turning
point in the history of attitudes toward death" with Freud as a key
figure. He transformed death from a subject of religious consideration to one of scientific investigation and explanation. In general, he
sought to make the study of the human mind and behavior analogous to the hard sciences, the disciplines of physics, chemistry, and
biology.[88] Although this pursuit was tempered somewhat at the time
he turned his attention to death later in his life, he still refused to
acknowledge that in investigating philosophical and moral questions
of death he had moved beyond the discipline of empirical psychology as he himself had defined it. He contended that he was dealing

strictly with "positive" facts and empirical observations about lower
biological, instinctual, and evolutionary processes.

Freud's followers do not always confess their indebtedness to
him. Yet most assume as did he that their commentary remains
morally neutral. Despite philosophical and religious entanglements,
they claim that their studies of death rest upon observation, experiment, and unbiased report.

What happens to the event of death when studied under the
auspices of such strict value neutrality? Ultimately, death is reduced
to a purely scientific, value-free experience. From Freud's perspective, death becomes simply a "return to inorganic lifelessness."[89]
He holds little regard for the moral qualities of its victims. He
thereby establishes a precedent for the sharp separation of fact from
value in psychological studies of death and for the general separation
of psychological studies from ethical reflection of any kind. The
pattern, set in *Beyond the Pleasure Principle*, is unfurled and reified
in his followers. They tend to consider ethics tangential or irrelevant. Death is understood within a new conception of reality in
which "psychological process" defines the whole of reality.[90] Dying
is psychologically predetermined and explained, whether by the
death instinct or some other exhaustive psychological category.

Yet what happens when psychology becomes *the* interpretative
framework to which people look when seeking counsel in the face of
death? Psychology loses its claim to value neutrality. Psychologists
began to see psychology as responsible as religion and philosophy
for examining the meaning of death and thereby deviated subtly
from Freud's original postulation of moral impartiality. Almost inevitably what is considered a purely investigatory study—the gather-
ing of data, the testing of hypotheses, the formulation of observations on human behavior—grows into normative recommendations
about how individuals and society should regard the fact of mortality. In shifting from explanation of human behavior based on early
childhood experiences to judgments about the other end of the life
cycle even Freud's "value-free" observations become value-loaded.
Psychological theory becomes a powerful means for controlling
human behavior. Yet seldom do the psychologists question the moral
paradigms that have crept into their work.

In a sense, we have avoided articulation of these paradigms,
much less explicit critique, for too long. The efforts of the "secular
theologists," as Rieff calls them, to "psychologize" death and rid
society of moralisms only eventuates in new moralisms. We need to

look more closely at those who took up the job of "completing" Freud's thought. If we do, we may discover that Freud's "trait-ethical egoism of a hedonistic kind" continues to influence us. Or we may find that others have reshaped his thought in more satisfying ways.

Footnotes to Chapter II

/1/   Don S. Browning, *Generative Man: Psychoanalytic Perspectives* (New York: Dell, 1973), p. 35.
/2/   Ibid.
/3/   Lionel Trilling, Introduction to Ernest Jones, *The Life and Works of Sigmund Freud*, ed. and abridged by Lionel Trilling (New York: Basic Books, 1961), p. vii; Robert White, "The Concept of Healthy Personality," *The Counseling Psychologist* 4 (1973), p. 4, cited by Browning, *Pluralism and Personality*, p. 23, n. 3; Philip Rieff, ed., with an Introduction to Sigmund Freud, *General Psychological Theory* (New York: Macmillan, 1963), p. 20.
/4/   Even as astute and thorough a moral theologian as Kenneth Vaux employs Freud's metaphors of Eros and Thanatos with little reflection on the positioning of these images within a psychological framework or on the difference between their psychological and their religious and moral use. Vaux, *Will to Live*, pp. 12, 15–16.
/5/   Tracy, *Blessed Rage*, p. 79.
/6/   Paul Ricoeur, *Freud and Philosophy: An Essay on Interpretation*, trans. by Denis Savage (New Haven: Yale University Press, 1970), pp. xi–xii.
/7/   Ibid., pp. 72, 63.
/8/   Ibid., p. 158.
/9/   Philip Rieff, *Triumph of the Therapeutic: Uses of Faith after Freud* (New York: Harper and Row, 1968), p. 34.
/10/   Sigmund Freud, *The Origins of Psychoanalysis*, trans. Eric Mosbacher and James Strachey, with an Introduction by Ernst Kris (New York: Basic Books, 1954), p. 355, cited by Ricoeur, *Freud and Philosophy*, p. 71.
/11/   Sigmund Freud, cited by Jones, *Life and Work*, p. 226.
/12/   Sigmund Freud, *The Question of Lay Analysis: Conversations with an Impartial Person*, trans. and ed. James Strachey (New York: Norton, 1962), pp. 104–105.
/13/   Freud, *Origins*, p. 141, cites by Ricoeur, *Freud and Philosophy*, p. 86.
/14/   Stuart H. Hughes, *Consciousness and Society: The Reorientation of European Social Thought 1890–1930* (New York: Random House, 1977), pp. 106–107.
/15/   Gregory Zilboorg, Introduction to Sigmund Freud, *Beyond the Pleasure Principle*, trans. and ed. James Strachey (New York: Norton, 1961), p. x; and Paul Roazen, *Freud and His Followers* (New York: Knopf, 1971), pp. 523–524.

/16/   Death had figured in his work as early as *The Interpretation of Dreams*. He openly confesses in the Preface to the second edition in 1908 the central role played by his reaction to his own father's death in 1896 in his writing this magnum opus. The death of the father is easily "the most important event, the most poignant loss of a man's life" (*The Interpretation of Dreams*, trans. and ed. James Strachey [New York: Basic Books, 1965], p. xxvi). And the problem of war inspires his "Reflections upon War and Death" in 1915 (in *Character and Culture*, ed. with an Introduction by Philip Rieff [New York: Macmillan, 1963]).

/17/   Historian H. Stuart Hughes warns us against drawing direct casual links but himself proposes similar reasons for what he calls "a dramatic change" or "apotheosis" in Freud's intellectual orientation:

> There are a number of possible reasons—the emotional and moral shock of the first World War, which had brought financial ruin and the collapse of the political system under which he lived; his own ill health, which made sustained clinical work increasingly difficult; perhaps more than anything else, the specter of death, which after 1923 was always with him (*Consciousness and Society*, p. 136).

For other similar arguments, see Gruman, "Historical Introduction," pp. 111–112, and Jones, *Life and Work*, pp. 391–392, 402.

/18/   For examples of theories about Freud's preoccupation with death, see Trilling, Introduction to *Life and Work*, p. xii; Jacques Choron, *Modern Man and Mortality* (New York: Macmillian, 1964), pp. 68–69; Ernst Becker, *The Denial of Death* (New York: Free Press, 1973) pp. 97–105; and Jones, *Life and Work*, pp. 198, 202, 226, 343–344, 349, 432.

/19/   Sigmund Freud, *An Autobiographical Study*, trans. James Strachey (New York: Norton, 1963), pp. 122–123. See Jones, *Life and Work*, pp. 437–444, for further description of the discovery of Freud's cancer of the jaw.

/20/   Freud, *Autobiographical Study*, p. 123.

/21/   Paul Ricoeur, "A Philosophical Interpretation of Freud," in *The Philosophy of Paul Ricoeur: An Anthology of His Work*, ed. Charles E. Reagan and David Stewart (Boston: Beacon, 1978), p. 174.

/22/   Ibid., p. 173.

/23/   Ibid., p. 255; idem., "Philosophical Interpretation," p. 173.

/24/   Ricoeur, *Freud and Philosophy*, p. 311.

/25/   Freud, *Pleasure Principle*, pp. 54–55, n. 1; idem., *New Introductory Lectures on Psychoanalysis* (New York: Norton, 1933), p. 95.

/26/   Freud, *Pleasure Principle*, pp. 32, 30.

/27/   Sigmund Freud, *The Ego and the Id*, trans. Joan Rivere, ed. James Strachey (New York: Norton, 1962), p. 49.

/28/   Ricoeur, *Freud and Philosophy*, pp. 289–290.

/29/   Even self-preservation instincts function as "myrmidons of death." They only assure that the organism dies in its own way by warding off "any possible ways of returning to inorganic existence other than those immanent in the organism itself" (Freud, *Pleasure Principle*, p. 33).

/30/ Ibid., p. 32.
/31/ Ricoeur, *Freud and Philosophy*, p. 290.
/32/ Sigmund Freud, *Civilization and Its Discontents*, trans. and ed. James Strachey (New York: Norton, 1961), p. 66.
/33/ Jones, *Life and Work*, pp. 406–407.
/34/ Freud, *Civilization*, pp. 65–66; idem., "Why War?" in *Character and Culture*, p. 141; idem., "Analysis Terminable and Interminable," in *Therapy and Technique*, ed. with an Introduction by Philip Rieff (New York: Macmillan, 1963), pp. 261, 264; idem., *New Introductory Lectures*, p. 95; idem., *An Outline of Psychoanalysis*, trans. and ed. James Strachey (New York: Norton, 1969), pp. 5–8.
/35/ Freud, *Civilization*, pp. 69, 80.
/36/ Ricoeur, *Freud and Philosophy*, pp. 156, 293.
/37/ Freud, *New Introductory Lectures*, p. 84; idem., "Why War?" p. 143.
/38/ Freud, *Ego and Id*, p. 36; idem., "The Economic Problem in Masochism," in *General Psychological Theory*.
/39/ Freud, *Pleasure Principle*, pp. 53, 31, 48.
/40/ Ibid., pp. 40, 43.
/41/ Freud, "Analysis Terminable," p. 264; idem., *New Introductory Lectures*, pp. 91, 94.
/42/ Ricoeur, *Freud and Philosophy*, pp. 258, 155.
/43/ Browning, "Religioethical Thinking," p. 150.
/44/ Ricoeur, *Freud and Philosophy*, pp. 312–313.
/45/ Ibid., p. 256.
/46/ Freud, *Ego and Id*, p. 44.
/47/ Ibid., p. 43. Emphasis added.
/48/ Ibid., p. 40.
/49/ Ricoeur, *Freud and Philosophy*, p. 306.
/50/ They are still not, however, positive attributes in Freud's eyes. The sense of guilt is simply the "price we pay for our advance in civilization" (*Civilization and Its Discontents*, p. 81). Ideally, under the guidance of the "impartial instrument" of psychoanalysis, we can replace moralistic demands with "rational explanation" and infantile wishes with an adult *"education to reality"* (*The Future of an Illusion*, trans. and ed. James Strachey [New York: Basic Books, 1965], pp. 36, 49).
/51/ Freud, *New Introductory Lectures*, p. 147, cited by Stanley Edgar Hyman, *The Tangled Bank: Darwin, Marx, Frazer and Freud* (Atheneum, N.Y.: Grosset and Dunlap, 1959), pp. 415–416.
/52/ Ricoeur, *Freud and Philosophy*, pp. 327–328. Freud recalls his astonishment as a child that his "Fate" was death. Only upon his mother's insistence did he "acquiesce" to the reality that "I was later to hear expressed in the words '*Du Bist der Nature einen Tod schuldig.*'" Not without significance, he misquotes Shakespeare's "Thou owest *God* a death" here as "Thou owest *nature* a death." (Freud, *Interpretation of Dreams*, p. 238; idem., "Reflections upon Death," p. 121. For commentary on this quotation, see Roazen, *Freud and His Followers*, p. 537).
/53/ Freud, "Reflections upon Death," p. 122.
/54/ Freud, *Future of an Illusion*, p. 17; idem., "The Theme of the Three Caskets," in *Character and Culture*, p. 76.

/55/   Freud, *Inhibitions, Symptoms and Anxiety*, trans. Alix Strachey, rev. and newly ed. James Strachey (New York: Norton, 1959), pp. 56, 66. For a summary of Freud's position on fear of death, see Choron, *Modern Man*.
/56/   Freud, *Future of an Illusion*, pp. 18–19.
/57/   Freud, "Three Caskets," p. 78.
/58/   Freud, "Reflections upon Death," p. 133.
/59/   Freud, *Future of an Illusion*, p. 50.
/60/   Rieff, *Triumph of the Therapeutic*, pp. 50, 24–25.
/61/   Browning, "Religioethical Thinking," p. 151.
/62/   Browning, *Pluralism and Personality*, p. 39.
/63/   Ricoeur, *Freud and Philosophy*, p. 336.
/64/   Ibid., p. 338.
/65/   Stefan Zweig, *The World of Yesterday* (London: Cassess, 1953), p. 422, cited by Roazen, *Freud and His Followers*, p. 537, n. 29.
/66/   Marthe Robert, *The Psychoanalytic Revolution: Sigmund Freud's Life and Achievement*, trans. Kenneth Morgan (New York: Harcourt, Brace and World, 1966), p. 339. For other similar examples, see idem., *From Oedipus to Moses: Freud's Jewish Identity* (New York: Doubleday, 1976), pp. 160, 164, 167; Gruman, "Historical Introduction," p. 113; Hughes, *Consciousness and Society*, pp. 28, 138–139, 364, 387–388; Paul Roazen, *Freud: Political and Social Thought* (New York: Knopf, 1968), p. 167; Jones, *Life and Work*, p. 530.
/67/   Ricoeur, *Freud and Philosophy*, pp. 290–291.
/68/   Lee Yearly, "Freud as Critic and Creator of Cosmogonies and their Ethics," paper presented at "Cosmogony and Ethics" Conference, University of Chicago, October 1982, p. 36. pp. 37–38.
/69/   Browning, *Generative Man*, p. 36.
/70/   For a brief, but thorough, summary of this argument, see Philip Rieff, Introduction to *Therapy and Technique*, pp. 8–24.
/71/   Rieff, *Triumph of the Therapeutic*, pp. 31–32, 81–82, 102.
/72/   Ibid., p. 34.
/73/   Philip Rieff, *Freud: The Mind of the Moralist* (New York: Viking, 1959), pp. ix, xxiv.
/74/   Rieff, *Triumph of the Therapeutic*, pp. 29–30, 46–47, 77, 87–89.
/75/   Eric Lindemann, "Sympomatology and Management of Acute Grief," in *Death and Identity*, ed. Robert Fulton (New York: Wiley and Sons, 1965), pp. 186–201.
/76/   Geoffrey Gorer, "The Pornography of Death," in *Death, Grief, and Mourning*, Appendix 4 (Garden City, N.Y.: Doubleday, 1965), pp. 192–199.
/77/   Herman Feifel, *The Meaning of Death* (New York: McGraw-Hill, 1959).
/78/   Jessica Mitford, *The American Way of Death* (New York: Simon and Schuster, 1963); Elisabeth Kübler-Ross, *On Death and Dying* (New York: Macmillan, 1969); Becker, *Denial of Death*.
/79/   Ibid. pp. ix–xi, 272–273, 284.
/80/   Ibid. pp. x–xi, 196.
/81/   Norman Brown, *Life Against Death* (Middletown, Conn.: Wesleyan University Press, 1959), p. 108.
/82/   Rieff, *Triumph of the Therapeutic*, p. 88.

/83/   Carl G. Jung, "The Soul and Death," in *The Meaning of Death*, pp. 4, 9.

/84/   Ibid., pp. 5, 14–15.

/85/   Ibid., pp. 7, 15.

/86/   Carl G. Jung, "The Stages of Life," in *The Structure and Dynamics of the Psyche* (New York: Pantheon Books, 1960), p. 403.

/87/   Jung, "Soul and Death," pp. 10–11.

/88/   See Browning, *Religious Ethics*, pp. 11–12, 32–34.

/89/   *Future of an Illusion*, p. 19.

/90/   Hughes, *Consciousness and Society*, p. 66.

CHAPTER III

ILLUSTRATIONS IN MEDICINE: THE SHIFT TO TECHNICAL DEATH

The State of the Art in the History of Modern Medicine

The "health-illness-medicine matrix,"[1] as Renée Fox labels it, has major impact upon how persons in modern society regard death. Persons commonly, if not exclusively, blame revolutionary advances in medical technology for raising ethical issues about death. While certainly technology plays a key role, it accounts for only a single dimension of much deeper historical and cultural shifts that create moral turmoil. The problems of death in medicine are, Fox insists, "as much an expression of metamedical, collective conscience issues as. . .a consequence of spectacular developments in medicine and biology."[2] The same questions of values, beliefs, and meaning that preoccupy the medical sector trouble many other sectors of society. These questions emerge out of a much broader process of change, what some call a "major transformation of the zeitgeist,"[3] that has carried American society "into a new stage of modernity."[4]

Some introduce, but then only tentatively explore this. Daniel Maguire exemplifies this tendency. In his writing on whether or not physicians should induce death, he begins by suggesting that to understand modern struggles with death we must understand "foundational" changes in "patterns of thought" in medicine. Then he proceeds to a narrower, limited examination of a "shorter-term" question.[5] Maguire and scholars like him leave the bulk of the work for others. Few serious studies exist.

Part of the problem lies in the state of the art of the history of medicine in general. Heretofore researchers have all too frequently ignored the role of cultural components. A book such as Iago Galdston's *Social and Historical Foundations of Modern Medicine* stands out as a lone exception. He complains in the first line about this situation: to the best of his knowledge "no historian of medicine has ever composed a history of medicine in which cultural factors are presented as major determinants."[6] A stroll through the library stacks confirms his charge. Books based on "the 'great man, great discoveries' view of medical history and medical progress" fill the shelves.[7] A book selected at random is usually written by a scientist who views medicine as another development in the history of science. Typically it contains a chronological compilation of facts and dates of modern medicine's success or "creation" story, its heroes and their discoveries, from Hippocrates, the "father" of medicine, to Pasteur's discovery of the germ theory. Historians who have tried to relate medicine to culture have been criticized for doing so.

I do not mean to imply that I want to challenge this literary genre or offer a comprehensive cultural history in its place. On a minor scale, however, I do intend a different sort of history. I hope to broaden the ordinary analysis in the direction of a sociology of medical knowledge which situates medicine within a wider cultural context. I want to delineate two main trends that play an important role in my story of the development of a problem in our moral attitudes toward death. First, in the last two centuries, technical, scientific understandings of death have replaced magical, moral, and religious understandings. The image of clinical, mechanical death has triumphed in hospitals and more subtly, in the very consciousness of society. Second, this first trend has become more apparent because of a second trend—renewed awareness of medicine's moral horizons. Persons have grown increasingly sensitive in recent years to the integral role of moral values in medicine. This has instigated new definitions of the relationship between moral responsibility, health, illness, and death. Broadly speaking, we can discern a very general movement from a "value-laden" to a "value-free" to a "value-mixed" view of death. There has also been a shift from earlier views of death as caused by supernatural forces to scientific explanations of death as a natural necessity to the latest view of death as significantly affected by personal behavior and, even, as a voluntary choice.

Precedent, as well as resources, for this chapter come from selected readings in the relatively new field of bioethics,[8] literature that itself illustrates the second trend. Its authors represent a wide diversity of backgrounds and disciplines (sociology, philosophy, medicine, biology, law, theology), unified around the conviction that the values of culture influence theories of medicine and conversely, that medicine has greatly affected mores. From this perspective, the history of medicine is not just another chapter in the history of pure science. Medicine has far greater historical and cultural relevance.

From "Magico-Moral-Religious" to Technical and Scientific Views

Prior to the rise of modern medicine, society relied upon what Fox describes as a "less scientifically developed" medicine "embedded in a general magicoreligious way of thought that [was] deterministic, closed, monistic." Religion, medicine, and human mortality were closely intertwined. Persons considered illness and health "products of supernatural powers and evil human intent."[9] They assumed a personal will which could be influenced by appropriate behavior. Their reasoning reflected heightened sensitivity to moral probity. That is, they viewed illness with an eye to its spiritual and moral rather than physical dimensions and expected to learn about themselves and their world from their misfortunes. "Relatively few experiences are regarded as neutral or without meaning; and virtually none are considered to be fortuitous."[10] Preliterate and ancient near eastern civilization, for instance, held that disease resulted from basic disharmony between the person and the divine, or between the person and the environment. Early Jews and Christians related illness to divine retribution for moral failings through more explicit ethical and theological reasoning.[11] Even Hippocrates who divested medicine of magical practices and introduced rational observation of natural causes seldom divorced medical judgments from moral and philosophical values.[12]

> The Hippocratic physician was acutely aware that his therapeutic powers were limited by the force of nature. The repetition and the austere tone of the injunction to restrain one's therapy in the face of the overwhelming power of nature and not to exceed the possibilities of the medical art *elevate the counsel beyond a suggestion about technique to a moral direction;* for the physician to have exceeded the possibilities of his art was to commit the sin of hubris.[13]

The circumstances of illness and death differed radically from modern conditions. Pre-industrial mortality rates were characteristically high. They fluctuated widely from place to place and time to time as a result of famines, wars, and epidemics.[14] Persons lacked control over death. Medical treatments belonged to popular folk practice and were apt to inflict as much harm as help. The doctor's ministrations therefore often functioned as nature's ancillary, helping a person to die as much as to get well and relieving anxiety more than curing.[15]

Scholars differ on where they locate the turning point between archaic and modern medicine, or between a pre-industrial and an industrial mortality. Some credit Francis Bacon with inaugurating an era in which persons began to seek natural causes to ill health through direct observation and experiment. He held that *regnum hominis*, "the conquest of nature for the relief of man's estate," was not only possible but a binding obligation. And "there is ample suggestion," Leon Kass observes, that Bacon "regarded mortality itself as that part of man's estate from which he most needs relief."[16]

Others believe Descartes established "victory over death" as the goal of the modern scientific project. He predicted that someday we would "free" society of "maladies" and "even possibly of the infirmities of age" through scientific advance.[17] Still others broadly mark the advent of mechanized industry, analytical science, and medicine as a profession toward the end of the Middle Ages and the beginning of the Renaissance as the commencement of modern medicine.[18]

No matter which person or period is chosen, there is general consensus that the modern medical model was firmly established by the nineteenth century. This consensus is based on a few key events: establishment of the mono-causal germ theory of disease, large-scale decline in mortality rates, and various advances in science and technology. In the late 1800s Louis Pasteur, Joseph Lister, Robert Koch, and other scientists succeeded in isolating the germs of one infectious disease after another. They solved the enigma of smallpox, cholera, the plague, typhoid, tuberculosis, and other diseases in the inner sanctums of bacteriology laboratories.

Alongside this phenomenon, medicine began to acquire the pretense of an exact science like chemistry or physics. Its success resided in its positivistic emphasis on exact diagnosis and prognosis, empirical tests and measurable signs of disease, and in its narrow physicological concept of disease as caused by specific invasive agents. Setting aside ultimate matters of meaning and value, medical scientists were able to discover the tubercle bacillus as the cause of tuberculosis. Physicians joined others in the search for the "holy grail" of modern Western thought—pure objectivity and value-free science.[19] According to Fox's definition, modern medicine is

scientifically oriented, to the point of formally excluding magical and religious explanations of health, illness, life, and death
from its orbit. Questions of meaning . . . are either silently
ignored, latently rather than manifestly acknowledged, or si-
phoned off to religious specialists. A confident and energetic
rationality prevails. It is felt that disease and premature death
. . . will progressively give way to scientific searching, robust,
targeted action, and informed, organized care.[20]

A Cartesian-like peace settlement established the boundaries between philosophy, theology, and medicine, allotting the physician
the body and philosophers and theologians the mind. Rather than
an art, medicine became a science and the practicing physician a
technician. The scientific doctor, concerned primarily with the visible world of quantitative precision, became the "prototype of technological man."[21] "Technological man" considers indirect communication through machines and technology more valuable and accurate
than immediate response to a patient's own "subjective" sense of her
illness based upon direct communication. Faith in such "objective"
procedures flourished despite evidence that the measurements
themselves were often liable to significant error and even dependent
upon subjective interpretations themselves.[22] This dedication resided in mistrust of knowledge based on intuition or on natural
senses unaided by machine. The "empirical gaze," Michel Foucault
notes, became the "depository and source of clarity."[23] Persons
deemed anything not visible to this "gaze"—the immaterial, terms
such as thought, mind, will, imagination—inconsequential.

Modern Clinical Death

Scholars attached an assortment of labels to the period from
1800 to 1980. It became known as the "bacteriological era," the "era
of epidemic-death prevention," or the "century of progress," "promise and aspiration" culminating in the "age of cure" in the 1930s.[24]
Fueled by the remarkable progress made in curing disease, medicine quested for virtual immortality. Death could not only be
controlled but conquered, not only mastered, but eradicated. Critic
René Dubos contends that the "Garden of Eden" or "the golden age
of humanity which had so long been placed in the inaccessible past
. . . was now promised by scientists for the near future." Medical
elimination of death would issue in "the millenium."[25]
Now that death was susceptible to scientific investigation, it

appeared intelligible, uniform, predictable. Scientists could exhaustively explain it in terms of a rational, scientific, morally neutral vocabulary, thereby eliminating questions of meaning, mystery, or moral imperative. The causes of death itself resided outside "personal" as well as "moral and religious responsibility" in microorganisms certified by the doctor.[26] In contrast to "a world where sudden and unexpected death remains a real and dreaded possibility in everyone's life experience," "a world in which lethal infectious diseases seldom seized a person suddenly in the prime of life . . . no longer stood in need of belief in Divine Providence to explain such deaths."[27] Persons considered not only religious *explanations* but theological and moral *meanings* superfluous. Physicians became interested in the question of "how," not "why." In essence, the culture of medicine had fashioned for culture at large an image of death as primarily an impersonal, technical matter or, more to the point, a failure of technology.

This evolution of the moral order of death exemplifies effects of Western secularization. Edmund Pellegrino and David Thomasma locate modern medicine's crisis in the "long process of secularization and rationalization."[28] Medical practitioners reductively relegated moral thinking to the private, subjective, or emotional realm. They perceived the latter as relative, capricious, and not a "proper" subject for a scientific discipline. More generally, David Mechanic argues,

> One of the most impressive characteristics of modern technological nations is the extent to which life [and death] concepts, previously within the province of morals and religion, have been removed to the technical sphere, and the authority of traditional institutions in molding these perspectives has been very much diminished.[29]

Ivan Illich, Eric Cassell, and Larry Churchill have applied this analysis to the specific question of death. Illich has been justly criticized for heatedly distorting the facts to support his ideological opinions. But he deserves credit as a "kind of lightening rod, picking up and conducting"[30] attention to the fact that "technical death has won its victory over dying." The "ideal of hospital death" or death "under intensive care" has transformed death "from a personal challenge" into a mechanical problem. This undermines the will and integrity of persons to meet suffering and express values.[31]

Cassell and Churchill temper their remarks with respect for

the contributions of technology. They prefer to establish clearer limits rather than eliminate medical advances entirely. But they agree with Illich that certain mechanical indications of death of the body—measurement of heartbeat and brain waves, for example—divert attention away from equally important and inherently immeasurable personal and social questions. The "temple of the technical order," the modern hospital, has lost a sense for valuational or "synthetic" over against "analytic" thought.[32] The "belief and ritual system" of this "temple" cuts persons off from the values of the dying by creating an artificial distance between the living and the dead and by imposing "technical armamentaria upon dying persons."[33]

In this setting, inherently human and moral problems for which no technological solutions exist are reduced to technological responses:

> Essentially moral problems—obligations to parents, for example—have become part of the technical order amendable to administrative or technical solutions. . . . Characteristically our society seeks solutions to these problems not by reasserting the moral, but by attempting technical solutions for moral imperatives.[34]

For example, persons mistake and even substitute social policies or legal statutes to protect the individual's right to die or right to refuse treatment or even the mechanics of placing a dying patient in a nursing home for deeper moral responsiveness. Moral issues and judgments are translated into the language of health.[35]

In brief, the modern medical world has a "profound effect in directing the course of behavior while, with an unbelievable conceit, claiming a neutral stand in the field of morals."[36] It promotes two questionable convictions that obscure the moral import of death: first, all problems, including death, are solvable by the power of technical rationality; and second, such analysis is morally neutral, or at least exempt from ethical critique.

Reawakening of the Moral Order

In the last two decades, medicine's so-called moral neutrality has come under attack. As Cassell contends, we have begun to acknowledge "that a way of seeing the world has failed us." For the

last century we "set aside" values "in hope that some new thing—
new religion, science—would make everything value-free, would
take away personal value judgments." Instead "the new religion—
science—failed,"[37] leaving us more conscious of the evaluative component of medical decisions.

Medicine, say persons like Pelligrino among several others, is
"at heart a moral enterprise";[38] it constitutes a "major normative
structure" that shapes culture and is itself dependent upon the
dominant morality.[39] Scholars have begun to question the idea of
medical science as a self-contained system alongside others, arguing
that it is not quite so objective and value-free nor religion and
philosophy so subjective. Their relationship is much more varie-
gated and convoluted. Both tell us something about the good life
and the nature of human well-being.[40] Medicine makes unquestioned moral assumptions that demand critical examination. As
Willard Gaylin demands, we must strip medicine "of its scientific
camouflage," "abandon the myth of a value-free science" and
"cleanly and clearly" label its moral presuppositions.[41] However,
Robert Morison aptly summarizes the moral paradox with which we
are left to wrestle:

> The pursuit of a "value-free" science and technology brings us
> to a whole new range of value-loaded questions. It also pro-
> vides us with another equally interesting paradox: the same
> science that has knocked many of the supports from the ethical
> structures of the past now demands a more thorough ethical
> understanding than could ever have been conceived of when
> the world operated according to God's will.[42]

These shared convictions imply a sharp break of confidence in
the modern medical model and may presage a "more radical so-
ciocultural change"[43] that Fox describes as "post-modern medicine." We can see this new "self-consciousness" in several changes.
Post-modern medicine is more concerned with existential and ethical deliberations and more open to the mystery and awe of life and
death. It is "less secular and more sacral than modern medicine,"
even "more religious" if that is understood sociologically as a preoccupation with questions of meaning. Moreover, post-modern medicine is conscious of the finitude and uncertainties of its own knowledge and of the need to delimit human expectations of its powers.
Finally, medicine is reevaluating and expanding its understanding of
causation and responsibility for disease to include social and psycho-

logical factors. Responsibility is "collectively defined, principally in biosocial and biocosmic terms."[44]

A Value-Mixed Post-Industrial Mortality

We can discern three basic changes in the understanding of death in post-modern medicine. First, death's necessity itself has been slightly altered. Second, and closely related to the first, the absolute commandment to prevent death has been modified. Third, a heretofore suppressed ambiguity about responsibilities and rights for securing health and warding off death has been resurrected.

The very nature of death, once considered immutable, has been altered. In modern medicine the hope to rid humankind of death was primarily utopian and idealistic. In post-modern medicine, the hope has become a live possibility: "Death no longer appears as a necessity belonging to the nature of life, but as an avoidable, . . . tractable and long-delayable, organic malfunction."[45] As Jonas notes, death is no longer simply a part of nature, but belongs to a "*trans-nature* of human making."[46] We have not only altered death, we have created a new reality. This transforms the nature of human action itself, demanding an entirely new kind of moral reflection. Persons have unforeseen options to what was once a definite term of the human condition. Death's "meaning has to be pondered in the sphere of decision." Our grandparents did not face the question of what "the desirable and *eligible* measure" of their life should be in quite the same way that our children will.

> [The] philanthropic gift of science to man, the partial granting of his oldest wish—to escape the curse of mortality—turns out to be to the detriment of man. . . . Already the promised gift raises questions that had never to be asked before in terms of practical choice. . . . No principle of former ethics, which took human constraint for granted, is competent to deal with them. And yet they must be dealt with ethically and by principle and not merely by the pressure of interests.[47]

Any possible trace of moral neutrality that might have graced modern death has been vanquished from post-modern death.

Wide-ranging questions are heatedly debated in this area. What are our duties and rights in the process of dying? Is it moral or legal to take direct action to induce death? "Could a moral obligation

. . . arise to terminate one's life responsibly" due to scarce resources, competing claims, and diminishing returns from high-cost
treatment? Can we justify "willful death-dealing," "death for
others," as Maguire suggests, "when . . . certain values outweigh
the need or right of others to remain alive"?[48] The uproar over a
Colorado governor's assertion that everyone has a "duty to die"
exemplifies the emotional flares and moral trepidation that these
questions raise. Considerable publicity followed his comment that
we should "get out of the way with all our machines and artificial
hearts and everything else like that and let the other society, our
kids, build a reasonable life."[49] This is not just a matter of how much
costly care society can afford. At a deeper level, it is a question of the
relation of death, moral duty, and rights (both personal and social).
Facing death in post-modern society is a poignant instance of the
monumental expansion of human responsibilities during the past
several years.

We do not, and perhaps cannot, solve these questions to
everyone's satisfaction. However, modifications in a second area offer
a partial response. The millinarian drive to transcend death, although not totally routed, has at least come under question. An
ethic of limits, prudence, and restraint has begun to replace the
ethic of unrestricted advancement of techniques to ward off death.
Beginning with the famous Quinlan case, a troubled public forced
this issue to the fore with the now familiar slogans of "death with
dignity," "quality of life," and "right to die." The protest challenged
prolongation of life and prevention of death as the single, or even
proper goal of medicine. Formerly scientists hoped that attainment
of this end would further another, that of human happiness. Now
this premise is doubted as well. Many realize that the enduring
problem of fulfillment is *not* a *medical* problem. Nor is it an issue
that is completely solvable by technical, scientific means. To make
death prevention or happiness the end of medicine perverts the true
intent of medicine to affect healing.[50] Solving problems of disease
and health, says René Dubos, is not, as medical scientists once
assumed, "the same as creating health and happiness." We ought to
pursue the state of health as a good in relation to the highest good,
but not as the highest good itself.[51]

In post-modern medicine, there have been fresh attempts to
limit medicine's efforts to the aim of health, and in turn, to limit the
definition of health itself and ultimately, to temper hitherto excessive expectations of the doctor's "powers." Persons mistakenly ex-

pected physicians and technology to satisfy every need and desire. Physicians face real limits to what they can and cannot do, and more importantly, to what they should do. The physician and the general public no longer consider various means of postponing death of unequivocal value. The doctor's "traditional discretionary latitude" of the last twenty years has gradually narrowed.[52] The doctor no longer acts as sole decision-maker or sacred authority. Health professionals can contribute to a "good" death. But, as Lewis Thomas states, they are "surely not in possession of special wisdom about how to live a life" or how to end one.[53] They can raise, but not resolve, queries about what kind of life and what kind of death are worth pursuing.

These first two changes affect, and are affected by, a third: "We are now in the midst of a nascent (if not actual) crisis about how 'health' ought properly to be understood, with much dependent upon what concept of health emerges in the near future.[54] Recent literature has only begun to address the manifold ramifications that a new conception of health may have for our sense of responsibility for health and illness. And the relationship between these ideas and our understanding of death receives even less attention. But the implications are there and cannot be avoided.

Health and disease are far more complex notions than previously believed. Dubos and others assert that the mono-causal explanation of disease as simply precipitated by a sole bacilli, which can be isolated, diagnosed, and cured by "magic bullets" is a myth of modern medicine. He even questions whether discovery of specific bacteria led to the decline in the death rate. This is itself an illusion promoted by medicine's scientific doctrine of disease causation. In reality, other factors—"pure food, pure water, and pure air"—led to death control. But the myth and the elimination of several infectious diseases fooled the public into hoping that age-old problems of disease would disappear and that factors of personal responsibility for health were negligible. Yet, despite the advances in control of disease and death, "people still fall ill and die," but now from other conditions. One set of fatal diseases is simply exchanged for another.[55] This has led to a new conclusion: not only is disease not easily solved, the "etiology of most disease is multifactional rather than specific."[56]

"Multifactional" has come to mean a whole host of factors from the narrow, neutral idea of environmental influences to value-loaded judgments about personal habits, behavior, life-style, and even

judgments about "the good life and the good society."[57] For example, some directly link cancer to a breakdown in social and parental
relationships, to feelings of anxiety, depression, hostility and
hoplessness, or to "self-injurious mechanisms."[58]

No matter how we define "multifactional," today's illnesses—
cancer, heart disease, and so forth—appear to result from a multitude of related factors, not all of which are strictly physiological.
Medicine can no longer remove culpability as before. Persons
used to experience a sense of blamelessness or non-responsibility
when the physician could find a natural cause outside the person
and deliver "absolution" of a sort.

> In the medical model, illness is seen as deriving from natural
> causes, rather than from any human action or intention. The
> most common alternative view of illness is the moral one in
> which the illness is precisely the patient's fault: it is punish-
> ment for immoral behavior. These two views always seem to be
> present, even in illnesses where one would expect the medical
> model to hold clear title.[59]

Once again, we are left with more questions than answers: Is it
"simply sinful," as Morison says, "for a middle-aged man with a
family to smoke cigarettes . . . clearly and willfully increasing the
probability that he would be unable [due to illness and death] to
fulfill his responsibility to his family or indeed, to society at
large"?[60] If persons have a right to health care on the one hand, and
yet personal habits and behavior can be shown deleterious to health
on the other hand, is the right limited in any way by considerations
of personal responsibility? Is the individual accountable?[61] Or, in
general, "How much sacrifice of individual health can society demand in the name of general health? How far must society go in
making use of medical means to satisfy individual and sometimes
idiosyncratic desires?"[62]

Opinions differ on whether widening the responsibility for
health and illness is harmful or helpful and range from fanaticism
about individual rights to a counter-fanaticism about individual responsibility. John Knowles makes a bold case that

> [Since] over ninety-nine percent of us are born healthy and
> made sick as a result of personal misbehavior and environmen-
> tal conditions the solution . . . involves individual respon-
> sibility, in the first instance, and social responsibility . . . in the
> second instance. . . . The idea of a "right" to health should be

replaced by the idea of an *individual moral obligation to pre-serve one's own health—a public duty* if you will.[63]

Similarly, but with greater caution, Engelhardt contends,

> It is hard to sift out the elements of moral responsibility with respect to disease. . . . Such responsibility is liable to increase as it becomes easier to predict what available actions will lead to or prevent disease. Thus, a smoker can be properly blamed for getting cancer. Further, if he or she required treatment that is a burden on the general community, one has a basis for saying that *he or she acted immorally with respect to the responsibility to avoid cancer and its public costs*. . . . They have a special duty to pay for the costs that have resulted from their acquiring a disease they could have avoided. They are to blame.[64]

Finally, more wary, Callahan recognizes the slipperiness of these arguments. These statements may easily degenerate into a "primitively moralistic view" since it is impossible to account for all the causal factors. Societal values and the media itself, for instance, heighten the glamor and appeal of smoking. Nor can we correlate smoking directly with irresponsibility: "no one has, at any rate, been able to show that smokers are, as a group, generally less responsible, less moral individuals than nonsmokers." Finally,

> Even if it were possible to work through some of these problems there would still be a final difficulty. While it has been shown that certain ways of life lead to higher incidence of certain diseases, it has also been shown that those same diseases can appear in the absence of all those causes. For that reason, if for no other, it would be impossible to *prove* that someone's disease was the result of his culpable, willful responsibility.[65]

Regardless, the unknown character of one's true culpability before illness and death remains a source of much personal anguish. "Who of us," even among the most rational adherents to modern medicine, Fox asks, "really believes his own bodily infirmities and the approaching death are a purely natural occurrence, just an insignificant event in the infinite chain of causes?"[66] Dubos describes this lingering, nagging apprehension as "something akin to shame arising from a subconscious sense of responsibility" for one's fate.[67] Persons inevitably persist in asking "why me?" No matter how well medicine accounts for the natural "hows" of the illness, persons ask, "What have I done to deserve this? Why does this have to happen to me?"

The modern medical model did a better job managing this question than the new model. Modifications in the concept of health and disease have caused profound anxiety to resurface. The strain becomes worse with the moral ambiguity of post-modern medicine's explanation of disease. Whether overtly acknowledged or not, the "good" patient who has purposively not smoked expects "reward" for her good behavior by being spared death by heart disease or lung cancer. And the person who gets one of these diseases is deeply troubled when the natural cause for it remains unknown. As Kenneth Vaux comments, when health becomes "a pursuit, an achievement, a reward of personal endeavor or of sociopolitical reform," the "loss of health" is even more likely to signal "moral failure."[68] When this line of thought is carried to its conclusion, persons with serious terminal illness open themselves to grave disillusionment and moral condemnation. As happens all too often, their illness "pursues a course unrelated to their compliant behavior" and "those around who are not so 'good' improve more quickly."[69]

In short, "the credibility and acceptability of death are both dependent upon one's knowing, suspecting, sensing or imagining the cause."[70] In post-modern disease and death patterns, however, causes are often elusive and complicated. The underlying physiological mechanisms and means to prevent, control, or cure continue to evade medicine. All it can offer is "half-way technologies," measures that palliate the manifestations of an already-established terminal disease, but seldom more.[71] The "violence" of death is always "in excess of expectation," "impersonal, unreasonable." The real dilemma, according to Frederick Hoffman, is that we lack the moral and religious resources to earnestly confront this problem. Persons no longer possess ways of dealing with failed responsibilities and guilt in the face of illness and death. They lack the "compensatory forces of remorse and penance" necessary to comprehend commission and atonement. They cannot "cast up [their] accounts" and adjust to the circumstances of their death. Moral responsibility for death is thrust upon them while they are directed "away from the moral, confessional, and willed levels" of moral development and understanding.[72] The "moral economy," Hoffman claims, is unbalanced and distorted: "the calculus of proper and reasonable judgment of death as a predictable result of understandable causes no longer obtains."[73] Without a developed "moral sense," without a way to account for "moral deficiencies," persons can no longer prepare for death. There is "little or no possibility . . . of calculating the moral, physical, and spiritual responsibilities for the event."[74]

We are left with questions that medicine itself has raised but cannot answer alone. Problems with death extend far beyond redefining the criteria of death or even determining when death has occurred. Medical questions open up into questions about individual and societal responsibility in the face of illness and dying and questions about basic moral understandings.

Footnotes to Chapter III

/1/ Renée Fox, "The Medicalization and Demedicalization of American Society," *Daedalus* 106, no. 1 (Winter 1977), p. 10.
/2/ Renée Fox, *Essays in Medical Sociology: Journeys into the Field* (New York: Wiley and Sons, 1979), p. 422.
/3/ Steinfels, Introduction to *Death Inside Out*, p. 2.
/4/ Fox, *Essays in Medical Sociology*, pp. 405–406.
/5/ Daniel C. Maguire, *Death by Choice* (Garden City, N.Y.: Doubleday, 1974), pp. 1–2; idem., "The New Look of Death," in *Science and Morality: New Directions in Bioethics*, ed. Doris Teichler-Zallen and Colleen D. Clements (Lexington, Mass.: Lexington Books, 1982), pp. 253, 259; idem., "Death and the Moral Domain," pp. 198–199.
/6/ Iago Galdston, *Social and Historical Foundations of Modern Medicine* (New York: Brunner/Mazel Publishers, 1981), p. 3. A recent exception is Paul Starr, *The Social Transformation of American Medicine* (New York: Basic Books, 1982).
/7/ Ibid., p. 134.
/8/ For further description of the appearance of the new field of bioethics, see Daniel Callahan, "The Emergence of Bioethics," in *Science, Ethics and Medicine*, ed. H. Tristram Engelhardt, Jr., and Daniel Callahan (Hastings-on-Hudson, N.Y.: Institute of Society, Ethics and the Life Sciences, 1976), p. x–xxvi.
/9/ Fox, *Essays on Medical Sociology*, pp. 527–528.
/10/ Ibid., pp. 516–517.
/11/ Darrel W. Amundsen and Gary B. Ferngren, "Medicine and Religion: Pre-Christian Antiquity," in *Health/Medicine and the Faith Traditions*, pp. 54–64. See also Edmund D. Pellegrino, *Humanism and the Physician* (Knoxville, Tenn.: University of Tennessee Press, 1979), pp. 38–53; and Lester S. King, "Some Basic Explanations of Disease: An Historian's Viewpoint," in *Concepts of Health and Disease: Interdisciplinary Perspectives*, ed. A. L. Caplan, H. T. Engelhardt, and J. L. McCartney (Reading, Mass.: Addison-Wesley, 1981), pp. 231–245, esp. p. 233.
/12/ Chester R. Burns, ed., Introduction to *Legacies in Ethics and Medicine* (New York: Science History Publications, 1977), pp. 1–2.

/13/   Stanley Joel Reiser, "Therapeutic Choice and Moral Doubt in a Technological Age," *Daedalus* 106, no. 1 (Winter 1977), 51. Emphasis added.

/14/   Goldscheider, "The Mortality Revolution," pp. 165–171.

/15/   McNeill, *Plagues and Peoples*, p. 209.

/16/   Kass, "Biology and Human Affairs," p. 2.

/17/   Ibid.

/18/   Amundsen and Ferngren, "Medicine and Antiquity," p. 113; Galdston, *Foundations of Modern Medicine*, p. 8.

/19/   Fox, *Essays in Medical Sociology*, p. 528.

/20/   Stanley Joel Reiser, *Medicine and the Reign of Technology* (Cambridge: Cambridge University Press, 1976), p. x.

/21/   Ibid., pp. 174, 183, 227–231.

/22/   H. Tristram Engelhardt, Introduction to *Knowledge, Value and Belief*, vol. 2, *The Foundations of Ethics and Its Relationship to Science*, ed. H. Tristram Engelhardt and Daniel Callahan (Hastings-on-Hudson, N.Y.: Institute of Society, Ethics and the Life Sciences, 1976), pp. 1–2.

/23/   Michel Foucault, *The Birth of the Clinic: An Archeology of Medical Perception*, trans. A. M. Sheridan Smith (New York: Pantheon Books, 1973), p. xiii.

/24/   Fox, "Medicalization and Demedicalization," p. 9; Tarlov, "Future Practice of Medicine," p. 1239; Morris Fishbein, *Frontiers of Medicine* (Baltimore: Williams and Wilkins, 1933), p. 77; Willard Gaylin, Foreward to *Moral Problems in Medicine*, ed. Samuel Gorovitz (Englewood Cliffs, N.J.: Prentice Hall, 1976) p. xv; Cassell, *Healer's Art*, p. 62.

/25/   René Dubos, *The Mirage of Health* (New York: Harper and Row, 1971), p. 19.

/26/   Fox, *Essays in Medical Sociology*, pp. 505, 528.

/27/   McNeill, *Plagues and Peoples*, pp. 227–228. See also Ronald L. Numbers and Ronald C. Sawyer, "Medicine and Christianity in the Modern World," in *Health/Medicine and the Faith Traditions*, pp. 139–140.

/28/   Edmund D. Pellegrino and David C. Thomasma, *Philosophical Basis of Medical Practice: Toward a Philosophy and Ethic of the Healing Professions* (New York: Oxford University Press, 1981), p. 158.

/29/   David Mechanic, "Health and Illness in Technological Societies," *Hastings Center Studies* 1, no. 3 (1973), p. 9.

/30/   Fox, *Essays in Medical Sociology*, p. 467.

/31/   Illich, *Medical Nemesis*, pp. 10, 127, 201–208.

/32/   Cassell, "Dying in a Technological Society," p. 35; idem., "Being and Becoming Dead," pp. 162–163, 173.

/33/   Churchill, "Attitudes about Death," pp. 171–172.

/34/   Cassell, "Dying in a Technological Society," pp. 32–33.

/35/   Daniel Callahan, "The WHO Definition of 'Health'" *Hastings Center Studies* 1, no. 3 (1973), pp. 82, 84; idem., "Biological Progress and the Limits of Human Health" in *Ethics and Health Policy*, ed. Robert M. Veatch and Roy Branson (Cambridge, Mass.: Ballinger, 1976), p. 160.

/36/   Willard Gaylin, "Medical Ethics: The Issues at Stake" in *The Teaching of Medical Ethics*, ed. Robert M. Veatch, Willard Gaylin, and Councilman

Morgan (Hastings-On-Hudson, N.Y.: Institute of Society, Ethics and the Life Sciences, 1973), p. 9.

/37/ Eric Cassell, Response to Richard A. McCormick, "Issue Areas for a Medical Ethics Program," in *The Teaching of Medical Ethics*, p. 115. Emphasis added.

/38/ Pellegrino, *Humanism and the Physician*, p. viii. For several other examples of this refrain, see Daniel Callahan, "Health and Society: Some Ethical Imperatives," *Daedalus* 106, no. 1 (Winter 1977), p. 33; Dubos, *Mirage of Health*, p. 178; Pellegrino and Thomasma, *Philosophical Basis*, pp. 22–27, 64, 77; Peter Sedgwick, "Illness—Mental and Otherwise," *Hastings Center Studies* 1, no. 3 (1973), p. 31.

/39/ Parsons, Lidz, and Fox, "Gift of Life," p. 387.

/40/ H. Tristram Engelhardt, "Human Well-Being and Medicine: Some Basic Value-Judgments in the Biomedical Sciences," in *Science, Ethics and Medicine*, p. 121.

/41/ Gaylin, "Medical Ethics," p. 13.

/42/ Robert S. Morison, "Preface," in *The Dying Patient*, ed. Orville G. Brim, et al. (New York: Russell Sage Foundation, 1970), p. ix.

/43/ Fox, *Essays in Medical Sociology*, p. 405.

/44/ Ibid., pp. 523–529.

/45/ Hans Jonas, *Imperative of Responsibility: In Search for an Ethics For the Technological Age*, trans. Hans Jonas with the collaboration of David Herr (Chicago: University of Chicago Press, 1984), pp. 18–19. Some argue that the aging process itself is unnecessary. See, for example, Arthur L. Caplan, "The 'Unnaturalness' of Aging—A Sickness Unto Death?" in *Concepts of Health and Disease: Interdisciplinary Perspectives*, pp. 725–737; Albert Rosenfield, "Are We Programmed to Die?," *Saturday Review*, October 2, 1976, pp. 10–17.

/46/ Jonas, "Philosophy of Technology," p. 40.

/47/ Jonas, *Imperative of Responsibility*, p. 19.

/48/ Maguire, *Death by Choice*, pp. 2, 6.

/49/ James M. Wall, "Combatting Science on Death and Dying," *The Christian Century*, August 1–8, 1984, pp. 731–732.

/50/ See Kass, "End of Medicine," pp. 11–42, esp. pp. 13–14, 16–18.

/51/ Dubos, *Mirage of Health*, p. 26.

/52/ Pellegrino and Thomasma, *Philosophical Basis*, pp. 156–158.

/53/ Lewis Thomas, "On the Science and Technology of Medicine," *Daedalus* 106, no. 1 (Winter 1977), p. 45.

/54/ Callahan, "WHO Definition," p. 83. See also Foucault, *Birth of the Clinic*, p. xv.

/55/ Dubos, *Mirage of Health*, p. 168.

/56/ Ibid.

/57/ Fox, "Medicalization and Demedicalization," p. 21.

/58/ Maguire, "New Look," pp. 257–258; John Knowles, "The Responsibility of the Individual," *Daedalus* 106, no. 1 (Winter 1977), p. 62; David Bakan, *Disease, Pain, and Sacrifice: Toward a Psychology of Suffering* (Chicago: University of Chicago Press, 1968), pp. 11–17, 25. Robert Morison goes so far as to argue that "Wesleyan" or "middle class virtues of

cleanliness, prudence, and moderation" and "a sense of individual responsibility for oneself and others" are among the significant factors behind high
health standards (Morison, "Rights and Responsibilities: Redressing the
Uneasy Balance," *Hastings Center Report* 4, no. 2 [April 1974], p. 3).

/59/   Miriam Siegler and Humphry Osmand, "The 'Sick Role' Revisited,"
Hastings Center Studies 1, no. 3 (1973), p. 46.

/60/   Morison, "Rights and Responsibilities," p. 4.

/61/   Vaux, "Theological Foundations," p. 222; Samuel Gorovitz, Introduction to *Moral Problems*, p. 6.

/62/   Callahan, "Health and Society," p. 24.

/63/   Knowles, "Responsibility of the Individual," pp. 58–59. Emphasis
added.

/64/   Engelhardt, "Human Well-Being," p. 128. Emphasis added.

/65/   Callahan, "Health and Society," pp. 31–32.

/66/   Fox, *Essays in Medical Sociology*, p. 510.

/67/   Dubos, *Mirage of Health*, p. 144.

/68/   Kenneth Vaux, *Health and Medicine in the Reformed Tradition: Promise, Providence, and Care* (New York: Crossroads, 1984), pp. 28, 114.

/69/   Siegler and Osmond, "'Sick Role' Revisited," pp. 51–52.

/70/   Frederick J. Hoffman, "Mortality and Modern Literature," in *The
Meaning of Death*, pp. 146–147.

/71/   Ivan L. Bennett, Jr., "Technology as a Shaping Force," *Daedalus* 106,
no. 1 (Winter 1977), p. 129. See also Thomas, "Science and Technology," pp.
37–43.

/72/   Frederick J. Hoffman, *The Mortal No: Death and the Modern Imagination* (Princeton: Princeton University Press, 1963), pp. 4, 5; idem.,
"Mortality and Modern Literature," pp. 138, 139, 146–147.

/73/   Hoffman, "Mortality and Modern Literature," pp. 134–135, 152.

/74/   Ibid., p. 135.

PART II

CONTEMPORARY RESPONSES

CHAPTER IV

THE DEATH AND DYING MOVEMENT: A SUBSPECIALITY IN PSYCHOLOGY

Part I demonstrated a confusion over the moral significance of death the source of which runs far deeper than the advance of technology alone. The culture of medicine has shaped a "post-industrial death" in which the nature of death's necessity itself has changed. We have new freedoms and responsibilities but not without coinciding moral ambiguities.

Yet we face these ambiguities without significant moral resources. Traditional responses, when considered at all, seem insufficient and outmoded. In contrast to the eras of Augustine, Calvin, and even Schleiermacher, when the Christian paradigm of death triumphed, religious institutions and beliefs have ceased to play the normative role in socializing us to the art of dying. Today we seldom link death, sin, and grace. Nor are we likely to perceive death as a spiritual or moral event. As with Freud, death is no more or less than the return of organic matter to an inorganic state. In the death and dying movement, the meaning and value of death became increasingly psychologized.

While this view is not erroneous in itself, it has coincided with an erosion of death's moral import. The general public lacks moral, religious, or philosophical language to incorporate the deeper moral meanings of their own finitude into their experience. Society has threatened the plausibility of moral understandings, but not removed the experiences that call for them. Part II turns to several implications and possible resolutions to this problem.

Of these implications, the appearance and appeal of a still relatively new genre of literature in psychology in the decade from approximately 1965 to 1975 is the most striking. The public looked to psychology for "how-to remedies" for its woes and quandaries about human finitude. Kübler-Ross and what I will classify for my purposes as the "Kübler-Ross discussion" filled the moral vacuum rather unself-consciously with partly inadequate ideals.

The moral overtones of this dramatic "turning point" demand critical attention. If the Kübler-Ross discussion belongs to the effort to "complete" Freud, heralding a "return of faith" and new moralisms, we cannot rest content with the luxury of sociological analysis "for the sake of analysis." When psychologists assume ethical authority in helping persons plan for their deaths, psychologies of death become, as Browning asserts, "candidates for evaluation" from the perspective of a critical moral philosophy.[1] This chapter initiates an evaluation which continues in the following chapters by juxtaposing a sampling of authors in the Kübler-Ross discussion with the reflections of psychologists Erik Erikson and Robert Lifton.

Views of the Moral Life in the Kübler-Ross Discussion, Lifton, and Erikson

Besides Kübler-Ross herself, I group within the Kübler-Ross discussion selected writings of Avery Weisman, Edmin Shneidman, Herman Feifel, Robert Kastenbaum, and Ruth Aisenberg. Their work reveals that consideration of death has become a subspeciality in psychology. It is not so much major figures who take up the problem, but minor figures whose works are specifically and solely on death. If persons recognize the authors at all, death is the singular expertise for which they are known.[2] By contrast, Erikson and Lifton entertain ideas about death within more extensive psychologies, within "a psychology of life" as Lifton likes to say.

Within the subspecialty, Kübler-Ross is the most renowned. Despite efforts to appear different, the others often begin by adopting a stance in relation to her. Their "uniquenesses" are primarily distinctions between one another and between themselves and her rather than major alternatives. Some have close working relations, sometimes co-authoring books.

But these characteristics are not the predominant factor that lead me to group several selected writings together as "the Kübler-Ross discussion." I have selected these figures because of their wholesale endorsement of one particular normative view of death, and because of the representative nature of their work as members of a larger discussion in psychology which Browning describes as the "culture of joy":

> By culture of joy, I have meant a loosely associated group of
> influential psychologists who share two common attitudes.
> First, they share a view of man that sees his inner biological
> makeup as full of rich and creative potentials which are strain-
> ing to express themselves. The release of these potentials
> brings enormous quantities of spontaneous joy and a deep
> sense of personal fulfilment. Second, they believe that these
> basic potentials will indeed express themselves if a warm en-
> vironment is provided and the oppressive hand of tradition and
> cultural expectations is stayed.[3]

Psychology becomes culture when it promotes encompassing orientations to life and normative images about what we *are* and what we
should be. The culture-making quality of these two basic assumptions about human nature makes the Kübler-Ross discussion a candi-
date for evaluation. Following in the footsteps of the humanistic
psychologies of Abraham Maslow, Carl Rogers, Fritz Perls, and
William Shutz, this discussion propagates an implicit normative goal
of personal fulfillment. It considers life, or death in this case, as an
ordinary fact of nature to be accepted and an occasion for the
unfolding of innate potentialities.

Lifton and Erikson resemble one another and differ from the
culture of joy in their adherence to an alternative interpretation of
the moral life which Browning names the "culture of care." Like
Erich Fromm, Rollo May, and William James, they are guided by an
"active care and concern . . . not only for oneself and one's progeny
but for the wider community." Browning defines the characteristics
of this culture in terms of James's idea of the strenuous life:

> It is a positive attitude of care—care for oneself, one's family,
> the wider community, and possible future communities which
> may extend beyond the limits of one's individual life. The
> strenuous mood entails a personal identification of one's self
> with a wider range of people and communities, both present
> and future. It involves heightening one's sympathies and over-
> coming what James called that "certain blindness" in human
> beings which makes it difficult for us to appreciate and respect
> the inner meaning of another's experience.[4]

Erikson and Lifton belong to the psychoanalytic "conflict
model." This model assumes that persons are

> continually and inevitably in the grips of the clash between two
> great, opposing, unchangeable forces. Life . . . is merely a

compromise, which at best involves a dynamic balance of the
two forces, and at worse a foredoomed attempt to deny the
existence of one of them.[5]

By contrast, the "fulfillment model" of the Kübler-Ross discussion
views conflict more as a failure in living than as an unavoidable fact
of life. If we lift external restraints and satisfy individual desires,
inner potentialities will naturally gain expression until we have
Rogers's "fully functioning person."

As this indicates, conflict and fulfillment models have distinctive views of morality. The fulfillment model perceives ethical
systems as external authorities or "conditions of worth" which
jeopardize the spontaneous unfolding of each person's internal "ge-
netic blueprint." If carefully attended to, subjective feelings will
prescribe one's special capabilities, and moreover, exactly what one
ought to do. Persons develop by moving *away from* environmental
norms toward personal preference and autonomy. When each person sheds the outer shell of conformity to social requirements, she
becomes "unique." Ideally, if everyone would actualize their own
individual potentialities, we would have a harmonious "complementarity of excellences" between persons, as moral philosopher David
Norton calls it.[6] That is, there would be a mutual and congenial
social balance of needs met and desires gratified as each person
successfully realized their own individual good.

For Erikson and Lifton, such harmony appears naive and
idealistic. Moral development is not a direct movement from external moralisms to internal feelings. They find room for both a narrow,
conventional, superego-dominated morality which can often foster
pathological conflict *and* for a higher ego-ruled ethics which allows
for the possibility of creative conflict. Development means incor-
porating the internalized external authorities from childhood into
the ego capacity to integrate and contribute creatively to ethical
principles in adulthood.[7] Both scholars are a great deal more sensitive to the contradictions of guilt, fear, despair—the "regressive"
or "underside" of human nature—than any of the culture of joy
scholars. These darker forces stand in dialectical tension with the
impetus to adapt, integrate, and symbolize. Success in balancing
the tension depends in part on the social and normative network in
which one is embedded. Persons must draw upon as well as care for
the rich resources of history and tradition.

Thus I have grouped the material to emphasize a distinction of contemporary moral philosophy. My classification highlights theories of obligation that operate in these various psychological interpretations of death, albeit often unacknowledged. The Kübler-Ross discussion is characterized by what moral philosopher William Frankena distinguishes as ethical egoism of a non-hedonic type. The principle of ethical egoism says that one ought to act so as to promote one's own welfare and advantage.[8] I am not saying that the Kübler-Ross discussion promotes an egotistic or even egoistic or selfish personality theory. Rather, implicit in the discussion is a type of ethical theory which says that an individual's one and only obligation is to promote for herself the greatest possible balance of good over evil, whether that person is self-effacing or selfish.[9] The good judged to be to one's advantage may be understood in any number of ways. Some define it hedonistically in terms of pleasure as we saw in Freud. The Kübler-Ross discussion defines the good more generally in terms of self-realization. It argues that I must learn to accept death in order to increase personal fulfillment. The only objective obligation I have is to live in such a way as to secure my own inner happiness and to develop, right up to the moment of death, my own unique potentialities.

Erikson and Lifton, on the other hand, represent variations on the theme of utilitarianism or the principle of utility. In Frankena's words,

> *Ethical universalism*, or what is usually called *utilitarianism*, takes the position that the ultimate end is the greatest general good—that an act or rule of action is right if and only if it is, or probably is, conducive to at least as great a balance of good over evil in the universe as a whole as any alternative would be, wrong if it is not, and obligatory if it is or probably is conducive to the greatest possible balance of good over evil in the universe.[10]

Like the Kübler-Ross discussion, Erikson and Lifton assume a teleological position that one ought to act so as to advance certain goods. Neither party endorses the alternative deontological theory of moral obligation—that "other grand class of deontological answers," as Browning says, "that say that we should determine what we are obligated to do not with reference to the increase of nonmoral value but on the basis of some self-evident moral first principle such as the command of God, authenticity, Kant's categorical imperative, or Rawl's 'justice as fairness.'"[11]

Erikson and Lifton differ from the discussion, however, over the question of whose good one ought to promote. For them, the ultimate end, even in approaching one's own death, is the greatest general good. The best way to integrate death into life is one conducive to the "balance of good over evil in the universe as a whole," or in Erikson's words, one guided by the *grand*-generative" function of mutual care and "meaningful interplay" between the cycle of generations.[12] According the Lifton, I can only transcend the unalterable brokenness of death through commitment to both my "biological fellows" and our common "history, past and future."[13]

Application of these various typologies to the modern discussion of death in psychology will attest that psychology is not robotically nor monolithically compelled as a discipline to repeat the normative vision of its forefather. It can align itself with other options besides Freud's ethical egoism of a hedonistic type. Moreover, to understand death psychologically does not necessitate an ethical egoist position. Other options are available. To demonstrate these claims, I bypass some of the unique contributions of individual psychologies, unless they illustrate particular normative biases. I do not claim to have treated them comprehensively. But I do not believe that I have distorted the evidence which shows the resemblance of the members of the Kübler-Ross discussion to each other and to the moral assumptions of the "culture of joy" and the possible alternatives of the "culture of care." By bringing such distinctions to bear, I also affirm the value of clearly distinguishing the psychological component from the ethical. These two kinds of statements, language, and understanding need to be more carefully identified and less freely confused. This is especially important in certain "psychological" considerations of death in which definite moral obligations and value judgments are promoted with little or no consciousness.

The Culture of Joy: Death as Opportunity for Personal Growth

If the reader hopes to gain from this chapter helpful advice on how to master fear of death or manage grief, you may be sorely disappointed. Such hope is natural since much literature today is clearly of this sort. In these matters psychology has assuredly acted as an aid to many troubled hearts and I respect these contributions. My focus, however, is the cultural and moral impact of these contributions. This is not to say that the articulation of an ethical system is or should be psychology's chief aim. But *my* interest is the moral stance shaping these psychologies and being shaped by them. Therefore I will more likely meet your expectations if you want to gain a more critical eye when you do read and apply a psychologist's advice on death and dying. And, I think, inadvertently, the former hopes may be partially met as well.

A few of the books and articles which I will look at more closely actually emerged before or around the same time as the acclaimed *On Death and Dying*. But the public was ripe for someone like Kübler-Ross specifically. She was in many ways fortunate enough to be in the right place at the right time. A research project undertaken at the instigation of a few seminary students forced open the closed doors of terminal wards and gradually evolved into regular seminars, books, tapes, and ultimately, a widespread public fascination with her five stages. She knew how to make the most of a ready market. Published in 1969, by 1972 her first book had sold over 100,000 copies in the paperback edition alone. In fact, "if there is a phenomenon akin to a 'death and dying movement' occurring in the United States. . .then Elisabeth Kübler-Ross is one of its charismatic leaders."[14] As "the American scholar most widely read and quoted" on the subject,[15] she sets the standard; the others play off against it. Nurses doing in-service training listened to her tapes; chaplains and pastors recommended her insights; laypersons came to know her stages without even having to read her books; people applied her stages to all sorts of grief-related phenomenon from suffering football injuries to having a miscarriage.

Surely we should commend Kübler-Ross for challenging a range of questionable assumptions in hospital medicine, some of which we explored in Chapter III. However, I want to do more than commend, or even summarize and review, her work. Instead, let us look at the ways in which it epitomizes the characteristics of the culture of joy and its moral assumptions.

For Kübler-Ross, any problems with death lie in the institutionalization of modern society, *never* in human society in its natural state. She nostalgically longs for her lost childhood, a romanticized past when good folk enjoyed the simple life of farm living "with its closeness to nature." They knew intuitively how to approach death with the "equanimity" due the rhythmic, harmonic changes of

season. Moreover, an uncontested confidence in the promise of
heavenly reward further supported their ease with death.[16]

Kübler-Ross has to take liberties with her education as a
Freudian psychiatrist to argue that people used to see death as a
natural part of life. Although she concedes that in our unconscious
we cannot conceive of our own death, in her romantic vision of the
past people did not shrink from talking about death "as an intrinsic
part of life just as they do not hesitate to mention when someone is
expecting a baby."[17] Death, she argues, "is as much a part of human
existence, of human growth and development as being born."[18] We
need not see death as sad, frightening, morbid, horrible, cata-
strophic, or destructive. We ought to see death as "a peaceful
cessation of the functioning of the body," like "watching . . . a falling
star . . . that flares up for a brief moment only to disappear into the
endless night forever."[19] Death is not "an enemy to be conquered
but an "expected" and "friendly companion on your life's journey."[20]

She must also take liberties with the more linear view of
history characteristic of her Western heritage. She views life as
cyclical in nature. We return in death "to the stage we start out with
and the circle of life is closed."[21] By likening death to birth, she
emphasizes this cyclical character as well as death's naturalness.

Others in the discussion see death through the same naturalistic lens. In almost identical words, Weisman and Kastenbaum
state that death is "as 'natural' as any other phase of life—as natural
as childbirth, for example."[22] Too often, and to our detriment, we
see death as a tragic, deplorable, or unnecessary and unmitigated
evil.

Instead of perceiving contemporary problems of death intra-
psychically as good Freudians might, Kübler-Ross places the blame
almost wholly on the "fall" of modern society. The "death-defying"
character of contemporary America, the "hostility, resistance, dis-
belief" encountered in hospitals where she sought entrance to talk
about death, and the "increasingly mechanical, depersonalized approach" of modern medicine obscure the self-evident facts of
nature.[23] Without hesitance, she contents, "I think most of our
patients would reach the stage of acceptance if it were not for the
members of the helping professions, especially the physicians who
cannot accept the death of a patient."[24]

Others in the discussion locate the problem in the external
world. They usually make three main points: first, in Feifel's words,
there is a "growing impersonality emerging from a technologically

dominated society"; second, we are alienated from all "traditional moorings," "conceptual creeds or philosophic-religious views with which to transcend death"; and finally, psychology needs to create fresh "strategies" to rescue modernity."[25]

Of the writers I selected, Weisman speaks out most adamantly about the increasing irrelevance of traditional values. He reiterates again and again his dissatisfaction with "unsubstantiated generalities which often sound more homiletic than scientific," "ceremonial supports that [our] forebears scarcely questioned," "platitudes," "moralisms and unwarranted universal dicta," and "global pronouncements."[26] He feels "obliged" as a psychiatrist to devise better ways to "cope" with death: "the problem is to find a death we can live with, to cope with the ongoing process by calling upon successful strategies."[27] Initially he believes that his strategies are morally neutral.[28] Awareness that he himself might be propagating his own moral or quasi-religious platitudes arises more as an after-thought in his later writings.[29] Even so, he still seems unable to distinguish when to stop psychologizing and "when to begin philosophizing."

In *The Psychology of Death*, Kastenbaum and Aisenberg agree that secularization has deprived us of resources for comprehending death: "*We no longer participate in a society that is dominated by tradition, lineage, or accepted dogma.* The older systems of social control within our culture have lost much of their ability to shape our behavior."[30] Their book attempts to offer a "worthwhile model" or a "useful guide" in light of the perceived vacuum.[31]

On a continuum with the others, however, they at least acknowledge the precarious tightrope which psychology walks. They observe the dangers of overstepping the discipline's necessary boundaries. By definition, psychology is limited in its ability to judge the "relative value" of different "strategies."[32] Even if it could establish "quantitative units" to evaluate these, there remains the deeper problem that "we just do not know what constitutes the most mature or ideal conception of death."[33] Such assessments represent "value orientations rather than inexorable conclusions" derived from psychological research:

> Perhaps this is a topic that will not yield much until we are more willing to examine the implicit value dimensions in what has been formulated, too readily, as an exclusively psychiatric or psychodynamic problem. From what standpoint can we say

> that one orientation of death . . . is "better" than another? Our
> own assumptions about the meaning of human life must be
> examined.[34]

Ultimate responsibility rests with other disciplines alongside psychology.

On our continuum, Feifel and Shneidman fall somewhere in the middle. Feifel believes that psychology must move beyond a narrow mechanistic framework into "the balliwick of moral issues and life choices." In fact, psychology is *the* discipline of choice to bring to the study of death "its philosophic and humanistic heritage in the context of its generic ideal of science."[35] He does not acknowledge that psychology's ideal of value neutrality may handicap it when it wants to entertain ethical and philosophical judgments.

The discussion's assessment of the problem of death in modernity exerts subtle moral influence through what Gerald Gruman describes as "a rather disguised, muddled, yet persevering drive towards 'secular salvation,' seeking to save mankind from sin and death by means of this-worldly activities."[36] The discussion strives "to make it easier to die," or, as Steinfels comments, to assure "a surefire progression to a happy ending."[37] It views the negative valence of death and the contrary emotions associated with it as unnatural, socially determined, and psychologically manageable. Fear of judgment or punishment is considered irrelevant or false; guilt is something the survivor might feel, but seldom the dying, and with the latter, it should be quickly and painlessly "worked through." Whatever the emotion, the psychologists suggest "coping techniques" by which persons obtain relief and maintain control over a dimension of life which always takes control out of human hands.

To bring death into their camp, these scholars must regard dying as a psychosomatic, psychosocial, or purely psychological event. As early as 1959, in his groundbreaking collection of essays, *The Meaning of Death*, Feifel had said, "I think that it is a much needed step forward in recognizing that the concept of death represents a psychological and social fact of substantial importance."[38] Only a few years later, Shneidman quotes this affirmatively and attempts to give death "a psychological, specifically introspective referent."[39] Likewise, Weisman argues that death results from psychological and social forces as much as from its reality as a "fact of nature."[40]

Kübler-Ross sets the stage for studying death as a psychological event. Her approach is to "tell the stories" of her patients. She truly believes that she offers "simply an account," unadulterated by any input or bias of her own, and that the five stages are inherent in the material, "discovered" in the telling. She and the seminary students did not read "any papers or publications on this topic so that we might have an open mind and record only what we ourselves were able to notice."[41] Her books are full of moving anecdotes with an open, honest, and even the confessional flavor that makes the stories difficult to discount. As a worthy newspaper journalist might, she weaves personal tale into believable fact. This art of story-telling disguises the line where illustration stops and commentary begins and lends a sense of legitimacy to her findings.

Others spy the effectiveness of this technique and exploit it. Weisman builds *The Realization of Death* around case studies. He claims it is a "dispassionate" or "candid discussion" with "the gentle neutrality of quiet dignity, seeking to learn, to understand, to participate."[42] In like manner Shneidman draws us into *Deaths of Man* by beginning the first chapter with "verbatim excerpts from four videotaped interviews."[43] How much closer to unadulterated "fact" can we get? Or, at least, this is the implication.

At the same time, the Kübler-Ross discussion tends to mock those who explicitly try to deal with "a philosophical, ethical, or religious aspect" of death "by philosophizing in an abstract manner."[44] Weisman asserts that "problems about death are neither as abstract as philosophy pretends" nor "as theoretical as religion professes."[45] They are concrete, self-evident, and empirically resolvable. All one need do, as Kübler-Ross likes to say, is "sit and listen," and then report.

Even in these seemingly neutral declarations about method, we find a hidden normative assumption operating. Freud's working maxim of the "talking cure" becomes an ironclad obligation. These psychologies presume that one of the fundamental needs, especially of those facing imminent death, is to talk. In Kastenbaum's words, "communication on the topic of death and bereavement is probably the most useful single prophylactic measure to avoid unnecessary suffering."[46] Feifel observes that "patients want very much to talk about their feelings and thoughts about death."[47] And Kübler-Ross claims "that those patients do best who have been encouraged to express their rage, to cry in preparatory grief, and to express their fears and fantasies to someone who can quietly sit and listen."

Typical advice runs like this: "Your pain may be all those swallowed feelings of anger and frustration. Get them out of your system without being ashamed and your pain will probably go away."[48] Clinical evidence demonstrates, according to Feifel, that those who ventilate experience "less depression, deviant behavior, and blame of others." "Further opening of channels of communication tends to attenuate feelings of inadequacy and guilt."[49]

These premises about emotional catharsis dictate the role the researcher or caregiver, whether nurse, relative, or friend, must take: to "sit and listen." Kübler-Ross strictly forbids people either to judge the feelings expressed or to impose their own values or perspective. She places a premium upon an accepting, non-judgmental environment. One must elicit needs and satisfy them. This, in fact, is the only "preconceived idea" that Kübler-Ross confesses she had: she hoped "to get a feeling for the terminally ill and their needs which in turn we were ready to gratify if possible."[50] "We have to elicit the patient's needs, hopes, and unfinished business, and then we have to find out who is able to gratify those needs."[51]

Each scholar has a further objective, however, beyond eliciting and fulfilling individual needs. Kübler-Ross listens to feelings and meets needs in order to enable the person to reach the final stage of acceptance. The others attempt to take a stand over against this by criticizing her stage theory. But in reality, their differences simply do not run that deep. In essence, they all promote a similar goal. *Each individual ought to achieve for herself or himself a more personally satisfying, "appropriate death," and be helped to do so.* They may endorse varying paths to this end, but, almost consistently, this is the final goal—personal satisfaction or self-realization in death and dying, a moral principle along the lines of what moral philosophers define as ethical egoism.

Kübler-Ross typically wraps up her overview of the five stages with statements like the following:

> If we can understand these people rather than judge or label them, we can be successful in helping them to the next stage. . . . If we can accept our patients' needs and do not project our own. . .the dying person will then reach the final stage of true acceptance.[52]

Or, again, "If we can accept our patients the way they are with denial, anger, bargaining, and depression, they will work through their unfinished business and reach a stage of acceptance enabling them to die in peace and dignity."[53]

Roy Branson and Larry Churchill have accused Kübler-Ross of confusing descriptive and normative categories. In part, Kübler-Ross foresaw the possibility of this criticism. She declares that "it has to be understood that not all patients go through these stages and certainly do not pass through these stages in this order."[54] She objects that she never intended to push people through all five stages to that of acceptance.

But as much as she prefaces her remarks with notes of caution, other statements strongly suggest, as Branson observes, "that in regard to her five-part scheme, Dr. Kübler-Ross does not simply report, she recommends."[55] Despite her disclaimers, when it comes right down to it, as she herself says, "a few common denominators . . . are worth keeping in mind."[56] For one, she has a specific order in mind that she indicates by her use of the category of *stages*. Branson perceives that the choice of this category, rather than *types*, is not accidental; she cannot accept any other conceptualization:

> She is committed to calling one response—acceptance—the final one. . . . Denial, anger, bargaining and depression are called "stages" because in Kübler-Ross's view, acceptance *ought* to be the last response to death. Her use of a terminology implying sequence has been dictated by normative considerations.[57]

The first four stages contain negative and potentially destructive emotions if not forsaken in order to reach the final stage of acceptance. Denial is "usually a temporary defense and will soon be replaced by partial acceptance"; relief of anger in the next stage is important primarily because it helps move a person "toward better acceptance of the final hours"; and depression is "necessary and beneficial if the patient is to die in a stage of acceptance and peace."[58] She describes herself as listening to "confessions" to further this process. In fact, she believes that being a priest would enhance her effectiveness.[59]

Kübler-Ross never defines precisely what she means by acceptance. But she does provide examples. She understands "true" or "genuine" acceptance to mean a final stage almost devoid of feelings. In particular, the dying person withdraws into herself and her inner world, regressing to the "primary narcissism" of early infancy, separating from all attachments and obligations, and experiencing "the self as being all."[60] When you accept death, your "circle of interest diminishes"; you wish to be "left alone or at least not stirred by the news and problems of the outside world."[61] Nothing should be asked of the dying; all should be given. Persons who have accepted death prefer to be solitary, silent, and sleeping.

She does not restrict acceptance to the imminently dying alone. We all should reach the stage long before our deaths:

> [Acceptance] is something we could teach our children even before they go to school. The stage of acceptance simply means that people live a different quality of life with different values, that they enjoy today and not worry too much about tomorrow, and that they hope that they still have a long, long time to enjoy this kind of life.[62]

We can learn an important lesson from those facing impending death: "we have only NOW—'so have it fully and find what turns you on, because no one can do this for you!' "[63]

Churchill demonstrates that a progressivist bias shapes this "tacit ethic of 'acceptance.'" "Progressivist thinking is the conviction that onward and upward movement is desirable and possible,"[64] a bias most apparent in the title of Kübler-Ross's later book, *Death: The Final Stage of Growth*. Death becomes a growth experience: "One of the most productive avenues for growth is found through the study and experience of death."[65] She does not mean just any kind of growth. She works from a peculiarly Rogerian definition. Confronting death frees you from conformity to external social expectations and values and allows you to "become more truly who you really are," "a unique and special person."[66]

The others in the Kübler-Ross discussion join Branson and Churchill in the somewhat voguish criticism of Kübler-Ross, although they owe the popularity of their books in part to her. They criticize her for making prescriptive rather than just descriptive observations. Nevertheless, even though they picked up this ethical perception, these psychologists seldom carry it further. Seldom do they identify and evaluate their own prescriptive biases. They have learned the content of one specific criticism, so to speak, but not the general method.

Their criticism betrays their own prejudices. Although Kübler-Ross herself is extremely concerned with the individual,

Kastenbaum, Shneidman, and Weisman contend that universal application of her stages ignores human individuality. As a result, they tend to be even more individualistic than she. Weisman, for instance, argues that her "schematic stages . . . are at best approximations, and at worst, obstacles to individuation." He suggests that, instead, we proceed case by case. Rather than stereotype and reduce people "to a least common denominator," we must "treat everyone as a special case."[67] Kastenbaum agrees that "rigid rules cannot be laid down," and that the stage theory "drains away individuality." Because everyone's desires and needs are unique, we can not "standardize" the way persons do or should die. The only standard that we can establish is that *the terminally ill person's own framework of preferences and lifestyle must be taken into account.*"[68]

As Parsons and Lidz observe, this institutionalizes decision-making in

> thoroughly *privatized* contexts, ones . . . defined as almost exclusively the "private matters" of the individuals involved. . . . The individual units must integrate their various commitments under the "supervision" of their own consciences, and the elements of the "public" affected by the decisions must rely upon the general quality of the plurality of private consciences.[69]

All resources for determining a "good" or "acceptable" death lie within, Weisman argues emphatically, although "psychosocial guidance systems" might help us uncover these.

> We have few resources beyond ourselves. . . . Traditional authorities, . . . precepts, policies, and principles, we see very clearly, are often exercises in self-serving rhetoric. . . . We have only our own reality and resources. . . . We are required to face ourselves, set into a mirror reflecting how life-styles might become death-styles. We have our own life to live and our own death to die. . . . We cannot trust established authorities.[70]

Individually the self totally creates the world in which it lives and dies. Then "death is whatever we choose it to be."[71] He defines an "appropriate death" as one in which we "confront our own mortality as if we had created it"; "an appropriate death is one we might choose, had we a choice."[72]

Futhermore, since a good death is only what is personally
suitable and internally desirable, what is suitable for one person
may not be for another.[73] "What might seem appropriate from the
outside, might be utterly meaningless to the dying person himself.
Conversely, deaths that seem unacceptable to an outsider, might be
desirable from the inner viewpoint of the patient."[74] In the end,
Weisman concludes, "the final judge is the patient—whether it feels
right to die at that moment."[75] There are no other possible criteria
or "ideals" for what might comprise a meaningful or valuable way to
die.

But Weisman himself does not remain completely true to his
position. In the end, he offers his own set of criteria for a better
death and ways in which psychologists, through "successful management" and "psychiatric intervention," can help persons achieve
this.[76] We have seen many of these guiding principles before in
Kübler-Ross: resolution of conflictual feelings; achievement of peace
and equanimity; satisfaction of "whatever remaining wishes" there
are; a "highly personal realization of completeness," perhaps even to
die "with greater self-esteem than was possible during life."[77]

Weisman works from a definition of "appropriate death" which
grew from a descriptive study in 1961 to a more expansive application of the idea in the 1970s. Based on empirical observations of the
dying process in five particular patients, initially he comments that
an "appropriate death" is a death which is

> not deplorable, but desirable as a means of attaining resolution
> of conflict, fulfillment of desire, and rewarding quiescence . . .
> one in which there is reduction of conflict, compatibility with
> the ego ideal, continuity of significant relationships, and con-
> summation of prevailing wishes. . . . It is not merely con-
> clusive; it is consummatory.[78]

In later publications he adds new, less descriptive and more philosophical concepts, such as *"significant survival"* or *"purposeful
death."* He defines these, as he did the idea of appropriate death, in
light of his ethical egoist assumptions. A purposeful death or significant survival should entail "a measure of fulfillment, quiescence,
resolution, and even traces of personal development."[79] These definitions help him address "questions that religion is supposed to deal
with," "questions about our human obligation to die."[80]

Shneidman thinks the idea of appropriate death is "illuminat-
ing, elevating, just right." The idea rates among the company of the
greats:

Every once in a while, some gifted student of human nature
enunciates an especially felicitous and powerful concept:
Freud's ideas of dreams as wish fulfillment. . . , Jung's arche-
types, Maslow's peak experiences. . . . Weisman's concept of
an "appropriate death" would seem to belong in such company.[81]

Everyone who interacts with a dying individual "should . . . help
that individual achieve a more appropriate"[82] or "a better death."
The dying ought to "live as fully and as richly as possible" and all
communication with them must "be tailored to specific human
needs."[83] He defines "maturity" itself, not just for the dying, but for
everyone, as the accomplishment of an appropriate acceptance of
death.[84]

Again and again we hear that personal emotions ought to be
expressed and individual needs met. How you feel should guide
your approach to death. The caregiver should only draw this out and
never impose her own views. Moral concerns are matters of personal
preference, aesthetic taste, or subjective feeling. Note, for a final
example, how Abraham Maslow defines a good death: "The right
moment for a good ending [is] a phenomenological sense of good
completion . . . entirely personal and internal and just a matter of
feeling pleased with myself."[85]

One problem with this line of thought is that individual desires
and feelings dictate needs and needs dictate rights and moral obligations. The psychologists in the discussion do not worry about this
escalation of needs to wants and wants to moral rights. By weighing
how you feel and what you want, you can discover the right course of
action as that which comes closest to satisfying all your needs in the
situation. As Vaux comments, "Ethics in this spirit is not motivated
by deep sympathy for fellow humans but by self-assertion and
advocacy of rights."[86] Personal happiness is synonymous with virtue.

The Culture of Care: Wisdom, Mutuality, and Continuity

A glimpse at how Lifton differs with the premises behind the
Kübler-Ross discussion is a good illustration of the distinctive per-
spective on death found among psychologies in the culture of care.
For Lifton, death does involve a psychic dimension, but not just

because of the death instinct or as an expression of a single life history. He asks us to consider several additional elements such as familial patterns of interaction, historical and cultural themes, random happenings:

> Even when there is a clear individual-psychological relationship to dying . . . one would have to explore the relationship of . . . individual psychology to historical and cultural factors . . . all in the context of general imagery around death and vitality as evolved through personal, environmental, and cultural influences, and . . . genetic-organic susceptiblities . . . and strengths. . . . Our formative-symbolic approach resembles what is sometimes called "general systems theory."[87]

Lifton uses a number of descriptors besides "formative-symbolic" to describe his approach—"shared-themes approach," "depth-psychological," "psychoformative," "psychohistorical." These qualifiers emphasize that his psychology includes historical, cultural, and ethical, as well as psycho-biological factors.

Lifton could never have reached this understanding without the impact of Erikson's psychosocial approach on his work. He himself comments that Erikson's "extensive influence on my work will be strongly evident"[88] and suggests "a sequence in psychological thought from Freud's model of instinct and defense, to Erikson's of identity and the life cycle, to an emerging paradigm of death and life-continuity taking shape in the work of a number of people including myself."[89]

Erikson demonstrates the significance of the relation of the ego to society. This is one of his chief contributions. Although he remains within the psychoanalytic conflict model, he integrates his view of intrapsychic conflict with ideas of the self as existing in mutual relationship with other selves in society. Even the title of his first book, *Childhood and Society*, and its layout in three interrelated parts dealing with biology, ego, and society, exemplifies a transformation of Freud influenced by ego psychology and by studies of child play, ethology, ecology, and anthropology. Just as Freud never totally freed himself from seeing the world through the eyes of his early training in biological research, Erikson's identity as a psychologist evolves out of the configurational orientation he had acquired as an artist.[90] He modifies Freud's specifically designated libido and death instinct by placing them within a broader canvas of instinctual patterns. Despite his desire to smooth over his diver-

gence from Freud,[91] Erikson gradually moves away from a fundamental indebtedness to orthodox psychoanalysis to create a psychology which hopes to "complement observations of childhood with a
view of adulthood, supplement a theory of libido with a concept of
other sources of energy, and fortify a concept of ego with insights
into the nature of social institutions."[92]

This approach strikes a chord with Lifton. He, too, flavors his
research with colorful field study—of Japanese youth, Vietnam, war
heroes, Nagasaki and Hiroshima. Yet, distinct from Erikson, he has
an eye toward discerning broader historical and cultural implications. These studies invariably lead him from empirical data to
comparative observations, and ultimately to speculation on the general principles of universal human nature. He expands Erikson's
tripartite network of biology, ego, and society to include, along with
"universal psychological elements" and *"cultural emphases and patterns,"* an emphasis on *"specific historical currents."*[93]

Lifton carries the configurational approach another step yet:
his most unique contribution beyond Erikson is his emphasis on the
human capacity for symbolization and its relationship to the ideas of
mortality and immortality. In this emphasis, he aspires to redefine
the central conflict of our age for which his "new psychology"
supplies a totally fresh psychological paradigm:

> Absurd death and discontinuity of life replace repressed and
> resisted sexuality [of Freud] and identity conflict [of Erikson]
> as the major source of our psychological impairments. The
> result is not so much a problem of relegating unacceptable
> ideas to the unconscious, or the experience of identity con-
> fusion. The more basic difficulty is the impaired capacity to feel
> and to give inner order to experience in general.[94]

The pervasive threat of nuclear destruction intensifies this problem.
By all measures of Thomas Kuhn's *The Structure of Scientific Revolutions*, we are experiencing a collapse of our previous thought
systems and a dire need for a new paradigm. Lifton professes to have
filled the "symbolic gap" with his "new paradigm" of death and
continuity.

In further contrast to the Kübler-Ross discussion, both Erikson and Lifton are acutely aware that psychology and psychoanalysis
often function as positive ethical sciences and must be judged on
that basis. Lifton's work in particular reflects the return of ethics to
greater prominence in the social sciences and public consciousness

in general in the late 1960s and 1970s. The psychological professions have, in his words, "outlived the period of ethical neutrality and the possibility of regarding their work and their place in society as being beyond moral scrutiny";[95] "psychologists do not simply interpret or analyze; we also construct."[96] Hence, they must avoid the "modern trap of pseudo-neutrality" by overtly admitting their commitments and moral passions—what he calls their "advocacy"—and by bridging "individual-psychological, ethical, and collective perspectives" through an openness to dialogue.[97]

Erikson himself was on the forefront of this new awareness. Psychoanalysts may initially have had no other choice, he notes, but to operate as modern scientists in order to free themselves from philosophy and theology. However, they must do "better justice to some aspects . . . than some of the causal and quantitative terms . . . of the founders."[98] A science which defines "normality" or "reality," a "science so close to questions of health and ethics," must include methods of self-observation and self-criticism, especially when it influences, whether intentionally or not, the process of history and culture.[99]

This is only a brief sketch of the general approach of two psychologies of the culture of care. Already we can see that their approach is quite distinct from the Kübler-Ross discussion. This has crucial consequences for their respective views of the moral horizons of death. In other words, if we are looking for a psychological analysis of the experience of death and dying, there *are* other models besides those in the specialized Kübler-Ross discussion. Moreover, which psychological model we choose has significant ethical repercussions not always readily apparent. Psychological approaches such as Erikson's may not be known for their consideration of death, for they do so within a more comprehensive theory of the personality. Yet this itself may be a positive attribute. And Lifton stands out as a notable exception in that he both has a reputation for giving prominent place to death *and* builds "an entire psychology of life." He believes that we cannot ignore the conceptual issue, but we need a comprehensive, integrated, albeit "death-oriented" psychology of life, not a narrow thanatology.[100] He hopes to compensate for the neglect of death in psychology, but not by making death the only subject or the sole explanation of human behavior.

So, what are some of the ethical ramifications of relying upon a Kübler-Ross or a Lifton, a Weisman, or an Erikson? Both Erikson and Lifton endorse the vision of the culture of care rather than the ethical egoist trend we observed above. They offer an alternative to psychologies which envision a lone individual who sees relationship as a means to the end of autonomous individuality and fulfillment; they offer another option to a discussion which often considers dependence upon, and even sacrifice for others an attempt to escape authenticity in "creating" one's "own" death. While the humanistic psychologies of the culture of joy place authentic selfhood in *separation* of the self from the influence of the social order, the leitmotif in Erikson and Lifton is that of *reciprocity* between subjective ego synthesis in the individual and ideological integration in the community.

Erikson is wary about discussing what he calles "the psychology of 'ultimate concern.'" But having said this, he goes on to affirm what he can talk about—the necessity of the complementarity of generations when facing "the great Nothingness": "If there is any responsibility in the cycle of life it must be that one generation owes to the next that strength by which it can come to face ultimate concerns in its own way."[101]

Lifton, on the other hand, states outright that he is prepared to "provide a framework for addressing this domain of 'ultimate concern'" which depth psychology has hitherto "abandoned to the theologians."[102] Since he writes about a decade after Erikson, he has a good deal more to say in direct response to the death and dying movement. The Kübler-Ross discussion, in his opinion, lacks appreciation for the psychological significance of a sense of transcendence and enduring continuity beyond the self.

Nonetheless, Lifton has at times an affinity with the culture of joy. For example, he proposes five "modes of immortality" by which persons transcend death. Sometimes it seems that the ultimate aim of these modes is to promote "maximum individuation."[103] They must be viable "so that they will continue to provide avenues for individual fulfillment."[104]

But by the publication of *The Life of the Self* in 1976 and *The Broken Connection* in 1979, he is better able to recognize his growing divergence from the narrow "stress on individual self-realization" that psychology inherited from Freud, and Freud from the Renaissance and Enlightenment. He distinguishes his "advocacy" from Freud's which he depicts as "somewhere in the libertarian tradition of John Stuart Mill."[105] Not until *The Broken Connection*, however, does he directly identify his misgivings with the Kübler-Ross discussion. Some of the psychologists, including Shneidman, Weisman, and Kastenbaum, are

> hampered by [a] form of literality that sees human beings as existing psychologically only in here-and-now relationships and underestimates the scope of the temporal imagination. . . . Without the theoretical framework that posits the anticipatory importance of enduring continuity beyond the self, the psychiatric theorist is apt to fall back on ad hoc impressions, moralistic sentiments or such psychoanalytic platitudes as "a primarily narcissistic orientation."[106]

Furthermore, they misrepresent death "by nervously and reductively invoking . . . clinical terms instead of examining the phenomenology of man's experience of his larger connectedness."[107]

Erikson does not have the "benefit" of the full Kübler-Ross discussion when he addresses the problem of death, but the discussion has the benefit of his work. Shneidman directly, and Kübler-Ross indirectly, refer to Erikson's idea of generativity. Yet their extrapolations of this concept, although they argue in opposite directions from each other, betray their ethical egoist bias and miss the point of Erikson's definition. Kübler-Ross implies that persons who are generative rather than materialistic or exploitative will experience greater personal "ease in accepting death."[108] Shneidman argues, on the other hand, that

> It does not mollify the terror of death to discuss it in the honorific and beguiling terms of maturity, postnarcissistic love, ego-integrity or generativity, even though one can be grateful to Erik Erikson for the almost persuasive way in which he has made a generative death sound ennobling and nearly worthwhile.[109]

Both these comments obscure Erikson's point. He does not propose the ideas of integrity, generativity, and wisdom as a means to assuage personal anguish, although granted a possible desirable side effect. For him, integrity and wisdom prior to death mean far more.

First of all, integrity is the epigenetic fruition of seven previous life cycle crises and their successful resolution in stagelike progression. That is, you cannot expect to face death with wisdom or integrity without constructively resolving the childhood conflicts of trust and mistrust, autonomy and shame, initiative and guilt, the adolescent conflict of identity and identity confusion, and the adult conflicts of intimacy and isolation, generativity and stagnation.

Second, the outcome of every age-specific conflict between the two polarities is never complete victory of the positive and vanquishing of the negative but delicate balance and synthesis of the two poles in favor of the positive. This synthesis gives rise to what Erikson calls "ego strength" or virtue. The decisional, "existentialized," or even moral character of the idea of crisis and resolution shares with Reform theology, according to Vaux, "a common perception that passages imply choice, and price, and pain—that they are transacted in a moral universe."[110]

Third, successful resolution of the conflict of integrity and despair in life's last stage can only occur, like every conflict, through mutual regulation and activation between the cycle of generations. In general, how life crises are faced and resolved depends to a great extent not only upon intrapsychic resources and mechanisms, but also upon human interaction with "significant others" in the self's social environment.

Finally and most important for our discussion, as the above point implies, every stage, including the last, is governed by an implicit moral principle of generativity. Browning calls this "the normative center of Erikson's thought."[111] For Erikson the highest good is "the preservation of life and the furtherance of well-being— the 'maintenance of life'" or the "regeneration of the cycle of generations."[112] Maintenance and regeneration mean explicit care for what has been created. On occasion he discusses this in terms of "mutuality," "an ecology of mutual activation,"[113] or even as a modern version of the Golden Rule:

> I would call mutuality a relationship in which partners depend on each other for the development of their respective strengths. . . .
> *Truly worthwhile acts enhance a mutuality between the doer and the other—a mutuality which strengthens the doer even as it strengthens the other.* . . . Understood this way, the [Golden] Rule would say that it is best to do to another what will strengthen you even as it will strengthen him—that is, what will develop his best potentials even as it develops your own.[114]

In contrast, Kübler-Ross states that her "golden rule" is "to help the ones who limp behind in the stages."[115]

Thus, in the integrity of life's final stage *two* cycles of life, not *one*, come to completion—"the cycle of one generation concluding itself in the next, and the cycle of individual life coming to completion"—and *both* must find reconciliation with the fact of human finitude.[116] The ego strength or virtue with which a person incorporates death into life includes *and* reaches beyond that person into "the beginnings of future generations."

> For it can only weaken the vital fiber of the younger generation if the evidence of daily living verifies man's prolonged last phase as a sanctified period of childishness. Any span of the cycle lived without vigorous meaning, at the beginning, in the middle, or at the end, endangers the sense of life and the meaning of death in all whose life stages are intertwined.[117]

The degree of an adult's integrity and wisdom in the face of death determines the infant's fear or trust:

> Webster's dictionary is kind enough to help us complete this outline [of the "eight ages of man"] in a circular fashion. Trust (the first of our ego values) is here defined as "the assured reliance on another's integrity," the last of our values. . . . And it seems possible to further paraphrase the relation of adult integrity and infantile trust by saying that healthy children will not fear life if their elders have integrity enough not to fear death.[118]

By actualizing integrity the individual becomes both a follower *and* a leader, a consumer of culture's rituals and traditions *and* a model, a ritualizer *and* a transmitter of traditional ideals and innovative ideas—in short, a link between the individual life cycle and the cycle of generations.[119]

Therefore integrity in the face of death must include a "*grand*-generative function":

> Only in him who in some way has taken care of things and people and has adapted himself to the triumphs and disappointments adherent to being, by necessity, the originator of others and the generator of things and ideas—only he may gradually grow the fruit of these seven stages. I know no better word for it than ego integrity.[120]

Ego integrity is not so much "a rare quality of personal character" as it is "above all a shared proclivity for understanding or for 'hearing'

. . . the integrative ways of human life" beyond oneself.[121] It is a "post-narcissistic love of the human ego" or of humankind and "not of the self" alone.[122] A person who possesses integrity can perceive a greater part of the whole and experience wholeness and use both of these abilities to understand, affirm, and even forgive herself, her parents, and others. She experiences a "comradeship" across barriers of race, time, age, and cultural differences. She transcends her own death through a "responsible renunciation" which paradoxically rests upon the ability to remain engaged in the sequence of generations. Such renunciation and participation fosters the virtue of "childlikeness seasoned with wisdom" which Erikson distinguishes from a Kübler-Ross-like "finite childishness."[123] The person lives and dies wisely—that is, with detached, yet active, concern *with life itself, in the face of death itself.*[124] And so, "death loses its sting."[125] The "sting of death" for Erikson is not the loss of life per se, but the loss of life's ideals—that is, loss of the chance to give the cycle of life meaning and value.

Psychologist Salvadore Maddi classifies Erikson as an example of the fulfillment model of the culture of joy.[126] In my estimation, however, his view of death is much more complex: the positive and the negative, the mature and the infantile, the progressive and regressive remain together. His vision of transcendence integrates rather than ignores the negative. Death is partially divested of its painful negativity without denying the reality of the doubts, fears, remorse, and guilt. In growing old, the individual must recognize the pain of

> time forfeited and space depleted but also (to follow . . . our [epigenetic] chart from left to right) for autonomy weakened, initiative lost, intimacy weakened, generativity neglected—not to speak of identity potentials bypassed, or, indeed, an all too limiting identity lived.[127]

Positive resolution of life's last hurdle necessitates "regression in the service of development"—that is, a return to any one of these earlier unresolved conflicts in a final attempt to achieve a more adaptive response. In the end, Erikson does not intend a comfortable self-actualization. Rather, genuine integrity and wisdom must comprehend the limitations of one's life and encompass the "often tragic or bitterly tragicomic engagement" in one's "one and only life cycle within the sequence of generations."[128] The aging must face the disgust and disquiet that is inevitably triggered by the "increasing

stage of being finished, confused, helpless."[129] Evelyn and James
Whitehead's personalized rewording of this tension is worth quoting
at length:

> Integrity does not eliminate despair. Despair is an appropriate
> response to my awareness of the limits of my own life and to my
> consciousness that this life is coming to an end. Not all the
> possibilities of my life have been realized. I know remorse and
> regret and guilt in the face of what I have done and what I have
> failed to do. My death will leave much unattended to—loved
> ones will be left behind; new possibilities in the world will go
> unwitnessed.[130]

In contrast to the acceptance of death in the Kübler-Ross discussion,

> Only an integrity that can be sustained in the face of these
> realities can bring my life to fruition. Without the tension that
> is engendered in the struggle to come to terms with despair,
> self-acceptance remains naive and one's integrity unconvinc-
> ing. It is the continuing interplay of both positive and negative
> possibilities that gives my self-acceptance conviction and
> efficacy. Without this dynamic, my affirmation of life can re-
> main an untested and empty optimism that is no service to me
> . . . nor to others.[131]

I would only add that without "continuing interplay" between the
generations neither self-acceptance nor affirmation of life is possible.

Lifton's retrieval of the concept of guilt in relation to death
illustrates the nuanced understanding that the culture of care can
lend. Kübler-Ross almost always relegates guilt to the problems of
bereavement. She recognizes it as "perhaps the most painful companion of death," but she is referring solely to family members left
behind to deal with their death wishes toward the deceased. Optimally we might reach "acceptance without guilt," or in Weisman's
words, "appropriate death without suffering" the torments of one's
"ego ideal."[132] Guilt, primarily an inappropriate emotion, ought to
be ventilated, worked through, and alleviated.

Lifton draws implicitly upon Erikson's view of morality and
explicitly upon Martin Buber's distinction between real and pathological guilt to formulate a more complex and adequate interpretation. Erikson does not assume, as does the Kübler-Ross discussion,
that societal norms are grafted upon the inherently asocial individual by the external threat of socialization or that they must be

outgrown through reliance upon one's internal valuing system. Rather, the child needs the superego and its primitive moral prohibitions to navigate through the tumultuous waters of youth and adolescence and to reach the level of ethical striving characteristic of maturity. Optimally, by adulthood the individual acquires the ego capacity to move beyond the archaic moralism of childhood and the ideologies of youth. The adult ego can selectively affirm certain traditions and values while revising and even criticizing others:

> Men could not become or remain moral without some such moralistic tendency; yet without a further development of truly *ethical* strivings, that is, a subordination of his moralism to the shared affirmation of values, man could never build the social structures which define his adult privileges and obligations.[133]

Thus as Browning observes, the capacity for ethics is an "emergent phenonmenon." Likewise, sensibility to guilt also has an emergent, epigenetic quality:

> Generative man is not without those residues of guilt which come from an internalization of familial and tribal limitations and moralities. Generative man knows that there is a place for those elemental limitations which come from one's own family and one's own province. Here Erikson would distinguish between guilt at the level of morality and that higher kind of existential guilt which comes from one's sense of failure or inadequacy in contributing to the general maintenance and strengthening of the cycle of generations.[134]

Lifton uses an essay by Buber, "Guilt and Guilt Feelings," to articulate more extensively this idea of the epigenesis of the sense of guilt in relation to death. Buber elaborates the "notion of noninfantile, nonarchaic, non-neurotic sources of our guilt." He distinguishes between *psychological guilt feelings* internally experienced as the transgression of ancient taboos, and *ontic guilt* resulting from an injury to the objective "human order of being." Each person stands in "objective relationship to others," sometimes developing an even closer "personal relation" that "can be injured. Injuring a relationship means that at this place the human order of being is injured. No one other than he who inflicted the wound can heal it."[135] While certainly some guilt has a neurotic, infantile character, the psychotherapist must not ignore the reality of individual responsibility for injury to the human order. Only from such a perspective can we recognize the significance of serious personal errors, betrayal of friend or cause, self-contradiction, and the real need for forgiveness, illumination, perseverance, and restoration.

Lifton draws on this distinction when he becomes interested in the problem of guilt and death as early as 1963 in his work with survivors of Hiroshima and Nagasaki. In these studies he recognizes that the sense of "the human order being injured" is not unique to such tragedies, but "may well be that most fundamental to human existence."[136] We need to retain certain Freudian insights about unduly harsh or neurotic guilt, but we must recast them in slightly different terms. We need an understanding of guilt centered

> not around the Oedipus complex . . . but rather, simply, around the issue of life and death itself insofar as we take responsibility for death and dying or for symbolic modes of killing or destroying aspects of others, whether literally their bodies or something more metaphorical in them or in ourselves. Separation, disintegration, stasis, are all symbolized forms of death imagery. So long as this goes on, we take on some responsibility for the fact of death and guilt is among us.[137]

Freud has some inclination of the import of guilt and death in the evolution of civilization despite his emphasis on the pathological. The Kübler-Ross discussion, however, lacks Freud's depth of vision. They see guilt as "simply a painful and harmful emotion, which must be analyzed and overcome."[138] Admittedly, self-lacerating, manipulative, or static guilt is "hopelessly mixed" with constructive, or what Lifton calls "animating guilt."[139] But to ignore the distinction that Buber lifts up is hardly helpful.

Lifton enumerates the positive moral possibilities opened up by consciousness of animating guilt. An animating relation to guilt heightens identification with and sensitivity to others and the hurt that we inflict. This relation to guilt is a "fulcrum" for transformation. The "anxiety of responsibility" propels us onto all sorts of creative, compensatory, or rectifying acts, insights, and renewals. One recognizes that "one must, should, and can act against the wrong and toward an alternative."[140] Thus, without ignoring the immobilizing quality of pathological guilt, Lifton retains the significance of "guilt in the evolutionary function of rendering us accountable" to "other's in one's human web":

> Guilt serves as a balancing principle, directly related to patterns of mutual dependency and to . . . harmonizing immedi-

ate and ultimate obligations . . . [and to] accountability to
those most integral to one's historical and biological roots.[141]

A key concept, "evolutionary responsibility," operates implicitly throughout this redefinition of guilt and clues us in to the
normative bedrock of Lifton's work. For him, ethical conflict and
guilt have "enormous survival value";[142] they contribute to human
perpetuation or to what Lifton likes to call human "vitality" or
"feeling alive."

In its extreme form, this idea leads to an ethics of survival.
Where Erikson values survival *for the sake of generativity*, Lifton
seems more enamored by survival *for the sheer sake of survival*.
Erikson comments that "Lifton has vastly clarified what it means to
be a survivor, but a person in adulthood must also realize . . . that a
generator will be survived by what he generated."[143] This is only a
slight divergence, however, in comparison with their commonality
as representatives of the culture of care. More than anything, this
difference reflects Lifton's horror at the possibility of nuclear holocaust.

Both assume as a bottom line an innate trust in the vitality of
life distinctively at odds with Freud's assumption that death super-
cedes life.[144] As Lifton says, "death does indeed bring about biological and psychic annihilation. But life includes symbolic perceptions
of connections that *precede and outlast* that annihilation."[145] Since
instinct is by its very nature an impulse toward life, Erikson finds
Freud's idea of a *death* instinct "a grandiose contradiction in
terms."[146] In place of the death instinct, Browning notes, Erikson
assumes that the human animal is guided by "a prudent avoidance of
premature death and an unconscious commitment to the preservation and continuity of the species."[147] Both Erikson and Lifton
presuppose that life triumphs over death.

To this Lifton adds the idea that humans are born with an
innate potential for death imagery and a *need* for a sense of immortality. The need is neither as pathogenic nor compensatory as Freud
contrives. Desire for deathlessness stems not from an illusory resistance to reality but from a drive for relatedness beyond the self to
biological, social, historical, and spiritual realities:

> Profound as Freud's words are . . . I believe it is more correct
> to say that . . . we are not absolutely convinced of our own
> immortality, but rather have a need to maintain a *sense of
> immortality* in the face of inevitable biological death; and that

this need represents not only the inability of the individual unconscious to recognize the possibility of its own demise but also a compelling universal urge to maintain an inner sense of continuous symbolic relationship, over time and space, to the various elements of life. Nor is this need to transcend individual biological life *mere* denial (though denial becomes importantly associated with it): rather it is part of the organism's psychobiological quest for mastery, past of an innate imagery that has apparently been present in man's mind since the earliest periods of his history and prehistory.[148]

All the various schemes that humankind has invented to assure immortality simply symbolize and express the need for continuity.

Lifton has a tendency to assume that innate biological needs or capacities should be moral prerequisites. He presumes, for instance, that the need for life continuity is as much a moral characteristic of the species as the "long neck of the giraffe."[149] He makes the natural physiological or psychological instinct a value to be attained. This conceptual leap needs greater ethical justification on his part.

But despite this rather unquestioned ethical naturalism, he avoids a narrow-minded biological determinism or innate-ism by suggesting a variety of "modes" of immortality through which we may express the drive for continuity—from biological propagation, cosmological immersion in nature, and creative achievements to spiritual attainment and transcendental experience.

He hopes that we can progress beyond a therapeutically-oriented obsession with "personal self-exploration:" to a "psycho-historical" perspective that is expansive enough to involve us in "a new relationship to the world."[150] In fact, Lifton wants viable "modes of immortality" for just this reason. Just as Erikson pictures integrity as "a comradeship with the ordering ways of distant times and different pursuits," all five modes of immortality emphasize what ethical theory calls the principle of universalizability or the ideal observer theory.[151] In one way or another, each mode permits the person to perceive "distant times and different pursuits." Each mode opens up to a perception of "the entirety of the larger universe and of one's own being within it," or one's "experience in relationship to the larger rhythms of life and death."[152] Persons use the various modes to situate themselves and their particular needs in time and space and yet ultimately, to detach themselves from their involvements in order to make judgments about events and principles beyond themselves. As he says, "one must psychologically travel outside oneself in order to feel one's participation in the larger human process."[153]

With this as an undergirding theme, Lifton retrieves modes of human connectedness which have lost their viability for modernity. For example, Freud made us overly conscientious about the harmful consequences of parental possessiveness or of excessive dependence upon one's children, parents, or siblings. By contrast, Lifton tries to return some semblance of meaning to the idea of biological and social continuity through one's family or "tribe" as a crucial factor for human survival and generativity. Similarly, he reclaims the idea of religious hope in life after death and the idea of ecstatic or mystical "losing oneself" as other valid modes of transcendence.

Death becomes a standard that measures progress in what Lifton calls the three subparadigms—integrity, connection, and movement. Death tests the strength of the *connections* we have made, particularly to people and groups of people; the meaning, *integrity*, and purpose for which we have lived; and finally, the completeness of the *movement*, development, and growth that we have inspired.

> People approaching death look back nostalgically over their whole lives, in what is in part a process of self-judgment sometimes called the "life review." They examine their lives around issues of integrity, connection, and movement and search for evidence of relationship to modes of symbolic immortality. The dying person may ask "Has my life been connected? Has my life had some significance? Has it had some ethical meaning that I can assert as I die? Has my life had movement or progress? . . . Do I live on in my family through what I have been to them, or in my works, or in nature, even though I now die?"[154]

More than Erikson or Freud, Lifton emphasizes that death as well as guilt can therefore become a source of further creativity and rebirth. Death calls forth the "capacity to confront . . . the most fearful aspects of experience and emerge with deepened sensibility and extended vitality and reach."[155] Guilt in the face of death signals our rightful responsibility for separation, disintegration, and stasis, and encourages compensatory reflections and action. While Lifton admits that in our unconscious we cannot fathom our actual physical demise, we can and do and even *should* imagine the ramifications of our impact on life after we have died:

While "I" will cease to exist (which is why I cannot imagine my
own death), elements of my "self"—of its impact on others . . .
will continue . . . as a part of the flow that absorbs and recre-
ates the components of that impact to the point of altering their
shape and obscuring their origin. I can well imagine *that*
process, and doing so contributes importantly to my acceptance of the idea of my own death. [156]

Suggestions for a Practical Theology of Death and Dying

Awareness of the implicit norms of psychological interpretations of death allows us to judge their moral adequacy in contribut-
ing to our conversation about a more adequate model of dying.
Erikson and Lifton recapture certain moral and religious meanings
of death and surpass the Kübler-Ross discussion in depth and com-
prehensiveness. Erikson emphasizes the developmental prerequisites for attaining certain moral attitudes towards death. A person
must resolve life's earlier crises to acquire the age-specific virtues or
ego strength necessary to face the complex ethical issues of death.
Only she who has genuinely cared for what she has generated, only
she who has lived and lives in mutual confidence with others in life's
vital network can approach death with integrity and wisdom. At the
same time, Erikson remains acutely aware of life's limits and the
moral ambiguities surrounding guilt and despair, a theme upon
which Lifton expands. Lifton, likewise, recognizes the importance
of human evolution in forming the kind of symbols that can integrate
death into life. In contrast with the Kübler-Ross discussion, he
creates formative paradigms which address not only the lone individual in her suffering, but the individual in her connectedness with
the larger stream of historical happenings and social meanings.

Both Erikson and Lifton incorporate Freud's cautious, negative view of morality and the dangers of a punitive, childish moralism into a more inclusive understanding of the importance of adult
ethics for shaping human care, generativity, and continuity. They
demonstrate the limits of an ethic based solely, as Kübler-Ross or
Weisman might say, on an individual's "inner valuing process" in
making decisions in the face of death.

The limits become more apparent when we look at the implications of the psychologies of joy and care for the dilemmas of
modern medicine. Lifton responds to what he calls "psychological
dislocation" or "psychic numbing" of technological society with a

renewal of our symbols for life continuity. In place of traditional images which no longer illuminate *and* future images of nuclear holocaust which desensitize and destroy the capacity to create symbols, he fashions new ways to reconceive death's meaning.

Nevertheless, there are problems with his ideal of "immortalizing visions," "immortalization," "immortalizing connectedness," and so forth. [157] Besides the problem of human lust for infinity, a criticism Augustine and Calvin might make, there are some practical problems. How, for example, can one recommend the mode of biological reproduction in a world plagued by overpopulation or, for that matter, to a 27-year-old person diagnosed with cancer of the colon but so far childless? Erikson's greater concern for care and generativity rather than survival and immortality alone at least provides more discretion in dealing with such complex issues. We saw in the earlier chapters that the quest for immortality through medical achievements can readily become perverted into an end in itself, an end that breeds insensitivity to other human goods. Obviously, the reassurance that one's self is "immortal" and that one's life survives past one's death does not justify certain actions.

Nonetheless, Lifton and Erikson bring more adequate ethical presuppositions to the complicated choices surrounding death than members of the Kübler-Ross discussion, whose implicit ethical assumptions operate subtlely in medical decision-making more often than we might like to admit. Unfortunately, the Kübler-Ross discussion stops with the question of individual desires, needs, and rights. This guiding principle cannot encompass complex situations. For example, this principle cannot adequately address the question of whether to provide the maximum artificial feeding to patients with rapidly degenerative intestinal cancer. Many patients may desire it to calm their fears of dying, but treatment is not always physically helpful, it is often very expensive, and funds and availability are limited. Although the psychologies of Erikson and Lifton are not equipped to resolve such a dilemma, nor even intended as such, they can at least more fully comprehend the issues. Lifton recognizes the dangers of decision-making that is guided by "personal salvation" or "technical-scientific transcendence." [158] He reminds us that in the midst of an "age of psychic numbing" we need to assume responsibility for our individual *and* our collective destinies.

Erikson, likewise, coaches us to win the game of technological progress, not through looking out for our own personal glory, but through teamwork. When he addresses a graduating class of medical

students, he does not shy away from the ethical complexities of the
hospital world that they will soon enter. He emphasizes that "every
technique has to be reconsidered from the point of a joint social
responsibility" for humanity's physical and mental health. Wisdom,
he continues to maintain, remains a valid term for the appropriate
response to death and the problems which it evokes, regardless of
whatever changes occur in the coming years or have already occurred since he first defined the term. Beyond this, medical advance calls for new rituals which affirm a continuous interplay
between those beginning life and those ending it. We need new
ways of insuring "some finite sense of summary and, possibly, a
more active anticipation of dying."[159] Above all, Erikson cautions us
against any illusory "one-way street to never ending progress" and,
as Browning points out, against *"irresponsible creativity* devoid of a
quality of enduring care."[160] He discourages uncontrolled and unquestioned technological expansionism. Beyond becoming "self-
made" persons, we must answer a deeper question on par with
genuine mature adulthood—"how to *take care* of what is being
appropriated in the establishment of an industrial identity."[161] In
Browning's rephrasing, we "must confront the forces of modernity
with *an advance*—an advance in humanness and an advance in
responsibility,"[162] an advance distinct from the personalistic advance in individual fulfillment proposed by the Kübler-Ross discussion. In Erikson's words, we need a new standard that acknowledges
"the responsibility of each individual for the potentialities of all
generations and of all generations for each individual and this in a
more informed manner than has been possible in past systems of
ethics."[163]

Whatever the contributions of Erikson and Lifton to the discussion, however, their ethical views remain inevitably unclear.
Their stance as scientists prevents them from systematically
thematizing the latent moral and religious dimensions of their
thought. Since they are psychologists, ethical discourse lies beyond
the recognized boundaries of their disciplines. For a more complete
practical theology, we will have to draw upon theologians Tillich and
Ramsey who state their moral and religious assumptions with a great
deal more self-consciousness.

Footnotes to Chapter IV

/1/ Browning, "Religioethical Thinking," p. 140; Don S. Browning, *The
Moral Context of Pastoral Care* (Philadelphia: Westminster Press, 1976), p.
13.

/2/   Lifton, in fact, describes this phenomenon as "the either-or approach":
theorists "either almost totally disregard death or focus on it so exclusively
that it becomes the definitive explanation of virtually all human behavior."
Robert Jay Lifton, Shuichi Kato, and Michael R. Reich, *Six Lives Six
Deaths: Portraits from Modern Japan* (New Haven: Yale University Press,
1979), p. 4.

/3/   Browning, *Pluralism and Personality*, p. 195.

/4/   Ibid., p. 41.

/5/   Salvatore Maddi, *Personality Theories: A Comparative Analysis*
(Homewood, Ill.: Dorsey Press, 1968), pp. 20–21.

/6/   David Norton, *Personal Destinies: A Philosophy of Ethical Individu-
alism* (Princeton, N.J.: Princeton University Press, 1976), pp. 306–309.

/7/   Browning, *Generative Man*, pp. 20–21, 30, 147.

/8/   William K. Frankena, *Ethics* (Englewood Cliffs, N.J.: Prentice-Hall,
1973), pp. 14–16. See also Browning, "Religioethical Thinking," pp. 144,
153–154.

/9/   Frankena, *Ethics*, pp. 17–18.

/10/   Ibid., pp. 15–16.

/11/   Browning, "Religioethical Thinking," p. 144.

/12/   Erik Erikson, *The Life Cycle Completed: A Review* (New York: Norton, 1982), p. 63.

/13/   Robert J. Lifton, *The Life of the Self: Toward a New Psychology* (New
York: Basic Books, 1976), pp. 31–34.

/14/   Fox, *Essays in Medical Sociology*, p. 421.

/15/   Churchill, "Experience in Dying," p. 24. See Introduction, pp. 6ff.,
above.

/16/   Kübler-Ross, *Death and Dying*, pp. 14–15.

/17/   Ibid., p. 141.

/18/   Kübler-Ross, *Final State of Growth*, p. x.

/19/   Kübler-Ross, *Death and Dying*, p. 276.

/20/   Kübler-Ross, *Final Stage of Growth*, pp. x, 6.

/21/   Kübler-Ross, *Death and Dying*, p. 120.

/22/   Avery D. Weisman and Robert Kastenbaum, *The Psychological Autopsy: A Study of the Terminal Phases of Life* (New York: Behavioral Publications, 1968), p. 2; see also pp. 42–43.

/23/   Elisabeth Kübler-Ross, "On Death and Dying," in *The Phenonmenon
of Death: Faces of Mortality*, ed. Edith Wyschograd (New York: Harper and
Row, 1973), pp. 18, 20; idem., "The Dying Patient's Point of View," in *The
Dying Patient*, ed. Orville G. Brim, et. al (New York: Russell Sage Foundation,
1970), pp. 157–158; *Death and Dying*, pp. 7–12, 23.

/24/   Elisabeth Kübler-Ross, *Questions and Answers on Death and Dying*
(New York: Macmillan, 1974), cited by Roy Branson, "Is Acceptance a
Denial of Death?" *The Christian Century*, May 7, 1974, p. 465.

/25/   Herman Feifel, "Death in Contemporary America," in *New Meanings
of Death*, p. 4; idem., "Attitudes Toward Death: A Psychological Perspective," in *Death: Current Perspectives*, p. 423.

/26/   Avery D. Weisman, *The Realization of Death: a Guide for the Psycho-
logical Autopsy* (New York: Jason Aronson, 1974), pp. 4, 22; Avery D.
Weisman and J. William Worden, "Psychosocial Analysis of Cancer
Deaths," in *Death, Dying, Transcending*, ed. Richard A. Kalish (Farm-

ingdale, N.Y.: Baywood Publishing, 1977), p. 55.

/27/   Avery D. Weisman, "The Psychiatrist and the Inexorable," in *New Meanings of Death*, pp. 108, 114.

/28/   Avery D. Weisman and Thomas P. Hackett, "Predilection to Death: Death and Dying as a Psychiatric Problem," *Psychosomatic Medicine* 23, no. 3 (1961), p. 247.

/29/   Weisman's Preface to *On Dying and Denying* implies that this belated recognition has caused a major delay in the book's publication. Avery D. Weisman, *On Dying and Denying: A Psychiatric Study of Terminality* (New York: Behavior Publications, 1972), pp. xii, xv, xvi.

/30/   Robert Kastenbaum and Ruth Aisenberg, *The Psychology of Death* (New York: Springer Publishing, 1976), pp. 163–164.

/31/   Ibid., pp. vii–viii. See also Robert Kastenbaum, "Death and Development through the Lifespan," in *New Meanings of Death*, p. 44; idem., *Death, Society, and Human Experience* (St. Louis: the C. V. Mosby Co., 1977), pp. v, 4.

/32/   Kastenbaum, "Death and Development," p. 38.

/33/   Kastenbaum and Aisenberg, *Psychology of Death*, pp. 4–5.

/34/   Ibid., p. 106. Kastenbaum comments, "How do people die? How *should* people die? These questions sometimes are jumbled together. It is difficult to keep our hopes and fears out of the picture long enough to determine the basic facts of the situation. . . . An entirely objective view may be an unattainable goal." *Death, Society, and Experience*, p. 183.

/35/   Feifel, "Attitudes: Psychological Perspective," pp. 423–424, 428.

/36/   Gruman, "Historical Introduction," p. 90.

/37/   Steinfels, Introduction to *Death Inside Out*, p. 3. See also Choron, *Modern Man*, pp. 90, 96; Crouse, "Fascination with Death," p. 137; Gutmann, "Dying to Power," p. 336; Warren A. Shibles, *Death: An Interdisciplinary Analysis* (Whitewater, Wis.: Language Press, 1974), p. 281.

/38/   Herman Feifel, "Attitudes Toward Death in Some Normal and Mentally Ill Populations," in *The Meaning of Death*, p. 128.

/39/   Edwin S. Shneidman, "Orientations Towards Death," *International Journal of Psychiatry* 2, no. 2 (1966), pp. 170, 173.

/40/   Weisman, *Realization of Death*, p. 189.

/41/   Kübler-Ross, *Death and Dying*, pp. xi, 22.

/42/   Weisman, *Realization of Death*, p. 7.

/43/   Edwin S. Shneidman, *Deaths of Man* (New York: Quadrangle/The New York Times Book Co., 1973), pp. 10–11.

/44/   Kübler-Ross, "Patient's View," p. 156.

/45/   Weisman, *Dying and Denying*, p. 11.

/46/   Robert Kastenbaum, "Death and Bereavement in Later Life," in *Death and Bereavement*, ed. Austin H. Kutscher (Springfield, Ill.: Charles C. Thomas, 1969), p. 51.

/47/   Feifel, "Attitudes: Populations," p. 123.

/48/   Kübler-Ross, *Death and Dying*, p. 119.

/49/   Feifel, "Attitudes: Psychological Perspective," p. 426.

/50/   Kübler-Ross, *Death and Dying*, p. 22.

/51/   Elisabeth Kübler-Ross, *Living with Death and Dying* (New York:

/52/   Elisabeth Kübler-Ross, "Dying as a Human-Psychological Event," in

The Experience of Dying, ed. Norbert Greinacher and Alois Müller (New York: Herder and Herder, 1974), pp. 51–52.

/53/   Kübler-Ross, "Patient's View," p. 169.

/54/   Kübler-Ross, "Dying as Psychological Event," p. 49.

/55/   Branson, "Is Acceptance Denial?" p. 464.

/56/   Kübler-Ross, "Patient's View," p. 168.

/57/   Branson, "Is Acceptance Denial?" p. 464.

/58/   Kübler-Ross, *Death and Dying*, pp. 40, 54, 88.

/59/   Kübler-Ross, *Living with Death*, p. 45; idem., *Death and Dying*, pp. 269–279.

/60/   Kübler-Ross, *Death and Dying*, pp. 119–120.

/61/   Ibid., p. 113.

/62/   Kübler-Ross, *Living with Death*, p. 48.

/63/   Kübler-Ross, *Final Stage of Growth*, p. xxii.

/64/   Churchill, "Experience of Dying," p. 25.

/65/   Kübler-Ross, *Final Stage of Growth*, p. 117.

/66/   Ibid., pp. x, 117, 164.

/67/   Weisman, "Psychiatrist and the Inexorable," p. 121.

/68/   Kastenbaum, *Death, Society, and Experience*, pp. 239.

/69/   Parsons and Lidz, "Death in American Society," p. 145.

/70/   Weisman, "Psychiatrist and the Inexorable," pp. 110–111.

/71/   Ibid., p. 109.

/72/   Ibid., p. 119.

/73/   Weisman, *Realization of Death*, p. 151.

/74/   Weisman, *Dying and Denying*, p. 37.

/75/   Weisman, *Realization of Death*, p. 151.

/76/   Weisman and Kastenbaum, *Psychological Autopsy*, pp. 35–37.

/77/   Weisman, "Psychiatrist and the Inexorable," pp. 118, 119.

/78/   Weisman and Hackett, "Predilection to Death," pp. 232–256, cited by Avery D. Weisman, "Discussion of Orientations Toward Death," *International Journal of Psychiatry* 2 (1966), pp. 191–192.

/79/   Weisman, *Dying and Denying*, p. 33.

/80/   Weisman, *Realization of Death*, p. 140.

/81/   Schneidman, *Deaths of Man*, p. 25.

/82/   Ibid., p. 11.

/83/   Schneidman, *Death: Current Perspectives*, pp. xiii, 227.

/84/   Feifel, "Death and Development," pp. 19, 35–36.

/85/   Abraham Maslow, "Abe Maslow Talks About Death," *Psychology Today*, August 1970, p. 16.

/86/   Vaux, *Reformed Tradition*, p. 107.

/87/   Robert Jay Lifton, *The Broken Connection: On Death and the Continuity of Life* (New York: Simon and Schuster, 1979), pp. 100–101.

/88/   Lifton, *Life of the Self*, p. 50.

/89/   Lifton, *Broken Connection*, p. 4.

/90/   Erik H. Erikson, "Autobiographical Notes on the Identity Crisis," *Journal of American Academy of Arts and Sciences* 99, no. 4 (Fall 1970), p. 744. See Robert Coles, *Erik H. Erikson: The Growth of His Work* (Toronto: Little, Brown and Co., 1970), pp. 22–23.

/91/   For more on the question of Erikson's thoughts about his affinity to and divergence from Freud, see Paul Roazen, *Erik H. Erikson: The Power and Limits of a Vision* (New York: Collier Macmillan, 1967), and idem., *Freud and His Followers,* pp. 513–517.

/92/   Erik H. Erikson, *Insight and Responsibility* (New York: Norton, 1964), p. 156.

/93/   Lifton, *Six Lives Six Deaths,* p. 6. See also *Life of the Self,* pp. 107–108, and *Broken Connection,* p. 6, n.

/94/   Lifton, *Life of the Self,* p. 81.

/95/   Ibid., p. 152.

/96/   Lifton, *Broken Connection,* p. 3.

/97/   Lifton, *Life of the Self,* p. 95.

/98/   Erikson, "Autobiographical Notes," pp. 741, 754.

/99/   Erikson, *Life Cycle,* p. 103.

/100/   Robert Jay Lifton, "On Death and Death Symbolism: The Hiroshima Disaster," in*The Phenomenon of Death,* pp. 92, 96. Others outside the Kübler-Ross discussion such as Ernest Becker or Norman Brown, who bring together death and psychology, still fall prey to the temptation to emphasize one at the expense of the other. *The Denial of Death,* for example, has only a sketchy dualistic personality theory behind its fascination with evil and death. *Life Against Death,* on the other hand, is actually more concerned with a psychology of remissiveness, not death per se.

/101/   Erikson, *Insight and Responsibility,* p. 133.

/102/   Lifton, *Broken Connection,* p. 35.

/103/   Lifton, "Death Symbolism," p. 100, n. 33.

/104/   Robert Jay Lifton and Eric Olson, *Living and Dying* (New York: Praeger Publishers, 1974), p. 94.

/105/   Lifton, *Life of the Self,* pp. 83, 153.

/106/   Liftoon, *Broken Connection,* pp. 101–102. See p. 440, n. 3.

/107/   Ibid., p. 35.

/108/   Kübler-Ross, *Death and Dying,* p. 265.

/109/   Edwin S. Shneidman, "The Enemy," *Psychology Today,* August 1970, p. 66.

/110/   Vaux, *Reformed Tradition,* p. 69. See also, Peter Homans, *Childhood and Selfhood: Essays on Tradition, Religion and Modernity in the Psychology of Erik H. Erikson* (London: Associated University Press, 1978), p. 236.

/111/   Browning, *Generative Man,* p. 181.

/112/   Erikson, *Insight and Responsibility,* p. 237.

/113/   Erikson, *Life Cycle Completed,* p. 21.

/114/   Erikson, *Insight and Responsibility,* pp. 231, 233.

/115/   Kübler-Ross, *Living with Death,* p. 47.

/116/   Erikson, *Insight and Responsibility,* pp. 132–133.

/117/   Ibid., p. 133. See also, idem., *Identity: Youth and Crisis* (New York: Norton, 1968), p. 141; and idem., "Dr. Borg's Life-Cycle," *Daedalus* 105 (1976), p. 23.

/118/   Erik H. Erikson, *Childhood and Society,* 2nd ed. (New York: Norton, 1963), p. 269.

/119/   Erik H. Erikson, "Ontogeny of Ritualization," in *Psychoanalysis—A General Psychology: Essays in Honor of Heinz Hartman,* ed. Rudolph M. Loewenstein, et al. (New York: International University Press, 1966), pp. 618–619.

/120/   Erikson, *Childhood and Society*, p. 268.
/121/   Erikson, *Life Cycle Completed*, p. 65.
/122/   Erikson, *Childhood and Society*, p. 268.
/123/   Erikson, *Life Cycle Completed*, p. 65.
/124/   Erikson, *Identity*, p. 140; idem., *Insight and Responsibility*, pp. 133–134, 157.
/125/   Erikson, *Childhood and Society*, p. 268.
/126/   Maddi, *Personality Theories*, pp. 39–40, 317.
/127/   Erikson, *Life Cycle Completed*, p. 63.
/128/   Erikson, *Identity*, p. 140.
/129/   Erikson, *Life Cycle Completed*, p. 61; idem., *Insight and Responsibility*, p. 134.
/130/   Evelyn Eaton Whitehead and James D. Whitehead, *Christian Life Patterns: The Psychological Challenges and Religions Invitations of Adult Life* (Garden City, N.Y.: Doubleday, 1979), p. 164.
/131/   Ibid., p. 164.
/132/   Kübler-Ross, *Death and Dying*, pp. 161, 180; Weisman and Hackett, "Predilection to Death," p. 254.
/133/   Erikson, "Autobiographical Notes," p. 753.
/134/   Browning, *Generative Man*, pp. 157, 185. Erikson heads in a direction that Ricoeur recommends, thereby negotiating a path ignored by Freud. Erikson suggests what Ricoeur describes as an "epigenesis of the sense of guilt." Guilt is not only regressive, but dialectically progressive: it occasions not only fixation and stagnation, but growth and restoration of new meaning.
/135/   Martin Buber, "Guilt and Guilt Feelings," *Psychiatry* 20 (May 1957), p. 120.
/136/   Robert Jay Lifton, "Psychological Effects of the Atomic Bomb in Hiroshima: The Theme of Death," in *Death and Identity*, p. 35; idem., "Death Symbolism," p. 89.
/137/   Leslie H. Farber, Robert Jay Lifton, et al., "Questions of Guilt," *Partisan Review* 39, no. 2 (Fall 1972), p. 518.
/138/   Lifton, *Broken Connection*, pp. 134–136.
/139/   Farber, Lifton, et al., "Questions of Guilt," p. 528. See also Robert Jay Lifton, *Home from the War: Vietnam Veterans: Neither Victims nor Executioners* (New York: Simon and Schuster, 1973), chap. IV, "Animating Guilt," pp. 97–133, and chap. XIII, "On Change," pp. 379–408.
/140/   Farber, Lifton, et al., "Questions of Guilt," pp. 519–522, 527–528; Lifton, *Broken Connection*, p. 138.
/141/   Lifton, *Broken Connection*, pp. 144–145.
/142/   Farber, Lifton, et al., "Questions of Guilt," p. 518.
/143/   Erikson, *Life Cycle Completed*, pp. 79–80.
/144/   See p. 47 ff., above.
/145/   Lifton, *Broken Connection*, p. 18.
/146/   Erikson, "Autobiographical Notes," p. 736.
/147/   Browning, *Generative Man*, p. 155.
/148/   Lifton, "Death Symbolism," pp. 93–94.
/149/   Lifton, *Broken Connection*, p. 7.
/150/   Lifton and Olson, *Living and Dying*, pp. 142–143.
/151/   See Arthur J. Dyck, *On Human Care: An Introduction to Ethics*

(Nashville: Abingdon, 1977), pp. 141–155.
/152/   Erikson, *Childhood and Society*, p. 268; Lifton, *Life of the Self*, p. 144; idem., "Death Symbolism," p. 110.
/153/   Lifton, *Broken Connection*, p. 34.
/154/   Lifton, *Six Lives Six Deaths*, pp. 14–15.
/155/   Lifton, *Life of the Self*, p. 20.
/156/   Lifton, *Broken Connection*, p. 8.
/157/   Lifton, *Life of the Self*, pp. 141–142.
/158/   Lifton, *Broken Connection*, p. 376.
/159/   Erik H. Erikson, "On Protest and Affirmation," *Harvard Medical Alumni Bulletin* (Fall 1972), p. 32.
/160/   Erikson, *Insight and Responsibility*, p. 132; Browning, *Generative Man*, pp. 27, 164.
/161/   Erikson, "Autobiographical Notes," p. 748.
/162/   Browning, *Generative Man*, p. 169.
/163/   Erikson, *Insight and Responsibility*, p. 157.

CHAPTER V
PAUL TILLICH AND THE RETRIEVAL OF THE MORAL COMPONENT

Foundations for a More Comprehensive Ethic

Paul Ramsey and Paul Tillich offer a response to Erikson's request for a more "informed" ethic for our time. Tillich sheds light on the theoretical question of the relation between death, sin, and the moral life, and Ramsey on the more concrete ethical issues of medicine and death.

Alasdair MacIntyre enumerates three general areas in which contemporary theologians must argue more convincingly if they wish those in the medical ethics discussion to take them seriously:

> First—and without this everything else is uninteresting—we ought to expect a clear statement of what different it makes to be a Jew or a Christian or a Moslem, rather than a secular thinker, in morality generally. Second, and correlatively, we need to hear a theological critique of secular morality and culture. Third, we want to be told what bearing what has been said under the first two headings has on the specific problems which arise for modern medicine.[1]

Measured by these three criteria, Tillich's work is weakest on the last, but strongest on the first two; Ramsey's scrutinizing attention to specific "rules of practice," by contrast, fills in the remaining gap. With the help of these two, therefore, we might begin to satisfy persons like MacIntyre and Erikson. Not only will we have approached a more systematic understanding of the moral order of human mortality, but we will have reappropriated some of the theological resources of our culture. Both scholars reinterpret traditional moral and religious views of death, sin, and grace in light of the shift to modern views, formulating a viable "non-moralistic" way to move beyond orthodox doctrines without losing significant moral meanings. Combining their theological perspective with the psychological perspective of the culture of care gives us a far more adequate ethic with which to approach "post-industrial" death than some of the normative images that currently control modern attitudes.

MacIntyre has reason to complain. While psychologists have made new forays into the realm of death to address and, indeed, to constructively resolve the moral confusion surrounding the modern deathbed, theology has seldom dared to tread too far or too deep. Churches, ministers, believers, and seminarians alike simply have not made questions of death and dying a primary concern. Or, if they have, the language and understanding of medicine or psychology, not the language and understanding of their respective faith traditions, often determine the controlling images.[2] The problem is, as Browning asserts, that when we inattentively borrow other understandings, we are "sometimes oblivious . . . that we appropriate . . . not only scientific information and therapeutic techniques but various normative visions of human fulfillment which are often neither philosophically sound nor theologically defensible."[3]

Other problems besides negligence plague modern theological views of mortality, some of which we touched on in previous chapters. We observed in chapter I that modern theologians since Schleiermacher have struggled to account for the traditional doctrines relating death, sin, judgment, grace, and eternal life, *and* for the modern view that death is a necessary aspect of being, not a flaw due to sin or a revolving doorway to heaven. When the ideas of authority, duty, punishment, and morality became increasingly unpopular, especially from the point of view of modern psychology, theologians ceased struggling with the relation between these ideas and death. The disappearance of the judgmental view of death has had its obvious liberating consequences. In the aftermath of Freud we can hardly help but affirm this. Yet, we witnessed in the last two chapters that total disregard for death's moral relevance leaves a vacuum that psychology and medicine fill with new moralisms. This is hardly a better solution from a religious or a secular perspective.

Related to this problem, many otherwise well-informed scholars rather superficially collapse the complex theological motifs that we saw in Augustine, Calvin, and Schleiermacher into one lone doctrine. They presume, for instance, that the Christian tradition sees death as simply an "unnatural evil resulting from moral evil," or that this view exhausts *the* Christian position. As Churchill laments, "contemporary thinkers—philosophers, physicians, and even theologians—frequently assume that once they have dealt with specific Christian doctrines on death, they have also dealt with the theological dimensions of death." These trends deprive us of "a portion of our moral resources" that we need "for assessing the meaning of our death and time of our dying."[4]

In addition, nontheologians define the moral problems of death and leave little room for theological answers. Many theologians completely shed their identity as theologians, adopt instead the categories of moral philosophy,[5] and disregard the impact of beliefs, loyalties, and the faith traditions on moral decision-making. Theologians themselves lack agreement about what would even comprise the subject matter of theology in this whole area. In the end, as James M. Gustafson notes, "we know what many of the *moral* issues are in technology and the life sciences [but] we are not sure what the "religious" or *theological* issues are."[6] Others err in the opposite direction. They retain the theological, but only as prophetic critique of the "idolatry" of the technological ethos, thereby limiting the possibility for conversation and failing to go beyond broad scale attack on the *zeitgeist* to specific, concrete cases.[7]

In spite of these various impediments, people still desire vibrant theological witness in the arena of biomedical ethics and in the area of death and dying. Veatch names the clergy as *the* most appropriate group to act as the dying patient's moral and religious agent, advocate, and covenantal partner. The dying patient "desperately needs counsel and guidance in the formulation of his conscience." The patient "has not only the right, but the duty, to express his own ethical theological views. It is only through training by the religious and philosophical leadership of the community that the patient is going to be prepared to carry out this awesome task."[8] Physicians and health professionals have neither the expertise nor the psychological and spiritual readiness to act as moral teacher, guide, counsel, or advocate. Clergy and churches must take on these roles. They desperately need foundational resources to do so.

Contributions from a Spokesman for Correlational Conversation

Tillich articulates "theologically defensible," "philosophically sound" moral counsel on approaching death. Some might argue that because of the abstract or methodological character of Tillich's work, his thought has little relevance for our dialogue. Moreover, one might say, the excitement of neoorthodox theology has grown stale, having made the names of the Niebuhrs, Barth, Tillich household words for an all-too-brief period of time. Tillich himself was nearing his own death at approximately the same time that psychology began to proliferate books on death and medicine to talk about something called "bioethics." He never made the subject of death a central concern. In addition, he worked more in the area of theology *per se* than in ethics, declaring that theology does not need a "special section for ethical theology." These factors could be construed as serious handicaps. Must we mine his magnum opus, the three-volume *Systematic Theology,* or rework his books, sermons, and articles in search of some random comment on the moral import of death?

While valid protests, his ideas have lived on, Tillichian school or no, and he does have a great deal to say about the problems I have discussed so far. Although he has no book or article on death specifically, hardly a page goes by without some mention of "being" and "non-being," the "boundary situation," the "abyss," finitude, estrangement in time and space. In one way or another, all of these ideas reveal that the problem of mortality and separation stands at the very heart of his thought. The seriousness with which he regarded existentialist writings on "being-towards-death" and psychoanalytic discussion of the "death instinct" further indicates his fascination with the subject.

This seriousness points to another factor that makes Tillich a compelling figure. His interest in Heidegger and Freud grows out of a correlational approach to doing theology. Of all theologians, he would undoubtedly have had keen interest in the "death and dying movement." Like the German classical school from which he emerged, he hoped to overcome the debilitating disjunction between religion and culture. He saw culture and religion as integrally related—religion is the "substance of culture" and culture the "form of religion."[9] Because of this conviction, "the problem of the relation between the theological and the psychotherapeutic understanding" moved "more and more into the foreground of my interest." Indeed, he concludes, "I do not think that it is possible today to elaborate a Christian doctrine of man, without using the immense material brought forth by depth psychology."[10] Religious thinking means "penetrating in an ultimate sense into what happens day by day, in labor and industry, in marriage and friendship, in ordinary social intercourse and recreation, and in meditation and quiet, and even in sleep,"—and we would add, even in death and dying.[11]

In a memorial tribute, Erikson observes that a basic theme in Tillich's life was "*Auf der Grenze sein*, Being on the Boundary": he lived "on the boundary" between the two temperaments of his parents—the "dutiful East-German" father and his "more sensual Rhineland" mother; he lived "on the boundary" between his homeland and a foreign country after his move to the United States in 1933; the name of the region where he originated *die Mark* itself means "the territory of the boundary" between the West and the Slavic East.[12] In a multitude of areas, he stood on the boundary between two elements, and inherited richly from both.

Almost by second nature, then, Tillich adopts the role of mediator. He certainly plays that role in our discussion. As Langdon Gilkey comments: "The main role of his thought has been to provide a point—on a surprising number of axes—where seemingly opposite positions come into a tense, comprehensible, relation. . . . In this sense, he continually mediates all over the place."[13] He mediates between culture and theology, philsophy and theology, Roman Catholic and Protestant, liberal and orthodox. For our conversation, he mediates between conservative views of death as unnatural and modern views of death as natural, and between death as part of the moral order and death as part of the natural order.

The Problem of Death in Contemporary Society

In contrast to the threefold schema of the Kübler-Ross discussion—triumph of technology, alienation from religion, and salvation through the "remedies" of psychology—Tillich does not locate the cause of denial of death in the decline of traditional religion, nor does he seek its solution in psychology. He agrees that denial and fear characterize modern attitudes, but he does not hold religion liable in the way that the Kübler-Ross discussion does.

Instead, "forbidden death" results from the attempts in the eighteenth and nineteenth centuries to transcend human limitation, including the bondage of finitude. Whereas, in the Middle Ages, "every room, every street, and more important, every heart and every mind were filled with symbols of the end," in the Enlightenment, "death and sin and hell were removed from public consciousness."[14]

Death and guilt disappear even in the preaching of early industrial society. . . . Man has shortcomings, but there is no sin and
certainly no universal sinfulness. The bondage of the will, of
which the Reformer spoke, the demonic powers which are
central for the New Testament, the structure of destruction of
personal and communal life, are ignored or denied. . . . Man is
pictured in a position of progressive fulfillment of his potentialities. . . . Their tragic and inescapable character is denied.
As the universe replaces God, as man in the center of the
universe replaces the Christ, so the expectation of peace and
justice in history replaces the expectation of the Kingdom of
God.[15]

Scientific developments in the last century further intensify
this attitude. People perceive the world as "calculable and manageable," as ameliatory "from the point of view of man's needs and
desires."[16] Guided by Adam Smith's collective *telos* of maximal
productivity, many persons in American society exclude the reality
of death from daily life, considering it in "poor taste" to mention it.
Funeral parlors across the land transform the dead "into a mask of
the living." Americans use a quasi-Platonic idea of the immortality
of the soul as a means of denying that there *is* an end,[17] or look to
the technical methods of therapeutic psychology to come to terms
with "the abyss of nothingness."

For a time, technological conquest of time and space stayed
the terror of human bondage to finitude.[18] Modern society thought
that it had destroyed death, not so much as "the natural end of life,"
but death as a power in and over life."[19] But the last several decades
have proved the hopes of modern civilization that it could conquer
finitude, sin, and tragedy simply "illusions of our period." After a
century of concealment,

the lid which we had fastened down over the abyss in our being
. . . was torn off. The picture of Death appeared, unveiled in a
thousand forms. . . . Our generation—the generation of world
wars, revolutions, and mass migrations—rediscovered the reality of death. . . . Death has again grasped the reins which we
believed it had relinquished forever.[20]

The title of the first chapter of James Luther Adam's book on
Tillich summarizes Tillich's alternative response to this situation—
"The Need for a New Language." The failure of religion to provide
meaning does not call for its demise, as with the Kübler-Ross
scholars, but demands earnest reinterpretation of its languishing

symbols. Like the symbol of God, he believes that the questions of death, sin, and forgiveness especially need redefinition:

> We need a translation and interpretation of this symbol, but not, as you [Carl Rogers] seem to indicate, a replacement. I don't believe that scientific language is able to express the vertical dimension adequately, because it is bound to the relationship of finite things to each other, even in psychology and certainly in all physical sciences. This is the reason why I think we need another language, and this language is the language of symbols and myths; it is a religious language. But we poor theologians, in contrast to you happy psychologists, are in the bad situation that we know the symbols with which we deal have to be reinterpreted and even *radically* reinterpreted.[21]

Throughout his work, Tillich retrieves the living meaning of "distorted and unintelligible" Christian doctrines, including those on death, in a way that appeals to those within theology *and* even those without theology who ordinarily dismiss Christianity as obsolete.[22]

Death, Sin, and the Myth of the "Fall"

Until Schleiermacher, people generally accepted the doctrine of Adam's "fall" into sin as the cause of death and evil. With the dismissal of this as an historically twisted and inaccurate view, persons also tend to dismiss the paradox of death as both natural and unnatural, or as both a part of the created order and the fallen order.[23] Tillich mediates the moral complexities involved in this tension. He retains death's moral character, yet affirms its reality as a natural, necessary part of life. He would agree with Reinhold Niebuhr that "while we have rightly criticized the view that links death exclusively to sin and fails to see that death is also implicit in finitude, nevertheless there is a profound truth in the thought of death as the consequence of sin."[24] In contrast to contemporary views of death in the cultures of psychology and medicine, Tillich affirms that we experience death differently as a result of sin and guilt. This leads to a more comprehensive understanding of human anxiety, freedom, and responsibility.

Like Schleiermacher, Tillich defines death as a natural, universal part of existence. He begins two sermons, "On Transitoriness of Life" and "The Destruction of Death," by observing its natural inherency as a basic element in the structure of being. Death is the

law of nature unto which God delivers us as "dust returns to dust."
In contrast to Augustine and Calvin, he interprets these words, "for
dust thou art and to dust thou shalt return," as a "statement of fact,"
not a "promise of future punishment."[25] As Niebuhr says, "The fact
that man dies is indubitable proof of his organic relation to the world
of nature and would seem to prove 'that a man hath no preeminence
above a beast.' "[26] Like grass, humans "withereth and fadeth."[27]

    Further, fear of death also belongs to the natural order of
being: "Anxiety about having to die belongs to the created order of
being quite apart from estrangement and sin. . . . It is rooted in the
structure of being and not in the distortion of this structure."[28]
Christ himself struggled in the Garden of Gethsemane with a fear
which was "neither neurotic nor connected with guilt," but which
was "the natural expression of everything finite when anticipating
the partial negation of suffering and the total negation of death."[29]
Tillich agrees with Kübler-Ross, Feifel, Becker, and others who
argue that fear of death is a mainspring of human behavior. It lies
behind all concrete fears and gives them ultimate seriousness.[30]

    Still, in both sermons, Tillich moves rapidly to a second point,
different from anything we saw in the Kübler-Ross discussion. Erikson and Lifton allude to this, but do not articulate it fully. Tillich asks
us to consider why our transitoriness is so troubling. If we are only
biological creatures who live and die, why is our anxiety over death
so disproportionate to its reality and our rebellion so excessive?
There seems to be "something more, profoundly mysterious," some
deeper reason lying at the root of these reactions that the natural law
"from dust to dust" alone does not explain. This "something more" is
"the feeling of guilt" and "God's wrath."[31] Guilt adds an "intensify-
ing element" to human anxiety that the Kübler-Ross discussion fails
to recognize. "It has been called by Paul the 'sting of death,' because
it adds to the natural anxiety of 'having to die' an anxiety which it
would not have without guilt, namely, the feeling of standing under
judgment."[32]

    On the one hand, we have to die because we are dust. That is
the law of nature. But, on the other, "we have to die because we are
guilty. That is the moral law to which we, unlike all other beings, are
subject."[33] Although natural to every finite being, death also stands
over against nature. Besides the order of growing and dying, we
belong as well to the "order of sin and punishment" and to an order
"uniting finiteness and sin" according to a "tragic law . . . which

ordains that human greatness utterly fall."[34] Like Augustine said, we are destined to be mortal and immortal at the same time.

Hence the fear of death is twofold as Calvin argued. Fear of death includes not only the "fear of extinction" but the "fear of judgment." The fear of extinction is rooted in the structure of our being. Psychology has made us quite familiar with this fear. But psychology cannot fully comprehend "fear of judgment," fear heightened by knowledge of our guilt and dread of God's wrath. As in Augustine and Calvin, we should not fear death so much as sin as the "sting of death."

> It is not that we are mortal which creates the ultimate fear of death, but rather that we have lost our eternity beyond our natural and inescapable mortality; that we have lost it by sinful separation from the Eternal; and that we are guilty of this separation. . . . We are slaves to fear, not because we have to die, but because we deserve to die.[35]

We ought not dismiss this second fear so quickly and easily. Tillich would disagree with Feifel that "fear of death no longer reveals fear of judgment," but simply "fear of total annihilation and loss of identity."[36] Granted, we no longer live in a society guided by medieval imagery of salvation, atonement, purgatory, and hell. Nonetheless, there remains an element of truth behind these images. Because we stand at the junction of nature and spirit, we err when we stop with the fear of extinction. We should even prefer the fear of judgment, Niebuhr implies, because it points toward that awareness in human nature of "the dimension of the 'Eternal'" and the freedom of the self to relate to this. Fear of annihilation grows out of the condition of finitude; fear of judgment demonstrates the "very substance" of nature and history—the mixture of sin, freedom, creativity, and transcendence.[37] As Karl Rahner observes, the "horror" has to do with sin manifest in "that death which alone is true death"—"eternal death."[38] We are lost and afraid "not in nothingness but in judgment."[39]

Erikson alludes to this fear. We fear death not because of an unresolved Oedipal conflict, as Freud claims, or, as the Kübler-Ross discussion contends, because we have failed to reach the "fifth stage" or to attain "appropriate death." We fear death when we cannot accept our one and only life "as the ultimate of life." We despair because death comes too soon.

Tillich goes a step further, however, and argues that because we are human and fallen, death *always* comes too soon.

> Acceptance of dying as the consummation of one's life . . .
> presupposed acceptance of one's previous life. . . . This is an
> area where we are never totally successful on our own account,
> because our life has always been to some extent a life of self-
> assertion and selfish rigidity.[40]

No matter how long we prolong life, we cannot bring about its consummation in any completely satisfactory way.

Donald Capps insinuates that even Erikson recognizes a final "nonacceptance of the finality of death borne of despair" which always overrides any simple acceptance. Only by a transcendence of "the limitations of our life cycle borne of 'ultimate concern'" (a term borrowed from Tillich) can we brace ourselves against despair.[41] In the end, we cannot accrue "ego integrity" because we forfeit responsibility for our actions at some point. The past is always present to us, Tillich states, "as a curse and as a blessing." And we are anxious about the future, not only because of its shortness and termination, but because of "its impenetrable darkness and the threat that one's whole existence in time will be judged as a failure."[42]

The view that Tillich offers in his sermons is not entirely consistent with that of *Systematic Theology*. In the former, he affirms the earlier Pauline tradition and more readily ascribes the "unnaturalness" of death and the "wrath of God" to human sinfulness. In part, his attempt to speak to at least two publics influences the tenor of his argument. He uses scripture to move the faithful in his sermons and philosophy to reason with the academy in his systematic enterprise.

In his sermon "On Transitoriness" he states that the law of nature and the moral law concerning death are both "equally true" and "stated in all sections of the Bible." Then a small shadow of doubt seems to sneak in and he adds, "If we could ask the psalmist or the other Biblical writers how they thought these laws are united, they would find it hard to answer."[43]

He offers one possible answer in the tri-part division of *Systematic Theology*. The first volume, like the first part of both sermons, establishes finitude and anxiety as natural elements in the structure of essential being, not flaws in nature. It is in the second volume on existence that he tries to explain what he calls in his sermons the "moral law" concerning death. But more than in his sermons, he aligns himself squarely within the philosophical tradition descending from Schleiermacher: "Sin does not produce death. . . . The idea that the 'Fall' has physically changed the cellular or psychological structure of man (and nature) is absurd and unbiblical."[44] He does not assert as he did in his sermons that we "have to die because we are guilty," or that "we deserve to die"— statements much closer to the traditional position. He favors Schleiermacher's interpretation that the world appears different as a result of sin. Sin destroys the "original harmony between the world and man." Hence we experience the "obstruction" of death as evil.[45] Similarly, Tillich argues, sin transforms the anxiety of essential being into the "horror of death." Death, a structure of being, becomes ineradicably evil, a "structure of destruction" or a "mark of evil"[46]—or as Niebuhr maintains, not an evil in itself, but an "occasion for evil."

But Tillich carries the analysis deeper than Niebuhr by emphasizing the demonic, tragic side of human brokenness—the "structures of destruction." The abuse that an idea such as the demonic has suffered in the hands of medieval superstitions or conservative Protestants does not warrant its complete abandonment. We need to retain, without diminishing all sense of moral responsibility, the idea of a structural and, therefore, inescapable evil that produces social and personal havoc "beyond the moral power of good will."[47]

Neibuhr fears that Tillich has gone too far in his desire to take the tragic structures of reality earnestly. He warns us of a tendency in Christianity to borrow dualistic understandings from the Greeks without proper discretion. The Hellenistic view of finiteness as evil has crept into Pauline and orthodox understandings of the relation between death and sin and obscures our organic connection to nature and our moral and spiritual responsibility over against finitude.

Tillich struggles to address this complex relation between freedom and the tragic structures of evil. In his sermons, as well as in the *Systematics*, he wants to maintain that although death is a "structure of evil," this does not release anyone from guilt or responsibility for this situation. At the same time, he adamantly wants to avoid the potential moralism of statements about the "moral law" and "God's wrath." To make all dependent on the moral state of our souls, as happens in some forms of American Protestantism, Tillich felt to be, as Gilkey says, "judgmental, heteronomous, moralistic, limited, unreflected, 'petit-bourgeois.'"[48] While death is the "work of Divine wrath," wrath does not refer to "a passionate act of punishment or vengeance" on the part of a furious tyrannical god. Rather, it is "the reestablishment of the balance between God and man, which is disturbed by man's elevation against God." God's wrath is not directed against special acts of disobedience or particular moral shortcomings (sins) in a narrow moralistic sense, but against the distortion of the inner law of our being (sin) due to human pride, arrogance, and the attempt to "become like God."[49] More than the mere "trespassing of a list of rules," sin is "our act of turning away from participation in the divine Ground from which we come and to which we go [and] the turning toward ourselves, . . . making ourselves the center of our world and of ourselves."[50] Tillich wants to retrieve the full meaning of this word without offending contemporary moral sensibilities:

> [We may not] like words such as "sin" and "punishment." They seem to us old-fashioned, barbaric, and invalid in the light of modern psychology. But . . . whether or not we call it sin, whether or not we call it punishment, we are beaten by the consequences of our own failures.[51]

In any case, we cannot abandon the concept of sin, especially in relation to death. The idea captures the freedom, albeit limited and often handicapped by destiny, that we have to determine or to fail to fully determine our destiny. This freedom becomes all the more earnest in the face of death. Tillich talks about this in terms of "question," "demand," and "decision." We must, as we stand above our existence as free beings, ask ourselves, "Is this true and good existence?" and we must make the demand that it be so. We must decide. We may wish to avoid the question and the demand altogether. But we should never fool ourselves into believing that we have thereby escaped the "demand to rise above [our] natural basis, to be free." Even our inaction betrays itself as a choice.[52] To live in freedom means acceptance of the unconditional demand to "realize the true and actualize the good." This is not a strange demand or law imposed from outside the person by society, by a tyrannical god, or by a psychological mechanism (as the Kübler-Ross discussion is apt to assert), but the expression of one's own being. Since we can never fulfill this demand in existence, awareness of having to die becomes the painful, guilt-ridden realization of the loss of the eternal for which one is *responsible*, despite its tragic universality.

Guilt, Despair, and the Place of Freedom and Responsibility

The Kübler-Ross discussion recognizes to varying extents the place of guilt and responsibility. Feifel, for example, observes,

> One leitmotif that is continually coming to the fore in work in this area is that the crisis is often not the fact of oncoming death per se, of man's unsurmountable finiteness, but rather the waste of limited years, the unassayed tasks, the lacked opportunities, the talents withering in disuse, the avoidable evils which have been done.[53]

Kübler-Ross also notes the struggles of the dying to "put their house in order," to make some final sense of life, to settle conflicts, to forgive wrongs.

Still the Kübler-Ross discussion has little appreciation for the full range of human freedom and responsibility. In part, this results from the negative view of morality as simply a grafting of society's norms upon the genetically asocial individual. The Kübler-Ross discussion naively underestimates the extent of human malevolence. In Niebuhr's words, "they believe that there is some fairly simple way out of the sinfulness of human history."[54] They do not conceive of death in any other way than as completely at one with the goodness of human nature. Death is, as Montaigne said, "just a moment when dying ends."[55] It is "sinful" in the same way "a 'glimpse of stocking was shocking' at another age"—that is, "sinful" is used rather thoughtlessly to signify an embarrassing social *faux pas*.[56] Beyond this the discussion considers the word rather meaningless. Likewise Weisman defines guilt in terms of having "fallen from the expectations of our ego ideal"[57] and Kübler-Ross in terms of the emotion that ministers inflict upon the dying. When one hears guilt in the "confessions" of a dying person, one should "find out if the patient feels . . . guilty for not attending church more regularly or if there are deeper, unconscious hostile wishes which precipitated such guilt."[58]

Tillich refuses to limit guilt to "irrational fears or the wish for punishment."[59] He wants to rescue the concept, like the idea of sin, from the state of disrepute into which it has fallen in modern psychology. "What was man [for Tillich]," Erikson asks in his memorial tribute, "without . . . the realization of his guilt in regard 'to acts for which,' as he [Tillich] put it elsewhere, 'responsibility cannot be denied, in spite of the elements of destiny in them?'"[60] Tillich asserts:

> I would still emphasize the problem of guilt more than anything else. . . . It is a fact that the problem of guilt, in spite of the problem of death and the problem of meaning, which are the three main problems—although the problem of meaning is, perhaps, externally the most conspicuous today—in the depths of everybody, the problem of guilt plays a tremendous role.[61]

Tillich says he owes part of his rediscovery of the meaning of sin and guilt to psychoanalytic understandings. Freud grasped the "demonic structures which determine our consciousness and our decisions"[62] better than many of his followers and critics.[63] Rogers, in particular, loses the depth of Freud's analysis when he contends that if simply provided with a warm, comfortable environment, humans will naturally fulfill their innate potentialities. Tillich does not believe persons have such "power."[64]

But unlike Freud and similar to Lifton, he distinguishes between "objective," "essential guilt-feeling," and "unhealthy guilt-feeling."[65] Objective guilt involves doing "something terrible—to [oneself], or to somebody else or to the order of life generally."[66] "We always do things which we should not have done and do not things which we should have done. . . . We are not what we essentially ought to be in a concrete situation."[67] We cannot reduce guilt in the face of death to unconscious wishes.

Distinct from Freud, Tillich understands guilt on more than the level of finitude. Humans have guilt which death itself cannot relieve. This guilt "points to the dimension of the ultimate . . . has eternal roots and demands a solution in relation to the eternal."[68] In essence, guilt culminates in a despair that is the ultimate threat to human existence, the "final index" of our predicament, the "boundary line" beyond which we cannot go and from which "even death cannot free us."[69] *In despair, not death, we come to the end of our possibilities:*

> Death may, to be sure, point toward the boundary situation; but it does not do so necessarily and death is not itself the

boundary situation. This is the reason that we feel death cannot give release from despair. The spiritual cleavage that is experienced in despair is not eliminated with the cessation of bodily existence. The boundary situation that is encountered in despair, threatens man on another level than that of bodily existence.[70]

It took the genuis of "the great Danish Protestant, Søren Kierkegaard," to discover this. Tillich, Niebuhr, and even Erikson, evidence Kierkegaard's influence. A closer look at his thought helps us see an important distinction that psychologies of death overlook.

For Kierkegaard, human nature is a synthesis of opposites— body and soul, finite and infinite, necessity and possibility, temporal and eternal. This synthesis is unthinkable without a third factor uniting the two poles. This third factor is "spirit," "freedom," the "eternal," the "self," to mention some of the expressions that he uses to designate the ambiguous power in the person of realizing the task of becoming in existence.[71] Psychology fails to perceive, attend to, or fully understand this third factor.

According to Kierkegaard, only if one recognizes this third factor can one understand human freedom, responsibility, guilt, and sin. He uses this understanding of the structure of selfhood to reinterpret, not many years after Schleiermacher, the relationship between sin, guilt, and death. In *The Concept of Dread* he considers the positive aspects of the traditional doctrine while rejecting the idea that Adam's sin at the start of human history made death our terrible punishment.[73] In human innocence, temporality is not evil, but belongs to the dialectical necessity and possibility of life. But once sin is posited, time and death become terrible in the dread which accompanies the power of being able to realize oneself in time. "The instant sin is posited, the temporal is sin."[74] Furthermore, there is a progression in the character of death's terribleness: dread of guilt takes up and surpasses dread of fate.[75] In John W. Elrod's words, for Kierkegaard, "Guilt . . . is the expression for a division within the structure of the self itself . . . an expression of a permanent rupture which characterizes . . . existence . . . a division in [oneself] which freedom seems powerless to close."[72] The more one seeks synthesis of body and soul in time, the more one tries to act responsibly in freedom by choosing oneself in relation to the "eternal," the greater one's guilt and the more dreadful one's death:

> From the characterization of the temporal as sinfulness death
> in turn follows as punishment . . . the more highly we value
> men, the more terrible death appears. The beast cannot prop-
> erly be said to die; but when the spirit is posited as spirit, death
> appears terrible. . . . At the instant of death man finds himself
> at the extremest point of the synthesis; the spirit cannot, as it
> were, be present, and yet it must wait, for the body must die.
> The pagan view of death . . . was milder and more attractive,
> but it lacked the highest element.[76]

Paradoxically the deeper the dread, the greater the person, for
dread is the very possibility of freedom:

> If a man were a beast or an angel, he would not be able to be in
> dread. Since he is a synthesis he can be in dread, and the
> greater the dread, the greater the man.[77]

Hence the fear of judgment indicates a "sharpening . . . *a genuine
step forward spiritually*"[78] as Niebuhr asserts. Fear of punishment
as part of the overall fear of death attests to the "height and depth in
the human spirit which nature as such cannot contain."[79] This is one
of Christianity's more remarkable contributions to the "pagan" view
of death. Christianity rightfully teaches us "to see death from the
point of view of eternity and to fear judgment more than death."[80]

Only if one understands all this can one arrive at the conclusion, as do Tillich and Kierkegaard, that despair over sin and
guilt, despair over having "lost the eternal and oneself," is a "sickness unto death" far worse than death or anxiety over finitude itself.
In despair, "even the last hope, death, is not available."[81] The
torment of despair is precisely "not being able to die." That is,
either one is not the person one should be, so one can go ahead and
die, or one does not have the power to "get rid" of oneself and
thereby to avoid the demand to become the person in freedom that
one does not want to be. Thus Kierkegaard declares, "I do not fear
death; like the Roman soldiers, I have learned there are worse
things."[82]

The Kübler-Ross discussion misunderstands the third factor of
the synthesis—spirit or freedom—and hence, renders guilt and
despair in the face of death negligible. In contrast, Tillich locates the
problem of death at the very intersection of body and soul, nature
and spirit, finitude and transcendence: we are creatures rooted
within history and time *and* creators able to transform and transcend
these necessities and make history. The Kübler-Ross discussion

underestimates the "height and depth" of the human spirit and overestimates the ability of human nature to conquer the terrors of existence. It exemplifies what Niebuhr calls modernity's "essentially easy conscience:" we can escape death's pathos by turning "from the daemonic chaos" of our spiritual lives "to the harmony, serenity and harmless unity of nature." One must merely "descend from the chaos of spirit to the harmony of nature in order to be saved."[83] Yet this reduces to the realm of the biological and the natural what is clearly a compound of nature and spirit. Our very sense of melancholy and our anxious brooding about death reveal the intersection of nature and spirit and point to that aspect of human nature which even death cannot resolve.

An Alternative Solution

Different understandings of the relation between death, guilt, freedom, and responsibility lead to distinctive approaches to death. The Kübler-Ross discussion suggests psychological mechanisms by which persons can obtain personal fulfillment, whether by proceeding through various stages to the "peace" and "equanimity" of acceptance, or by realizing an "appropriate death." Erikson talks about resolving life's final conflict in the direction of integrity and wisdom. Lifton creates new paradigms to assure communal survival.

Tillich, on the other hand, concludes in one of his sermons that "within Christianity there is only one 'argument' against death: the forgiveness of sin and the victory over him who has the power of death."[84] Adequate response must answer not only the fear of extinction but the fear of judgment and the reality of guilt and sin in relation to finitude. Niebuhr reaches a similar conclusion. The condition of finiteness and freedom, sin and creativity, he notes, is "a problem for which there is no solution by any human power."[85] The ultimate culmination of history requires "divine completion of human incompleteness" and "a purging of human guilt and sin by divine judgment and mercy."[86] For Tillich, a comprehensive answer to death necessarily involves the response of salvation, that is, "a judgment which declares that we do not deserve to die because we are justified"[87] and that divine wrath and human guilt have been conquered.

As a first step, Tillich challenges the "Myth of a Meaningful Death"—the pretensions in psychology and in medicine that we can completely manage the experience of death. The "Protestant princi-ple" announces the seriousness of the "boundary-situation" by pro-claiming the ambiguity and the limited usefulness of all human remedies and securities.[88] Psychologies of death might remove neu-rotic self-contradictions, but they cannot fully comprehend existen-tial dread, guilt, and despair.[89] They might alleviate guilt feeling, but they "cannot overcome the feeling of a bad conscience, after real guilt."[90] Even Lifton assumes that his solution can overcome the "boundary situation." He divides the person into two parts—not a body/soul division exactly, but into a part that perishes in death and a part that is unassailable, a substitute for ourselves that lives on after we die through one of the five modes of immortality. The "Protestant principle" reveals the partiality and fallibility of this human attempt to assure security as well.

But if Christianity only insists upon the "boundary-situation" in all situations, we are left with a "spiritual vacuum": "It's message becomes nothing more than a stentorian 'No' to all human endeav-ors, nothing more than a proclamation of the threat to human existence."[91] We cannot simply toss aside answers such as Lifton's as inadequate. New idols merely fill the emptiness. Into this situation, Tillich contends, the "'something more' of a 'Yes,'" which includes, but goes beyond the "No," speaks. The "Yes" of salvation is

> not based upon anything that we have done . . . but . . . on something that Eternity itself has done, something that we can hear and see, in the reality of a mortal man who by his own death has conquered him who has the power of death.[92]

Sounding like Kierkegaard, he says that the "Yes" is "the coming of the Eternal to us, becoming temporal in order to restore our eter-nity."[93] In Kierkegaard's words, the eternal itself has entered time, "is born, grows up, and dies."[94] The eternal overcomes the rupture in ourselves that makes death "terrible" by constituting the syn-thesis between the temporal and the eternal in time in those who, so believing, make a "leap" of faith. Thus "the opposite of being in despair is believing"[95] in the paradox of an undeserved, absurd forgiveness, the paradox of the "God-man." The "peace" of faith does not occur as an inner psychological change, but, as Helmut Thielicke emphasizes, "initially takes place outside of [us] in the objective peace with God by virtue of the reconciliation in Christ."[96]

Reconciliation involves repentance or a turning away from sin in judgment and a turning toward God. The "message of a new being" involves, as Augustine claimed, more than the promise of psychological peace or naturalistic acceptance of death.

In *The Courage to Be*, Tillich explores how this message surpasses other solutions, including the answer of Stoicism, the "only real alternative to Christianity in the Western world."[97] The answer of the Stoic, similar to the Kübler-Ross discussion, fails to address the whole of human experience since it does not fully recognize human brokenness or evil as a matter of personal responsibility and guilt. Therefore the Stoic does not face death with the "utter desperation" so characteristic of the full human experience:

> One must ask, has the Stoic as a Stoic reached the state of "utter desperation"? Can he reach it in the frame of his philosophy? Or is there something absent in his despair and consequently in his courage?

Tillich's answer to this last question is yes: "The Stoic as Stoic does not experience the despair of personal guilt."[98] Stoic courage solves the problem of fate and death, *but not that of sin, guilt, and condemnation*. The latter problem suggests the need for salvation instead of renunciation:

> According to Christianity we are estranged from our essential being. We are not free to realize our essential being, we are bound to contradict it. Therefore death can be accepted only through a state of confidence in which death has ceased to be the "wages of sin." This, however, is the state of being accepted in spite of being unacceptable. Here is the point in which the ancient world was transformed by Christianity.[99]

Furthermore, adequate answer to death in contemporary society must also include response to the anxiety which determines our period—not the anxiety of fate and death nor that of guilt and condemnation, but that of emptiness and meaninglessness. Tillich analyzes the forms of anxiety and courage throughout civilization by applying to history a threefold typology of the kinds of "nonbeing"—ontic, moral, or spiritual. Whereas ancient Greece and Rome reputedly were obsessed with the ontic problem of death and the Middle Ages, with moral imagery of purgatory, hell, and moral condemnation, we moderns are burdened by a beleaguered spiritual state. Spiritual anxiety is by far the most worrisome:

> For the anxiety of meaninglessness undermines what is still
> unshaken in the anxiety of fate and death and of guilt and
> condemnation. In the anxiety of guilt and condemnation doubt
> has not yet undermined the certainty of an ultimate respon-
> sibility. We are threatened but we are not destroyed. If, how-
> ever, doubt and meaninglessness prevail one experiences an
> abyss in which the meaning of life and the truth of ultimate
> responsibility disappear. . . . Even in the despair of having to
> die and the despair of self-condemnation meaning is affirmed
> and certitude preserved. But in the despair of doubt and
> meaninglessness both are swallowed by nonbeing.[100]

In such a situation, "there is one possible answer, if one does
not try to escape the question: namely that the acceptance of despair
is in itself faith and on the boundary line of the courage to be."[101]
Today's world demands an "absolute faith" or a "courage to be *in
spite of*" meaninglessness. A courage "in spite of" takes the threat of
non-being "into itself" and promises the possibility and power of
being *even in the face of radical non-being*. Again, the idea of
"absolute" faith "in spite of" comes in part from Kierkegaard. He
talks abut the impossible possibility of an absolute "leap" of faith
which does not annihilate dread, but continually develops "itself out
of the death throe of dread."[102] Tillich's dialectic theology, however,
puts Kierkegaard's understanding into more systematic, rational
concepts without losing the paradoxical complexities.[103] The "leap"
of faith does not rest on belief in certain tenets or doctrines, nor on
theoretical affirmation or opinion. Rather, faith comes from "being
grasped by the power of being which transcends everything that is
and in which everything that is participates."[104] Humans are subject
not only to *the law of nature* and to the *moral law,* but to "a *higher
law,* to *the law of life* out of death by the death of Him who
represented eternal life."[105]

In modernity we must also reformulate the traditional answers
to the other two anxieties of guilt and death. The traditional promises of forgiveness and hope need to be reinterpreted without "the
safety of words and concepts" of former times. Tillich suggests the
word "acceptance" as preferable to the phrases "forgiveness of sins,"
"justification by faith," righteousness, absolution, pardon of guilt,
and so on—terms which have all taken the same course in modernity as the idea of sin.[106] Still, he adopts more psychological language
cautiously: being accepted does not mean that guilt is denied. He
warns psychotherapists and others who use similar terminology:

> I think we should not make it too easy . . . to swallow the
> problem of acceptance. [Persons] must come into community
> with objective transpersonal powers of forgiveness or of accept-
> ance in order to be able to accept themselves. Otherwise, it is
> simply a self-confirmation in a state of estrangement.[107]

In greater detail:

> It must be emphasized that neither for religion nor for psycho-
> therapy is self-acceptance an easy-going process of "forgiving
> and forgetting." Religion has made this clear in the traditional
> doctrines of atonement, showing the heavy price which had to
> be paid and the tremendous toil which was required for our
> salvation.[108]

Acceptance does not occur through "suspending judgment." But
neither does it mean "continuing and strengthening moral demands." Rather, "there must be acceptance without suspending
judgment." Judgment, acceptance, and transformation must be held
together in rather close proximity.[109] Only then is "the cycle of dust
to dust, from sin to wrath . . . broken."[110]

Reflections on the Moral Life

The contrasting solutions reflect distinct normative horizons.
We noted in the previous chapter that normative images of ethical
egoism of the non-hedonic type implicitly govern the Kübler-Ross
discussion. One should act so as to promote one's own greatest good,
desires, or preferences. Both Erikson and Lifton espouse a more
utilitarian perspective. One should act so as to promote the greatest
possible balance of good over evil in terms of generativity or evolu-
tional responsibility. On the one hand, Tillich articulates more self-
consciously the normative images that govern his view of death. On
the other, his ethical premises resist simple classification since they
are embedded in the more extensive project of his theology.

In terms of the categories of moral philosophy, I shall classify
Tillich's moral position *very roughly* as an "ethics of love." This
position maintains that there is only one basic principle—to love—
and that all the others are derived from it.[111] As Tillich states, "all
laws are summed up in the law of love by which estrangement is
conquered."[112] The interpretation of this law varies greatly, how-

ever, depending upon the theologian. In one particular sermon, "Love is Stronger than Death," he brings the problem of death and the imperative of love together. "Death" in this instance includes not just personal mortality but estrangement in nature and in society—"the death of nations, the end of generations, and the atrophy of souls." Every death means parting, separation, estrangement, isolation, opposition. Only love "overcomes separation and creates participation in which there is more than that which the individuals involved can bring to it."[113] He defines love as the "drive toward the unity of the separated" or the "reunion of the estranged." Love binds us responsibly to other persons as well as to ourselves, and ultimately overcomes what Tillich calls the "greatest separation"— the "separation of self from self."[114] Its ultimate source is God, the ground of being which takes non-being into itself. God's *agape* makes love between persons possible. Love for others includes a desire to make the other's need one's own. Only this kind of love conquers disintegration and death. It "creates" anew, "bears" up, "overcomes," "rescues."[115] When we are separated from this love by guilt, "we cannot face death, because the sting of death is sin." The power of the love which triumphs over death lies in its "ultimate victory over separation."[116]

Tillich has in mind a love that is both life and world-affirming. Love affirms the self in its individuation, and it affirms the world in which selves participate. This love can transcend the courage that a person might muster to face death based on her own internal resources (e.g., the Kübler-Ross discussion) and the courage that membership in a community instills through its symbols and traditions (e.g., Lifton and Erikson). The love that conquers death unites both of these forms of affirmation in one dialectical whole.

Alongside this and at odds with it at times, we find a normative emphasis on individual self-affirmation or fulfillment not all that different from that of the culture of joy. John J. Carey describes Tillich's approach as an "ontological self-realization ethic" that focuses on the actualization of individual potential.[117] Tillich believes that a person ought to actualize her own being as a centered person. Death makes the unconditional demand to become an actual person or to realize one's essential being in existence all the more urgent and agonizing. Death brings despair precisely because individuals in their freedom have lost and are responsible for having lost their unique potentiality in estrangement. In these conclusions, he has more concern for the individual in relationship to God than for justification of the community as co-workers with God in the realization of the kingdom.

Albeit accurate, this characterization of Tillich's normative position ignores other moral themes. His attention to the anxiety of guilt and condemnation itself attests that he has an eye toward the brokenness that exists not only in the self but also within the human community and between the community and God. Characterizing his ethic as simply an ethic of self-realization stresses one part of a whole which he himself would not want to divide in exactly this way. The moral command is to become what one potentially is, a person *within a community of persons.* The individual is a self only in relation to a world; to be is to-be-in-the-world or in dialectical tension between "individuation" and "participation." Moral action includes concern not only for oneself but for person-to-person encounter, the encounter of social groupings, and ultimately, the encounter in the "sphere of the holy."

> The aim is . . . "to become the way in which God sees us, in all our potentialities." And what that now practically is, is the next very important question. . . . To become social . . . I would call it love, in the sense of the Greek word *agape* . . . which accepts the other as a person and then tries to re-unite with him and to overcome the separation, the existential separation, which exists between men and men.[118]

Tillich's marked departures from Rogers's and Erich Fromm's narrower definitions of freedom and "self-love" demonstrate the greater adequacy of his normative positive. He agrees with Rogers that "openness" to one's own inner experiencing, "becoming more fully [oneself]," and the freedom of personal self-determination are important considerations. To a certain extent, then, persons should preside over the rites of their dying in the manner they individually deem most appropriate.

But he asks Rogers about "the aim" of this openness and freedom. For Tillich, it must include not only self-realization and freedom from arbitrary norms, but also the imperative "to become social." The ideal of human personality exemplified in the Kübler-Ross discussion suffers because it "tends to cut the individual off from his existential roots, from the social group, its traditions and symbols."[119] Freedom is not only "freedom *from* something"; it is also freedom *for* something.[120] We should not reduce autonomy in treatment decisions, for example, to freedom from external authorities and vindication of all manner of private action. As important as the prerogative for autonomy is its direction or aim in relation to others and to God.

> The perversion of freedom ensues when decision involves only decision for the infinity of one's own desire; when vital power is made to predominate over rational mutuality; when man attempts to place himself at the depth or the center of being rather than relate himself to it; when man, who is dependent upon the primal "given" creativity of being, sets up his own creaturely and conditioned character as unconditioned. It appears, in short, when he tries to make his own finiteness infinite.[121]

Autonomy separated from the ultimate ground beyond itself goes astray.[122]

Similarly, Tillich reorients the concept of "self-love" in the direction of communal motifs. He reprimands Fromm for his narrow use of the term. The idea of self-love presupposes a natural and relatively neutral self-affirmation.[123] But there is also a negative form of self-love which turns against others and uses them in "self-affirming" selfishness as a means to other ends. Finally, there is a "self-love" of an entirely higher order: an acceptance of one's self which is repentant of one's selfishness and "which cannot be produced by ourselves intentionally [but] needs the power of the community, which has ultimate sources, and then, finally the ultimate power itself in order to enable somebody to accept himself."[124]

> Self-affirmation of our essential being [is] unconditional. . . . This is quite different from an affirmation of one's self in terms of one desires and fears. Such a self-affirmation has no unconditional character; ethics based on it are ethics of calculation, describing the best way of getting fulfillment of desires and protection against fears. There is nothing absolute in technical calculation. But morality as the self-affirmation of one's essential being is unconditional.[125]

Tillich would question the psychology of the Kübler-Ross discussion in which needs become confused with desires, desires with needs, and both with rights that the larger community must satisfy. His normative stance has more affinity with the emphasis on mutuality and continuity in Erikson and Lifton. The appeal of their models lies in their attempt to place individual needs and desires into some sort of balanced relationship with those of the larger community and cosmos.

Philosophical critique of ethical egoism questions whether the egoism of the Kübler-Ross discussion is even an "ethical" stance, much less an adequate one. We do not need an ethic to reinforce what is already a natural drive to look out for ourselves. An adequate "ethical" stance determines how this drive should be controlled in light of the impact of actions, disposition, intentions, traits upon other sentient beings, and on human interaction as a whole. Kant argues that, "One has no moral duty to promote one's own happiness, even if one does have such a duty to cultivate one's talents, respect one's own dignity, and not to commit suicide."[126] Tillich himself states that self-affirmation need not become a "commandment"; we presuppose self-love as an inherent tendency. As Frankena argues, although it is a bit arbitrary to define moral duty only in terms of the good of others and to exclude duties and the application of the principles of beneficence and justice to oneself, "because we humans are already so prone to take care of our own welfare . . . it is practically strategic for us in our ordinary moral living to talk, think, and feel as if we do not have a duty to do so."[127] According to Kurt Bauer, a "moral point of view" precludes, by definition, being egoistic: "one is taking the moral point of view if one is not being egoistic, one is doing things on principle, one is willing to universalize one's principles, and in doing so one considers the good of everyone alike."[128] These observations challenge the adequacy of a Kübler-Ross-type stance unless supplemented with a more explicitly ethical point of view. Frankena concludes,

> It seems to me . . . that prudentialism or living wholly by the principle of enlightened self-love just is not a kind of morality. . . . This is not to say that it is immoral though it may be that too, but that it is nonmoral. . . . The moral point of view is *disinterested*, not "interested."[129]

Tillich's attempt to preserve the relevance of traditional theological understandings enhances his model as a viable alternative to what Ariés calls the "hedonist attitude toward death."[130] Death has a moral and theological significance that transcends it. Valid response to it, therefore, must have an interpersonal, even transnatural character. While we might wonder whether Tillich would be more critical today of his tendency toward an "ontological self-realization ethic," his understanding of this kind of self-love surpasses the nature of the ethical egoism of the Kübler-Ross discussion. He also articulates more clearly and carefully some of the unspoken ethical assumptions that operate covertly in Erikson and Lifton.

Nonetheless, we still lack something. Granted Tillich has shown other moral virtues or obligations worth considering besides prudence. But, as Frankena argues,

> Not all our prima facie obligations can be derived from the principle of beneficence any more than from that of utility. For the principle of beneficence does not tell us how we are to distribute goods and evils; it only tells us to produce the one and prevent the other. When conflicting claims are made upon us, the most it could do . . . is to instruct us to promote the greatest balance of good over evil and . . . we need something more.[131]

While I commend Tillich for articulating aspects of the principle of beneficence, he does not give us entirely what we need, especially as modern society faces increasingly complex questions of death and dying. "Conflicting claims" and distribution of goods are central issues these days. To become potentially what we should be within the community of persons simply does not answer the problem of who receives what among the many new and costly improvements in health care. In addition, Tillich's wariness of moralism prevents him from giving concrete ethical advice. Conscience, as he understands it, "calls us to what we essentially are, but it does not tell with certainty what that is."[132]

An adequate approach to death, therefore, still needs further refinement, extension, and rigor in relation to the technical aspects of death. For this I turn to Paul Ramsey's "rules of practice" and his morality of "agent agape" or, in medical ethics, "agent care," developed to address particular questions about death and dying. We do well both to heed Tillich's caution about moralism and to investigate what Ramsey might have to offer.

Footnotes to Chapter V

/1/   Alasdair MacIntyre, "Theology, Ethics, and the Ethics of Medicine and Health Care: Comments on Papers by Novak, Mouw, Roach, Cahill, and Hartt," *The Journal of Medicine and Philosophy* 4, no. 4 (1979), p. 435.
/2/   Robert Fulton and Gisbert Geis vividly illustrate this "continuing attrition of the sacred orientation" toward death. They note that in a

memorial issue on death of the *Register* of the Chicago Theological Seminary, the entire content "is devoted not to a theological discourse on death . . . but to the practical essentials of 'Religion and Social Work.'" The issue contains, "among other things, down-to-earth hints for ministers. . . . The advice is not to recommend faith . . . but to establish contact with a family casework agency, a mental health clinic, or similar agencies, all of which can provide 'expert help for the person.'" (Fulton and Geis, "Death and Social Values" in *Death and Identity*, pp. 70, 72).

/3/   Don S. Browning, "Pastoral Theology in a Pluralistic Age," in *Practical Theology*, ed. Don S. Browning (San Francisco: Harper and Row, 1983), p. 188.

/4/   Churchill, "Attitudes About Death," p. 175.

/5/   Vaux, "Topics at the Interface," pp. 197–198.

/6/   Gustafson, "Theology Confronts Technology," p. 387. See also, Gustafson and Hauerwas, "Editorial," pp. 345–346.

/7/   Gustafson, "Theology Confronts Technology," pp. 389–390.

/8/   Robert M. Veatch, "The Clergyman as the Dying Patient's Agent," in *Death and Ministry: Pastoral Care of the Dying and the Bereaved*, ed. D. J. Bane (New York: Seabury, 1975), p. 155.

/9/   Paul Tillich, *Theology of Culture*, ed. Robert C. Kimball (London: Oxford University Press, 1959), p. 42.

/10/   Paul Tillich, "Autobiographical Reflections," in *The Theology of Paul Tillich*, ed. Charles W. Kegley (New York: Pilgrim, 1982), pp. 18–19.

/11/   Paul Tillich, *Religiöse Verwirklichung* (Berlin: Furche, 1930), p. 61, cited by James Luther Adams, *Paul Tillich's Philosophy of Culture, Science and Religion* (New York: Schocken, 1970), p. 12.

/12/   Erik H. Erikson, "Memorial Tribute to Paul Tillich," *Harvard Divinity Bulletin* 30, no. 2 (1966), pp. 13–14. See Tillich, "Autobiographical Reflections," p. 8.

/13/   Langdon Gilkey, "Tillich: The Master of Mediation," in *The Theology of Paul Tillich*, p. 27.

/14/   Paul Tillich, *The New Being* (New York: Charles Scribner's Sons, 1955), pp. 165–166.

/15/   Tillich, *Theology of Culture*, p. 44.

/16/   Ibid., p. 43.

/17/   Paul Tillich, *The Courage to Be* (New Haven: Yale University Press, 1952), pp. 42, 110, 169.

/18/   Paul Tillich, *The Eternal Now* (New York: Charles Scribner's Sons, 1956), p. 71.

/19/   Tillich, *New Being*, p. 170.

/20/   Ibid., p. 171.

/21/   Paul Tillich, *The Meaning of Health: Essays in Existentialism, Psychoanalysis, and Religion*, ed. Perry Lefevre (Chicago: Exploration Press, 1984), p. 199.

/22/   Ibid., p. 53.

/23/   Some, such as Helmut Thielicke in *Death and Life*, Karl Rahner in *On the Theology of Death*, and Kenneth Vaux in *Will to Live, Will to Die*, have tried to address this tension and reinterpret the meaning of death, creation, and sin. Vaux, for example, talks about a "root tension between living and dying" or between the "will to live" and the "will to die" (Vaux, *Will to Live*, pp. 15–16). We have a drive to live (eros); we have an urge toward death (thanatos). We live, we die. But, by stressing the natural and failing to relate this to symbols of sin and death, he tends to collapse the tension in the direction of a psychological or more naturalistic view, a danger we saw foreshadowed in Schleiermacher. He overlooks the moral complexities of death as they occur within the natural order.

At the same time, later in the book, Vaux rather reductionistically equates the Jewish and Christian tradition with the view of death as the "payoff" for sin, and therefore, as "unnatural," an "enemy" (Ibid., pp. 56–57, 102, 106). Perchance he read someone like Oscar Cullman or Helmut Thielicke. Cullman denounces all attempts to see death as a natural phenomenon: "Death is not something natural, willed by God, as in the thought of the Greek philosophers; it is rather something unnatural, abnormal . . . a curse." (Oscar Cullman, "Immortality of the Soul or Resurrection of the Dead," in *Immortality and Resurrection*, ed. Krister Stendahl [New York: Macmillan, 1965], cited by Roy Branson, "Is Acceptance Denial?" p. 466).

Likewise, Thielicke sets "the Biblical view" completely over against natural philosophy, his covert opponent in *Death and Life*. As a result, he creates a gulf almost too wide to bridge between biological death and the Christian view. He disagrees with the orthodox argument for a direct causal relationship between the fall and death, but still argues that death is not a part of creation or the natural rhythm of life. Death is life's "enemy, a contradiction." (Helmut Thielicke, *Death and Life*, trans. E. H. Schroeder [Philadelphia: Fortress Press, 1970], pp. xx–xxii).

> *Human death is simply unnatural*. At no time and in no place is it the expression of any sort of normality of nature, as if it signified the necessary ebb in the rhythm of life. Death is rather the expression of a catastrophe . . . directly opposite . . . nature. (Ibid., p. 105.)

To allow for this *and* leave room for the biological reality of death, he must argue dualistically. The two realms are "totally different." Biological death belongs to an entirely different "dimension," "field," "plane," or "level" than human death (Ibid, pp. 1–2, 149, 186). He disregards the significance of the physical experience of death as a deeply-felt loss of a body to which we are so intimately connected. We also must wonder about the theological and scriptural accuracy of his argument. It convinces, only if we buy his original premise, that there is strict division between nature and spirit, animal and "personhood."

Those unable to enter the narrow circle of Thielicke's belief that we can only understand death from the perspective of "Biblical theology" might find Rahner's Catholic reading more compatible. For him, revelation occurs through natural processes, rather than outside and over against them. In explaining the place of death in creation, however, he turns to a Catholic response that he otherwise carefully avoids: natural explanation only goes so far, then revelation must take over. Biology has not completely settled the question of why we die with its answers about the physiology of old age. And

> since we do not really know why all living things composed of many cells, and man in particular, do die, the reason offered by faith (that is, the moral catastrophe of mankind in its first parents) is really the only available explanation of the incontestable universality of death. (Karl Rahner, *On the Theology of Death* [New York: Herder and Herder, 1961] pp. 14–15).

Nevertheless, I appreciate Rahner's affirmation of the utter necessity of death's "natural essence" (Ibid., pp. 36–38). Although death is more than this, it *is* a natural process. For theological reasons among others, we must recognize in death "some common element, neutral, so to speak," for otherwise it could not even be an event of salvation, much less damnation (Ibid., p. 56).

/24/   Reinhold Niebuhr, *Principles of Christian Theology* (New York: Charles Scribner's Sons, 1966), cited by Branson, "Is Acceptance Denial?" p. 466.

/25/   Reinhold Niebuhr, *The Nature and Destiny of Man: A Christian Interpretation*, 2 vols. (New York: Charles Scribner's Sons, 1941–1943, 1964), vol. 2, pp. 174–175.

/26/   Ibid., vol. 2, p. 7.

/27/   Paul Tillich, *The Shaking of the Foundations* (New York: Charles Scribner's Sons, 1948), pp. 18, 68, 170–171.

/28/   Paul Tillich, *Systematic Theology*, 3 vols. (Chicago: University of Chicago Press, 1951–1963), vol. 1, p. 194.

/29/   Tillich, *Meaning of Health*, p. 190.

/30/   Tillich, *Courage to Be*, p. 38. See also, idem., *Systematic Theology*, vol. 1, pp. 193–194; and idem., *Shaking of the Foundations*, pp. 169–170.

/31/   Tillich, *Meaning of Health*, p. 190; *Shaking of the Foundations*, pp. 64–75; 169–172.

/32/   Tillich, *Meaning of Health*, p. 190.

/33/   Tillich, *Shaking of the Foundations*, p. 70.

/34/   Ibid., p. 19.

/35/   Tillich, *Shaking of the Foundations*, p. 171.

/36/   Herman Feifel, "The Problem of Death," in *Death: Interpretations*, ed. H. M. Ruitenbeck (New York: Delta, 1969), p. 126.

/37/   Niebuhr, *Nature and Destiny*, vol. 2, pp. 292 (n. 6), 294; idem., "A View of Life from the Sidelines," *Christian Century*, December 19–26, 1984, pp. 1197–1198.

/38/   Rahner, *Theology of Death*, pp. 100, 194, 54–55.

/39/   Thielicke, *Death and Life*, pp. 100, 194.

/40/   Gisbert Greshake, "Towards a Theology of Dying," in *The Experience of Dying*, pp. 96–97.

/41/   Donald Capps, *Life Cycle Theory and Pastoral Care*, in Theology and Pastoral Care Series, ed. Don S. Browning (Philadelphia: Fortress, 1983), p. 29; Erikson, *Childhood and Society*, pp. 268–269.

/42/ Tillich, *Eternal Now*, pp. 127, 124.

/43/ Tillich, *Shaking of the Foundations*, p. 70.

/44/ Tillich, *Systematic Theology*, vol. 2, p. 67.

/45/ Schleiermacher, *Christian Faith*, vol. 1, p. 315.

/46/ Tillich, *Systematic Theology*, vol. 2, p. 68.

/47/ Paul Tillich, *The Protestant Era*, trans. James Luther Adams (Chicago: University of Chicago Press, 1959), pp. xvi–xvii.

/48/ Gilkey, "Master of Mediation," pp. 47–48.

/49/ Tillich, *Shaking of the Foundations*, pp. 70–71; *Theology of Culture*, p. 123.

/50/ Tillich, *Eternal Now*, pp. 52, 56.

/51/ Tillich, *Shaking of the Foundations*, p. 19. See also *Eternal Now*, pp. 50–51.

/52/ Tillich, *Protestant Era*, pp. 118, 197–198; Adams, *Tillich's Philosophy*, pp. 24–25.

/53/ Feifel, *Meaning of Death*, p. 127.

/54/ Reinhold Niebuhr, *Christianity and Power Politics* (New York: Charles Scribner's Sons, 1940), p. 3, cited by William C. Placher, *A History of Christian Philosophy* (Philadelphia: Westminster, 1983), p 298.

/55/ Kübler-Ross, *Death and Dying*, p. 268. See Choron, *Death and Western Thought*, pp. 98–102.

/56/ Shneidman, *Death: Current Perspectives*, p. 69. Fulton states that "Death . . . in such a secularly-oriented society as ours is no longer the wages of sin; the medical insinuation is that it is the wages of loose living. The fear of death no longer is the fear of judgment but, psychiatrically, the expressions of a neurotic personality." (Robert L. Fulton, *The Sacred and the Secular Attitudes of the American Public Toward Death* [Milwaukee: Bulfin Press, 1963], p. 8).

/57/ Weisman, "Psychiatrist and the Inexorable," p. 114.

/58/ Kübler-Ross, *Death and Dying*, p. 270.

/59/ Ibid., p. 84.

/60/ Erikson, "Memorial Tribute," p. 15.

/61/ Tillich, *Meaning of Health*, p. 244.

/62/ Tillich, *Theology of Culture*, pp. 123–125; idem., *Meaning of Health*, p. 117.

/63/ Tillich, *Systematic Theology*, vol. 2, p. 54.

/64/ Tillich, *Meaning of Health*, p. 196.

/65/ Ibid., pp. 234–235.

/66/ Ibid., p. 212.

/67/ Ibid., p. 234.

/68/ Tillich, *Systematic Theology*, vol. 2, p. 76.

/69/ Ibid., vol., 2, p. 75; idem., *Protestant Era*, p. 198.

/70/ Tillich, *Protestant Era*, p. 197. See also, *Courage to Be*, pp. 54–57; *Systematic Theology*, vol. 2, pp. 75–76; vol. 1, p. 201.

/71/ Søren Kierkegaard, *The Concept of Dread*, trans. Walter Lowrie (Princeton, N.J.: Princeton University Press, 1941), pp. 39–40. See also, Mark C. Taylor, *Kierkegaard's Pseudonymous Authorship: A Study of Time and the Self* (Princeton: Princeton University Press, 1975), pp. 86–94, 109–

122; John W. Elrod, *Being and Existence in Kierkegaard's Pseudonymous Works* (Princeton: Princeton University Press, 1975), pp. 29–32.

/72/ Elrod, *Being and Existence*, p. 179.
/73/ Taylor, *Kierkegaard's Authorship*, pp. 269–276.
/74/ Kierkegaard, *Concept of Dread*, p. 82
/75/ Ibid., pp. 92–98.
/76/ Ibid., pp. 82–83 (note).
/77/ Ibid., p. 139.
/78/ Søren Kierkegaard, *Journals and Papers*, ed. Howard and Edna Hong (Bloomington, Ind.: Indiana University Press, 1967 ff.), vol. 1, p. 338.
/79/ Niebuhr, *Nature and Destiny*, vol. 2, p. 10.
/80/ Kierkegaard, *Journals*, vol. 1, p. 523.
/81/ Søren Kierkegaard, *The Sickness Unto Death*, trans. Walter Lowrie (Princeton: Princeton University Press, 1941), pp. 146, 150–154, 195.
/82/ Kierkegaard, *Journals*, vol. 1, p. 523.
/83/ Niebuhr, *Nature and Destiny*, vol. 1, p. 24.
/84/ Tillich, *Shaking of the Foundations*, p. 172.
/85/ Tillich, *Systematic Theology*, vol. 2, p. 295.
/86/ Niebuhr, *Nature and Destiny*, vol. 2, pp. 287–288.
/87/ Tillich, *Shaking of the Foundations*, p. 74.
/88/ Tillich, *Protestant Era*, pp. 195–205.
/89/ Tillich, *Theology of Culture*, pp. 122–123.
/90/ Tillich, *Meaning of Health*, p. 213.
/91/ Adams, *Tillich's Philosophy*, p. 40.
/92/ Tillich, *Shaking of the Foundations*, p. 172.
/93/ Ibid., p. 172.
/94/ Søren Kierkegaard, *Concluding Unscientific Postscript*, trans. David F. Swenson, completed with an Introduction and Notes by Walter Lowrie (Princeton University Press, 1941), p. 513.
/95/ Kierkegaard, *Sickness Unto Death*, p. 182.
/96/ Thielicke, *Death and Life*, p. 74 (note).
/97/ Tillich, *Courage to Be*, pp. 9, 101.
/98/ Ibid., p. 17.
/99/ Ibid., pp. 169–170.
/100/ Ibid., p. 174.
/101/ Ibid., p. 175.
/102/ Kierkegaard, *Concept of Dread*, p. 104.
/103/ Walter M. Horton, "Tillich's Role in Contemporary Theology," in *The Theology of Paul Tillich* p. 65.
/104/ Tillich, *Courage to Be*, pp. 173, 176.
/105/ Tillich, *New Being*, p. 178. Emphasis added.
/106/ Tillich,*Meaning of Health*, p. 198.
/107/ Ibid., pp. 231, 244; 56. See also, idem., *Courage to Be*, p. 166
/108/ Tillich, *Meaning of Health*, p. 56.
/109/ Ibid., pp. 119–121.
/110/ Tillich, *Shaking of the Foundations*, pp. 73, 156.
/111/ Frankena, *Ethics*, pp. 56–59.

/112/   Tillich, *Systematic Theology*, vol. 2, p. 47.

/113/   Tillich, *New Being*, p. 173.

/114/   Paul Tillich, *Love, Power, and Justice: Ontological Analyses and Ethical Applications* (New York: Oxford University Press, 1954), p. 25.

/115/   Ibid., p. 10.

/116/   Tillich, *New Being*, pp. 57–58.

/117/   John J. Carey, "Morality and Beyond: Tillich's Ethics in Life and Death," in Tillich Studies: 1975 Papers Prepared for the Second North American Consultation on Paul Tillich Studies, Tallahasse, Fla.: Florida State University, 1975. pp. 107–109.

/118/   Tillich, *Meaning of Health*, p. 201.

/119/   Tillich, *Protestant Era*, p. 130.

/120/   Tillich, *Meaning of Health*, p. 14.

/121/   Adams, *Tillich's Philosophy*, p. 32.

/122/   Although Tillich does not use this concept, Gilkey suggests the idea of a *"theonomous death."* In theonomous death, one depends upon a power beyond oneself, but not in a way that crushes one's own "creative powers, standards, goals, and projects, [one's] own *arete* and fulfillment." Death is "at once real, significant, freed and creative; but also . . . points beyond itself," and in so doing, death's negative, annihilating power is transcended. (Gilkey, "Meditation on Death," pp. 29–31).

/123/   Tillich, *Meaning of Health*, p. 223.

/124/   Ibid., pp. 225–226.

/125/   Tillich, *Theology of Culture*, pp. 136–137

/126/   Frankena, *Ethics*, p. 54.

/127/   Ibid., p. 55.

/128/   Ibid., p. 113.

/129/   Ibid., pp. 19–20.

/130/   Ariès, "Reversal of Death," p. 157.

/131/   Frankena, *Ethics*, pp. 19, 48.

/132/   Tillich, *Theology of Culture*, pp. 138–139.

CHAPTER VI

PAUL RAMSEY AND COVENANT LOVE
EVEN UNTO DEATH

Paul Ramsey has much to offer to public conversation about moral questions of death and dying. Similar to Tillich, he shares an appreciation for what James Childress calls the deeper "trends in our social ethos." But, distinct from Tillich, he investigates this ethos specifically as a Christian *ethicist*, not only as a theologian. In Childress's words, Ramsey "primarily wants to analyze and reform the ethos and state of moral discourse in our society."[1]

On one front, he criticizes the sloppiness of Protestant ethics and its tendency toward relativism and situational ethics. In contrast to the Roman Catholic tradition, Protestants are "in danger of making a virtue of the lack of rigor and substance." Where Tillich resists establishing a special field of "Christian ethics," Ramsey believes that "it is high time we . . . attempt to say with exactness and rigor what we mean in the field of Christian ethics."[2] As a result his work lacks a certain depth of systematic theological understanding, but attends to complex moral issues in contemporary society. Whereas Tillich's appeal lies in his constructive theological and theoretical synthesis, Ramsey's lies in his thorough, if not at times overly detailed, treatment of particular problems of human conduct.

Related to his interest in particular problems, Ramsey pursues reform on a second front. In *The Patient as Person*, he explores the bearing of religious ethics on medical practice. Health care professionals, too, should become more ethically literate.[3] They can no longer rely upon surface intuitions to determine what is good and right practice. Neither can vicarious transmission of values from practicing doctor to training intern, nor faith in the personal integrity of physicians substitute for careful deliberation about complex ethical decisions.[4] In the area of death he seeks reform in light of two extremes, that of relentless treatment of the hopelessly dying and the opposite extreme of encouraging active euthanasia. In *The Pa-*

tient as Person Ramsey responds to the former, troubled by an era at "'war without retreat and without quarter' against Almighty God for the last shred of sentient life."[5] In *Ethics at the Edges of Life*, written only eight years later, the other extreme, recent glamorization about choosing death, draws his critical attention. Several articles appearing between these two books, such as "The Indignity of 'Death with Dignity'" and "Death's Pedagogy," reveal that he positions his argument differently in polemical response to whichever extreme he finds annoying. Mostly cautious and conservative, he tends to search for a safe "middle ground." Or, as he says, he "leans against" certain excesses toward which humans, especially in our modern age, are inclined.

But it would be misleading to infer from this that Ramsey responds haphazardly to issues. Rather, certain basic convictions about the moral ethos and his particular response to its problems undergird his grievances. He agrees with the assessment that technology is not the sole culprit of the problems that surround modern death:

> If there are moral dilemmas in modern medicine, . . . this is not because of recent triumphs in medical research or the great promise and grave risks stemming from medical technology. The fundamental reason is rather the *continuing moral crisis in modern culture generally*, which reverberates throughout all professions. It can no longer be assumed in the human community that we are agreed on moral action guides, the practice of virtue, the premises and principles of the highest, most humane, most bracing ethics, or what a moral agent owes to anyone who bears a human countenance.[6]

In our "era of 'lapsed links'" a general erosion of moral bonds between persons, generations, one moment and another across time, shakes the ground beneath medicine.[7] We "can no longer rely upon ethical assumptions in our culture to be powerful enough or clear enough to instruct the professions in virtue."[8]

In response, Ramsey formulates a Christian ethic of convenantal love which reconnects the moral agent with other agents and with society, and which links individual moral acts with other moral doings in a sustaining, protecting web of relations, obligations, and duties, and in a history of past and future actions. Indirectly he challenges the personalistic, relativistic ethic of the Kübler-Ross discussion and its influence upon medicine through the death and dying movement.

However, Ramsey explores different issues than the Kübler-Ross discussion. For him, the area of death raises crucial moral dilemmas that demand specific decisions. He formulates answers from an ethical, theological, and Christian perspective. Kübler-Ross and her cohorts investigate the far more diffuse cultural problem of modern attitudes toward death through descriptive, psychological analyses of causes and consequences. Still there is good reason to bring the two views together as different approaches to understanding death. Both parties articulate possible normative models for mortality. We need a unified model that can encompass wide-ranging approaches—dynamic, ethical, and religious—as well as the average dying experience.

Covenant Love and Agent Care

Ramsey brings a deep-felt Christian faith to medical ethics and to the problems of death, not abstract religiosity as "some hypothetical common denominator."[9] He prefaces his books by declaring that he writes "as a Christian ethicist," and that "religious warrants need not be silenced in order to engage in fruitful moral discourse."[10] He allows, as Lisa Cahill notes, the "theological context of his reflection to furnish normative obligations which remain central and vibrant."[11]

In *Ethics at the Edges*, Ramsey nicely summarizes the key principles:

> I . . . invoke ultimate appeal to scripture or theology and to warrants such as righteousness, faithfulness, canons of loyalty, the awesome sanctity of a human life, humankind in the image of God, holy ground, *hesed* (steadfast covenant love), *agape* (or "charity"), as these standards are understood in the religions of our culture, Judaism and Christianity.[12]

These warrants amplify and refine a basic premise of *Basic Christian Ethics*, his earliest and only systematic treatment of the subject:

> The central ethical notion or "category" in Christian ethics is "obedient love"—the sort of love the gospel describes as "love fulfilling the law" and St. Paul designates as "faith that works through love."[13]

In *Patient as Person* he talks about "the Biblical norm of *fidelity to covenant,*" and again in *Ethics at the Edges* "covenant fidelity to the life and interests of another."[14]

Ramsey's definition of love in terms of covenant is perhaps the sharpest contrast between himself and Tillich. He characterizes God's righteousness as the "main theme" of Biblical revelation and the basis and the norm of covenant. God enacts righteousness with the chosen people and in the *kenotic* love of Christ. Because God makes this covenant with persons, they have an obligation to be faithful. Fidelity to God's action requires responsive love which includes love of neighbor and fidelity between persons. God's righteousness measures the rightness and wrongness of action like a "plumb line." We know the meaning of the "good" or the "right" by "how God brought us up out of the house of bondage," or by "how God first loved us."[15] Persons ought to treat their neighbor as one for whom Christ died.

Tillich restricts the term "covenant" to revelatory events in the history of Israel.[16] He believes that our "love of God . . . cannot be equated with obedience." In fact, he seldom uses the words obedience, love, and faith in the same sentence or paragraph in any positive vein. The idea of "obedience of faith" confuses faith and love with heteroneous subjection to authority.[17] Love has only become a command under the conditions of estranged existence. Love "cannot be commanded . . . because it is the power of that reunion which precedes and fulfills the command before it is given."[18] He warns against reducing *agape* to a mere "moral concept" or a detached act of obedience. "Love without its emotional quality is 'good will' toward somebody or something, but it is not love."[19]

Ramsey, on the other hand, warns against obscuring "the single covenant-meaning of love."[20] He defines love completely in terms of obedience. Obedience means no more than love, and love fulfills every legitimate obedience.[21] He considers Tillich's Hegelian idea of love as reunion one of his fundamental mistakes. If Tillich would simply change this word and take the Biblical meaning of love as covenant-faithfulness seriously, his definition would be far more accurate.[22] But Tillich understands love as an ontological, as well as a moral, category. It is a state of affairs, the reunion of the separated in God and more a noun than a verb. Ramsey considers love a rule-term, an active verb or an adverb qualifying an obedient action. Love is more a matter of will, intention, intellect than a matter of the ontological ground of being or of emotion or feeling.

Ramsey's definition of love as "covenant obedience," rather than as a striving toward a *telos* of reunion, has other implications. In his eyes Christian ethics is fundamentally deontological. According to Frankena, deontological theories

> assert that there are other considerations that may make an action or rule right or obligatory besides the goodness or badness of its consequences—certain features of the act itself other than the *value* it brings into existence, for example, the fact that it keeps a promise, is just, or is commanded by God or by the state. . . . For [deontologists] the principle of maximizing the balance of good over evil, no matter for whom, is either not a moral criterion or standard at all, or, at least, it is not the only basis or ultimate one.[23]

In *Deeds and Rules in Christian Ethics*, Ramsey directly challenges Frankena's characterization of Christian ethics as teleological or utilitarian. Ramsey believes that Christian ethics is "radically non-teleological" because it does not establish its principles upon a scale of values, nor by aspiring toward union with the highest possible good. It requires an absolute standard in morality—absolute obedience to God and single-minded love of neighbor. The "reduction of Christian ethics to teleology is nearly the same thing as abandoning it."[24] *Agape* means "ready obedience" to the *present* reign of God. Teleological calculus of consequences plays a role, but such calculation always remains subordinate to determining the right or obligatory act of love for the neighbor as part of the inbreaking of the Kingdom. We cannot derive the meaning of obligation from any good end to be obtained. Moral obligation means to seek nothing but to love the neighbor, "no matter what the morrow brings," single-mindedly, not because the neighbor is worthy, but for her "*own sake*." We are called to "entirely non-preferential regard for whomever happens to be standing by," desiring nothing nor making any claims in return.[25]

From his idea of covenant love, Ramsey eventually derives "rules of practice." He modifies Protestant rulelessness by adapting the categories of several moral philosophers. Borrowing from Frankena, he reasons that "act-agapism drives on to rule-agapism of some sort" and "summary rule-agapism drives on, or is open, to pure rule agapism."[26] Inspired further by John Rawls's renowned essay, "Two Conceptions of Rules," he argues, "agape can and may or must work through rules and embody itself in certain principles which are

regulative or the guides of practice."[27] He likes Rawls's analogy of
the rules of the game of baseball as illustrative of how "rules of
practice" govern an institutionalized structure of activity, such as the
"game of caring." One asks "what love requires to be *practiced*, as it
were, *as a practice*, or as a *societal* rule."[28] We should not consider
individual acts of love outside the umbrella rules. A proper "exception" does not weaken the original principle, but extends and ampli-
fies it. Rules of practice offer stability, continuity, and consistency
without falling prey to legalism or absolutism. In his extensive
specification of moral rules, he hopes to correct the "far too elastic"
or "far too woolly" reliance of Protestant ethics upon intuitive insight
and affectivity.[29] He encourages us to seek instead increased clarity
in moral judgments.

Death, Dying, and the Obligation to Care

All this would not help much with the problems of death in
modern society if Ramsey did not also believe that the Christian
principle of *hesed* translates into language of natural morality and
nonreligious values. Without qualifying his revelational ethic, he
transposes his ethic of "agent agape" into common human experience in terms of an ethic of "agent care." Phrases such as "sanctity of
life," "respect for persons," or "claims" of persons upon others,
illustrate "nonreligious replacement[s]" for religious categories. The
"natural" relations entered at birth, as well as the institutions or
roles entered by choice throughout life, implicitly exemplify the
principle of "covenant-fidelity."[30] Every person, simply by being a
person, places a demand on another human being. Obligation to
remain faithful to others characterizes *all* relations. Through this
translation, he attempts to qualify the "original particularistic position" of his Christian ethic and bridge the gap between it and the
secular world of human action.[31]

But "Just how is the Gospel a lamp unto our feet and a guide
on the pathways of the modern world"[32] in regards to particulars of
death and dying? What is the meaning of faithfulness of one human
being to another in dying? At its broadest level,the response paral-
lels the response of Ramsey's general ethics: act always so as to
exhibit faithfulness. "Do what is called for and what is fitting, do that
which is most caring," not as a means to further ends, but as
"fulfillments of the *categorical* imperative" to never abandon care.

He gives the "rule of practice" of caring greater specificity in terms of what best demonstrates "care, comfort, and human company" to the dying.

In *Patient as Person*, Ramsey implicitly suggests a revised image of the life cycle. Life is not simply an arch from point X, birth, to point Y, death. Life is a continuum along which there comes a point Z where the process of dying irreversibly begins. The former image leaves little ethical choice except relentless attempts to cure right up until the end. The alternative allows for a two-tiered decision-making process. First, medical expertise and experience must determine point Z according to the objective facts of each patient's dying process. Second, once the physician decides that a patient has reached such a point, persons make ethical judgments about treatment "in accord with the facts." If the process of dying has begun, obligations change. Pretended remedies, officious treatments, palliative operations are more an offense than an obligation. Instead, we are obliged to learn to practice the principle of *only* caring for the dying and even obligated to intervene "against many a medical intervention that is possible today."[34]

When medical assessment defines the dying process as irreversible, we must heed one categorical imperative in particular: "Never abandon care!"

> Acts of caring for the dying are deeds done bodily for them which serve solely to manifest that they are not lost from human attention, that they are not alone, that mankind generally and their loved ones take note of their dying and mean to company with them in accepting this unique instance of the acceptable death of all flesh. An attitude toward the dying premised upon mature and profoundly religious convictions will display an indefeatable charity that never ceases to go about the business of caring for the dying neighbor.[35]

The assertion, "there is no duty to use useless means, however natural or ordinary or customary in practice," illustrates another universal rule of the game called "caring."[36] So does the statement that the physician should make a human presence felt to the dying, or that we have a "duty to respect with simple acceptance the dying process" of others.[37] Never "intend another to fall short of the call of charity (no, never) for the sake of any goods that are lesser, as all are."[38] All these statements define the exceptionless or unbreakable rules of the game of fidelity between persons. None of the rules are means to other ends. They simply demonstrate in concrete actions what it means to practice care and to keep covenant with another person. We may abandon care only when the person becomes entirely oblivious to human presence, if this ever happens. And then, such an exception must be universalizable extension of the rule of fidelity itself.

Ramsey revises some of this in *Ethics at the Edges*. He focuses more on the duty not to kill or hasten death than on never abandoning the dying. Drawing extensively upon the work of Arthur J. Dyck, he articulates another categorical imperative: never choose death as an end or as a means. To do so is to claim dominion over life where we have none. God, the trustworthy gift-giver, inexplicably offers us life as a "gift and a trust."[39] As stewards and trustees, not owners, we ought not take it lightly or pridefully. This idea distinguishes Stoic from Jewish and Christian views:

> The Stoic heritage declares that my life and my selfhood are my own to dispose of as I see fit and when I see fit. The Jewish and Christian heritage declares that my life and my selfhood are not my own and are not mine to dispose of as I see fit. In the words of H. Richard Niebuhr, "I live but do not have the power to live. And further I may die at any moment but I am powerless to die. . . . We can choose among many alternatives; but the power to choose self-existence or self-extinction is not ours."[40]

To directly choose death repudiates the meaning of life and severs human relationships prematurely.[41]

Instead, decisions in the face of death always should be choices, as Dyck says, "of how to live while dying." "Dying well enough" involves "life choices" that serve life, not death. When one chooses to quit useless treatment and to care for, rather than to seek to cure, the "still-living dying," one is *not* choosing death, nor performing passive euthanasia. Rather, one is simply allowing the cause of death to advance by the disease itself.[42]

In *Ethics at the Edges of Life*, Ramsey suggests "a medical indications policy" as a more refined means to determine point Z. We can reduce distinctions such as that between ordinary and extraordinary treatment to this policy almost without remainder. It entails objective comparison of treatments by the physician to decide whether treatment is indicated or whether it will no longer affect the curative process and will only prolong dying. While Ramsey acknowledges the importance of a patient's "free and informed participation in medical decisions," he emphasizes that this does not mean meeting *all* desires and wishes—something that the Kübler-Ross discussion has encouraged:[43]

> A competent conscious patient has no moral right to refuse [certain medically indicated treatments], just as no one has a moral right deliberately to ruin his health. Treatment refusal is a relative right, contrary to what is believed today by those who would reduce medical ethics to patient autonomy and a "right to die". . . .
>
> Instead, a patient's need and real claims upon our care have to be read from the human and medical reality of his case, not from his expressed wishes alone. . . . Not yet have we assigned the right to die, the right to choose death as an end . . . the same moral status as the right to life.[44]

Ramsey has several concerns operating here. He hopes to prevent the physician from becoming an "animated tool" of patient desires. He also favors a particular definition of human autonomy that counters those that enthrone "an arbitrary freedom" or "subjective voluntarism" by making medical intervention dependent upon individual whims and transforming free choice into a relativism of personal preferences.[45] "Treatments are not electable because elected, desirable because desired."[46] Freedom must include restraints. This directly challenges some of the attitudes that Kübler-Ross and her followers promote.

He also challenges decisions based on assessment of quality of life, in particular Richard McCormick's "quality-of-life judgments" and Joseph Fletcher's fifteen criteria of differentiating "humanness" from "subpersonal" life. We "have no moral right to choose that some live and others die" based upon a person's capacity for meaningful relationship or on a person's potentiality for values, happiness, or fulfillment "when the medical indications for treatment are the same."[47]

> Persons are not reducible to their potential. Patients are to be loved and cared for no matter who they are and no matter what their potential for higher values is, and certainly not on account of their responsiveness. What they are, in Christian ethical perspective, is our neighbors. They do not become nearer neighbors because of any capacity they own, nor lesser neighbors because they lack some ability to prevail in their struggle for human fulfillment.[48]

We cannot judge a particular life worthless because a person lacks certain qualities or potential for certain earthly achievements. Life escapes such quantitative definition. "While there may be some meaning in speaking of the 'untimely' death of the young," he asserts, "I see no conclusive reason for saying that six months of babyhood or two years of infancy are any less ultimate worth than sixty years of manhood or womanhood."[51] Each day or year holds equal worth, for each life is a "value" in and of itself. As a gift from God, and in God's image, human life always has "unrepeatable, non-interchangeable significance,"[49] an incommeasurable goodness. To measure the quality ignores the intrinsic, inviolable worth of each life. We lack "standing" in the moral universe to judge one life worth living and another not. God makes no distinction based on estimations of individual qualities; nor should we.[50] Indeed, if anything, God shows special care for the helpless and needy.

Some, however, would not agree, including those in the Kübler-Ross discussion, as well as Erikson, Lifton, and even Tillich. These scholars propose valid considerations. From the ethical perspective I have classified as "teleological," they demonstrate that moral decisions in the face of death require at least some consideration of human potential and consequences. They raise sound questions: is a deontological ethic fully adequate, and, if not, how do teleological concerns fit in? Erikson and Lifton demonstrate that we dare not ignore future generations in resolving conflicts. Consideration of the value of certain ends might compel persons to choose an action that promotes the common good before an act required by the principles of covenant fidelity, and for equally valid and rationally acceptable motives and reasons. Ramsey tends to relegate the need to safeguard the common good and the desire for personal fulfillment to subsidiary positions at best, and at worst does not deal with them at all. Although we found the emphasis on personal satisfaction in the Kübler-Ross discussion ethically limiting, Ramsey overlooks individual yearning for personal wholeness and its place, if any, within a Christian ethic of death and dying. Moreover, is Christian ethics as purely deontological as Ramsey would like to argue?[52] Is Biblical morality strictly a deontology of covenant love? Gustafson suggests that "certain actions which love does not permit for Ramsey can be argued as permissible from other theological ethical grounds, and . . . actions which love requires for Ramsey can be questioned from another theological perspective."[53]

A deeper tension between the good of the individual and the

common good is at stake in this debate. As Cahill states, "Ramsey leaves aside the question of community as more than a mechanism for reconciling claims of individuals."[54] He almost rules out individual sacrifice for the common good. We must not compromise the sacredness of the individual out of consideration for certain benefits, or formidable long-term consequences for others or for society.[55] He has greater concern for the bonds of covenant between individual and individual than for those of the community as a whole. Leon Kass suggests that this may be one reason why Ramsey finds himself, to his chagrin, aligned with those who want to transform the horror of death into "death with dignity":

> Indeed, I would suggest that Ramsey's predicament of finding himself in bed with too many partners may stem in part from the fact that both he and they give too much emphasis to "uniqueness," to the subjective, to the individual human soul in its "individuation." Could it be that the stress on the "unique worth of the individual" connects together the mainstream of today's secular thought and its severed theological source, from which Paul Ramsey still takes his watering?[56]

The developmental psychologies of Erikson and Lifton and the ontology of Tillich make self *and* society or individuation *and* participation more essential ingredients to a well-balanced ethic than Ramsey. He separates the idea of covenant love between individuals from the responsibilities of individuals as part of a more extensive network of relationships. With death in particular, enduring transindividual values and species-directed concerns require a kind of consideration which he seldom gives them.

The Last Enemy

In Ramsey's eagerness to clarify moral concerns, he bypasses critical theological issues.[57] Beside Tillich's reflections on the relation between death, sin, and grace, Ramsey's work appears rather elementary. But it is worth looking at, not to prove these remarks, but because the ideas occur in articles which address the ethos surrounding death and indirectly the psychologies of death that shape that ethos.

Even the title, *The Patient as Person*, reflects the impact of the Kübler-Ross discussion. A genuine caring tenor and person-oriented quality characterizes this literature. Like Ramsey, Weisman states, "If cure is impossible, then care and safe conduct ensure a dignified exitus. It is our mutual obligation."[58] Similarly, Kübler-Ross asserts, "The primary physician does not desert the patient. This simply means that we still care for him as a human being, when a patient's condition cannot gratify the physician's need to cure, to treat, to prolong life."[59]

Nonetheless, the foundational justifications behind these statements, the moral objectives, and the practical consequences differ dramatically from Ramsey's. For him, we care for others in obedient responsiveness to the One who has given the gift of life. For the Kübler-Ross discussion, we care because this will nurture the seed within each individual and allow it to grow to its full potential. If faced with proper acceptance, death is a means to enhanced growth. Ramsey strictly forbids choosing death as a means or end. Under no circumstances ought we seek death as a good that will benefit us. We have definite duties which we must not reduce to enhancing the dying experience or to satisfying individual desires. We must not compromise our steadfast concern for the neighbor for the sake of benefits, whether for the individual or for society at large.

Ramsey passionately attacks modern attempts to beautify death in "The Indignity of 'Death with Dignity.' " and in "Death's Pedagogy" and indicates his theology of death. The polemical nature of these pieces makes the task of interpretation difficult. Would he state his case so strongly apart from the need to attack an inviting opponent? Yet these articles reiterate ideas from an earlier sermon, "Death's Duel," written under more tranquil circumstances. The current situation simply calls them forth in more rhetorical language. Together, all three treatises give us a general sense of his position.

Ramsey objects to the "widespread chatter" on how to rationally "manage death" and manipulate sentiments. This turns "mysteries to be contemplated and deepened . . . into problems to be solved." The same outlook that promoted "calisthenic sexuality," when "addressed to 'the last taboo' can only lead eventually and logically to the same thing: to 'calisthenic dying.' "[60] The calisthenics of "pre-death morticians" obstruct genuine care and avoid death's tutelage, "the instruction of facing death as an alien power."[61]

For Ramsey, from a Christian perspective death is the "last enemy." It is always a "threatening, bracing Other," an "ultimate (noncomparative) indignity."[62] He does not conceptualize this idea in terms of a systematic theology but bases it on existential evidence and certain theological doctrines.

Existentially we experience death as dreadful:

> [Death] cannot fail to be . . . an irreparable loss, an unquenchable grief, the threat of all threats, a dread that is more than all fears aggregated together, an approaching "evil" which annuls every ordinary distinction between good and evil . . . a murmuring music rising to a cacophony and then receding which, not written in the score, we hear behind all themes of life whether well or poorly sung.[63]

Unlike Erikson and Tillich, or even Augustine and Calvin, the problem is not guilt and despair, but loneliness. "The dread of death is the dread of oblivion,"[64] not dread of judgment. Death means terrible severance from human community, from "every loved one, . . . everything that constituted the self in its world, . . . every experience [and] . . . nothingness beyond."[65] "The sting of dying is *solitude*," not guilt. "*Desertion*," not despair, "is more choking than death, and more feared. The chief problem of dying is *how not to die alone*."[66] Instead of reinterpreting the traditional view that "sin drew death after," he focuses on the existential argument that "death draws sin after." Anxiety about death *produces* sin; it provokes selfishness and bitterness; it alienates us from love of others and from love of God: it fills our hearts with "madness" and "evil," thereby supplying the "internal setting or precondition for sin."[67]

Existentially Ramsey has made death the source of evil. To correct this, he returns to doctrinal argument. For Jewish "consciousness," the problem of sin is the central theme, for the Greeks the problem of death, and for Christianity the two come together in a unique way:

> In the new religious consciousness uncovered when the New Testament joined sin and death together, death is our last enemy, not the first; and sin brings death, not death sin. A *second* look at that way of ordering the connection of sin with death should make it plain that this was never merely an odd theoretical explanation of why all men are mortal.[68]

He oversimplifies the distinctions between views and presents the traditional position as *the* Christian view, without revision and with little concern for resonance with modern world views. Death is punishment for sin and not a natural part of life.

While he does not wholly deny death as a part of nature, he does not develop this idea. Instead, he ridicules those who attempt to appease the terror by saying that "death is simply a part of life." Death is no more natural or acceptable than disease, injury, and congenital defects or even murder, rapine, and pillage. Nor does it matter to the dying individual that death is "an evolutionary necessity" since everyone transcends the species, stands alone in fear and trembling before death, and "happens not to be evolution."[69] To make death equal with birth, growth, and natural selection "smacks more of whistling before the darkness descends and an attempt to brainwash one's contemporaries to accept a very feeble philosophy of life and death."[70] From this perspective, he has no trouble quickly dismissing psychological schemas: "So much for the consolations of 'social immortality' or Robert Jay Lifton's 'surrogates for immortality' needed in the modern age."[71]

Only the gospel introduces a positive factor into this fearsome situation. Christ conquers the twin foci of misery—death and sin. Apart from relieving fear, however, this does not alter death's negativity, even for the believer. Death is far from a positive event, except on the other side of redemption.

Nonetheless, Ramsey discusses an important positive outcome. Where fear of death remains, care of the dying is stymied. In Christ, "Death the Enemy" is "conquered," and love is perfected. Release from fear allows moral agents to minister to one another:

> The essence of love is respect for the shadow of death upon the face of another. It means powerful compassion for another doomed soul, respect for the shadow of death that falls across everyone who bears a human countenance. Love means acknowledging that, while all men reach a natural death, they do not die naturally and no matter how they try will never learn to perish like things.[72]

Living according to the love of God frees persons from the power of death and the selfishness, hatred, strife, and estrangement that it instills. No longer striving for "modes of immortality" to insure continuity "against the day which is to come," they can cease trying to give themselves life. The ethical person "may always gird" herself "to oppose this enemy, but not the religious ethical" person.[73]

Implications for the Moral Life

These sweeping images influence Ramsey's ethic. If our greatest fear is to face death alone, then the presence of human company becomes imperative. All "still living dying" must have companionship before this "alien power." And while some good may come from death, even at its best it is still a "good evil."[74] Death then can never be a goal or a positive choice in the best interest of anyone. Death, as evil, should never be chosen as an end.

Robert Morison and Leon Kass respond to Ramsey's article, "The Indignity of 'Death with Dignity,'" with highly critical remarks. Both argue that it is absurd to maintain that death is an indignity, existentially, theologically, or philosophically. In fact, from Kass's perspective, there is something *un*dignified about defying death's rightful place in nature.

> *Death is natural and necessary and inextricably tied to life.* . . . To decline and die are necessary parts of the *life cycle.* . . . Living things have in themselves a principle of growth *and decay.* Decay and decline are not "affronts from outside" [as in Ramsey] but are natural processes *built into* the principle that causes life.[75]

To put it bluntly, Ramsey "fails to give nature her due."[76]

Ramsey's polemic leaves Morison, a self-confessed "latter-day pagan" and biologist, with the impression that to be Christian means to believe that divine spite curses us with death as a punishment for sin. He can only conclude that he wants nothing to do with theological attempts to relate death and sin.[77] Fortunately Kass has the breadth of scholarship to confront Ramsey for asserting this as *the* Christian view. Kass calls this a gross oversimplification. He demonstrates other interpretations in the Jewish and Christian traditions in which death belongs to the created order of being, and is, as such, good. Death promotes regeneration and permanence of being. It is surpassed by what may turn out to be greater evils, such as current biochemical research on retarding the process of aging.[78] Considering the negative ramifications of such studies, far from being a curse, mortality may, indeed, be a necessary condition, even a blessing and a value, for the welfare of individuals and for a decent human community.[79] Kass knows Ramsey's other writings well enough to believe that Ramsey himself would likely agree. He is doubly disappointed, therefore, when Ramsey's main advice to the reader is to fight always and forever against death's arrival.

These judgments raise once again the deeper issue of the adequacy of Ramsey's overall interpretation of Biblical resources. Is the relation between death and sin that he portrays *the* Christian perspective or *the* Biblical view? Rather there are many different interpretations of God's actions and many different kinds of language that describe the moral life. The "religious consciousness" of the scriptures and traditions is more complex than Ramsey allows.

Perhaps we can understand his argument best in its narrower intent as a polemic against an extreme that he perceived dangerous. Indeed, I welcome his emphasis on death's alien nature, despite all attempts to mollify fears and doubts, as a healthy balance to the opposite extreme which reductionistically embraces death as good simply as part of nature or as a psychological growth experience. The latter obscures many of the moral and spiritual problems. We may find dying fulfilling, but he impresses upon us that that is not all or even part of what death means.

By stating his case so vigorously, however, Ramsey leaves his respondents and his readers with the half-truth that for Christians, death is *entirely* evil or *solely* an enemy. One could easily suppose, as Kass suggests, that Christians would favor always resisting its advances. Preserving life becomes an absolute end in itself, no matter its quality or nature, circumstances or consequences.

Certainly Tillich agrees that death has its demonic dimensions, but he achieves, in part as a result of more careful ontological analysis, a more balanced perspective. Christ does not deliver us from death alone, but more importantly, from the "sickness unto death," from hopelessness, and from despair worse than any loss of life. If anything, the medical sciences need reminders that humans are mortal and fragile, that death will and must come sooner or later, and not always as a defeat or failure. [80] Death *is* an integral aspect of life, as even the Kübler-Ross discussion helps us see despite its limitations.

More significantly, because death is an ambivalent event, we cannot achieve the kind of moral certainty that Ramsey wants or that we want in order to feel comfortable in a horribly complex world of fundamental moral risks. At the same time, Ramsey reminds us that we should never use this as an excuse to forfeit critical moral inquiry. Although his single-rubric approach has its limitations, the motif of covenant love permits skillful handling of a number of diverse and complicated questions.

Footnotes to Chapter VI

/1/   James F. Childress, "Ethical Issues in Death and Dying," *Religious Studies Review* 4 (July 1976), p. 180.
/2/   Paul Ramsey, *Nine Modern Moralists* (Englewood Cliffs, N.J.: Prentice-Hall, 1962), p. 3.
/3/   Paul Ramsey, "The Nature of Medical Ethics," in *The Teaching of Medical Ethics*, p. 123.
/4/   Ramsey, *Patient as Person*, pp. xv–xviii.
/5/   Ibid., pp. 119, 135.
/6/   Paul Ramsey, "Conceptual Foundations for an Ethics of Medical Care: A Response," in *Ethics and Health Policy*, p. 35.
/7/   Paul Ramsey, "Responsible Parenthood: An Essay in Ecumenical Ethics," *Religion of Life* 26, no. 3 (Autumn 1967), p. 343, cited by Paul F. Camenisch, "Paul Ramsey's Task: Some Methodological Clarifications and Questions," in *Love and Society: Essays in the Ethics of Paul Ramsey*, ed. David H. Smith and James T. Johnson (Missoula, Mon.: Scholars Press, 1974), p. 81.
/8/   Ramsey, *Patient as Person*, p. xviii.
/9/   Paul Ramsey, "The Indignity of 'Death with Dignity,'" *Hastings Center Studies*, 2, no. 2 (May 1974), p. 56.
/10/   Paul Ramsey, *Ethics at the Edges of Life: Medical and Legal Intersections* (New Haven: Yale University Press, 1978), pp. xiii–xv; *Patient as Person*, p. xi; idem., *Basic Christian Ethics* (Chicago: University of Chicago Press, 1950), p. xiv.
/11/   Lisa Sowle Cahill, "Within Shouting Distance: Paul Ramsey and Richard McCormick on Method," *The Journal of Medicine and Philosophy* 4, no. 4 (1979), p. 415.
/12/   Ramsey, *Ethics at the Edges*, p. xiii.
/13/   Ramsey, *Basic Christian Ethics*, p. xi.
/14/   Ramsey, *Patient as Person*, p. xii; idem., *Ethics at the Edges*, p. 161.
/15/   Ramsey, "Kant's Moral Philosophy or a Religious Ethics?" in *Knowledge, Value and Belief*, pp. 62, 66.
/16/   Tillich, *Systematic Theology*, vol. 1, pp. 125, 143, 227.
/17/   Ibid., vol. 1, p. 287; vol. 3, p. 132.
/18/   Tillich, *Systematic Theology*, vol. 2, p. 81.
/19/   Ibid., vol. 3, pp. 136–137. See also, Paul Tillich, *Morality and Beyond* (New York: Harper and Row, 1963), pp. 40–41.
/20/   Ramsey, *Nine Modern Moralists*, p. 185.
/21/   Ramsey, *Basic Christian Ethics*, p. 34.
/22/   Ramsey, *Nine Modern Moralists*, p. 184.
/23/   Frankena, *Ethics*, p. 15.
/24/   Paul Ramsey, *Deeds and Rules in Christian Ethics* (New York: Charles Scribner's Sons, 1967), pp. 108–109.

/25/   Ramsey, *Basic Christian Ethics*, p. 39.
/26/   Ramsey, *Deeds and Rules*, p. 114.
/27/   Ibid., p. 5; John Rawls, "Two Concepts of Rules," *Philosophical Review* 64 (1955), pp. 3–32.
/28/   Ramsey, *Deeds and Rules*, p. 7.
/29/   See James M. Gustafson, *Protestant and Roman Catholic Ethics* (Chicago: University of Chicago Press, 1978), p. 43.
/30/   Ramsey, *Patient as Person*, pp. xii–xiii.
/31/   Cahill, "Within Shouting Distance," pp. 399–400.
/32/   Paul Ramsey, "Faith Effective Through In-Principled Love," *Christianity and Crisis* 20 (1961), p. 76.
/33/   Ramsey, *Patient as Person*, pp. 151, 153, 159.
/34/   Ibid., p. 118. Cf. Ernie W. D. Young, "Reflections on Life and Death: The Theological Imperative in Medicine is Being Seriously Called into Question," *Journal of Theology for Southern Africa* 18 (March 1977), pp. 48–55.
/35/   Ramsey, *Patient as Person*, p. 153.
/36/   Ibid., p. 132.
/37/   Ibid., p. 125.
/38/   Paul Ramsey, "Incommensurability and Indeterminacy in Moral Choice," in *Doing Evil to Achieve Good*, ed. Richard A. McCormick and Paul Ramsey (Chicago: Loyola University Press, 1978), p. 134.
/39/   Ramsey, *Ethics at the Edges*, p. 148.
/40/   Arthur J. Dyck, "An Alternative to the Ethic of Euthanasia," in *Ethics in Medicine*, p. 534 (also citing Niebuhr, *Responsible Self*, pp. 114–115).
/41/   Ibid., p. 533.
/42/   Ramsey, *Ethics at the Edges*, p. 151.
/43/   In an earlier 1977 article, "Prolonged Death: Not Medically Indicated," he includes a second consideration alongside the medical indications policy—"a patient's right to refuse treatment" (*Hastings Center Report* 6 [February 1976], p. 15). He modifies this in *Ethics at the Edges*.
/44/   Ramsey, *Ethics at the Edges*, pp. 156–158.
/45/   Ibid., pp. 157–159.
/46/   Ibid., p. 158. See also Dyck, "Alternative to Euthanasia," p. 531.
/47/   Ramsey, *Ethics at the Edges*, p. 192.
/48/   Ibid., p. 227. For an example of Ramsey's application of the medical indication policy, see pp. 181–188.
/49/   Paul Ramsey, "Death's Pedagogy," in *Death, Dying and Euthanasia*, ed. Dennis J. Horan and David Mall (Washington: University Publications of America, 1977), p. 341.
/50/   Ramsey, *Ethics at the Edges*, pp. 194, 203, 205.
/51/   Ibid., pp. xii–xiii.
/52/   See Gustafson, *Ethics and Theology*, p. 90.
/53/   Ibid., p. 89.
/54/   Cahill, "Within Shouting Distance," p. 406. See also, Camenisch, "Methodological Clarifications," pp. 67–89.
/55/   Cahill, "Within Shouting Distance," p. 402.
/56/   Kass, "Dignity in Death," p. 69.
/57/   "Anthropology and the doctrine of sin, in particular," David Smith agrees, "play a very small part in Ramsey's handing of conflict situations"

(David Smith, "Paul Ramsey, Love and Killing," in *Love and Society*, p. 7). Charles Curran points out that Ramsey does not consider seriously human nature or ontological structures as possible loci of ethical norms (Charles Curran, "Paul Ramsey and Traditional Roman Catholic Natural Law Theory," in *Love and Society*, p. 51).

/58/   Weisman, *Realization of Death*, p. 190.
/59/   Kübler-Ross, *Living with Death*, p. 25.
/60/   Ramsey, "Death's Pedagogy," p. 343.
/61/   Ibid., p. 331.
/62/   Ibid., pp. 331, 338; idem., "Indignity of 'Death with Dignity,'" p. 52.
/63/   Ramsey, "Death's Pedagogy," pp. 340–341.
/64/   Ramsey, "Indignity of 'Death with Dignity,'" p. 50.
/65/   Ibid.
/66/   Ramsey, *Patient as Person*, p. 134. Emphasis added.
/67/   Paul Ramsey, *Death's Duel*, (University Park, Pa., 1961), Sermon delivered in University Chapel, Pennsylvania State University, January 8, 1961, unpaginated. Also published in *Motive* (April 1962).
/68/   Ibid.
/69/   Ramsey, "Indignity of 'Death with Dignity.'" pp. 48–49.
/70/   Ibid., p. 52.
/71/   Ramsey, "Death's Pedagogy," p. 336.
/72/   Ibid.,; see also, idem., "Indignity of 'Death with Dignity,'" p. 56.
/73/   Ramsey, *Patient as Person*, p. 132.
/74/   Ramsey, "Indignity of 'Death with Dignity,'" p. 58.
/75/   Kass, "Dignity in Death," p. 75.
/76/   Ibid., p. 76.
/77/   Robert Morison, "The Last Poem: The Dignity of the Inevitable and Necessary," *Hastings Center Studies* 2, no. 2 (May 1974), p. 66.
/78/   Kass, "Dignity in Death," pp. 77–80; idem, "Biology and Human Affairs." Cf. Idem, *Toward a More Natural Science*.
/79/   Ibid.; idem, "Man's Right to Die," p. 76.
/80/   See Richard Landau and James M. Gustafson, "Death is Not the Enemy,": *Journal of the American Medical Association* 252 (November 2, 1984), p. 2458; Kass, "End of Medicine," p. 18.

CONCLUDING REMARKS: A PROPADEUTIC TO A PRACTICAL THEOLOGY OF DEATH AND DYING

David Tracy characterizes death as one of life's "limit situations."[1] By this he means that death is an existential boundary which evokes perennial questions about the limits and meaningfulness of experience. Culture's attempts to understand these quandaries almost invariably possess what Tracy calls a "religious dimension." I have analyzed and compared a number of ways culture "houses" this dimension in religious or quasi-religious forms in the Kübler-Ross discussion, Erikson, Lifton, Ramsey, and Tillich. This leads to several implications for the further step of formulating an approach to death. To limit and organize the many possible comments, my observations fall into two general categories: theological questions of death's nature and ethical questions about death's moral import. In both of these areas I do not attempt to resolve all the issues, particularly between Ramsey and Tillich, or to suggest any final solution to how we should live in the face of death. Rather, I intend primarily suggestive remarks that flow naturally from my critical analysis of culture.

Death the Enemy, Death the Friend: A Debate with Moral Implications

Is human life "just a collection of molecules, an accident on the stage of evolution, a freakish speck of mind in the mindless universe, fundamentally no different from other living—or even non-living—things?"[1] If this is so, is death nothing more than the simply the passing from physical vitality of one more mass of cells in the evolution of the human species? We cannot understand these questions of the nature of life and death apart from their roots in religious and social forces and the history of philosophical and theological thought. Not only do religion and theology answer these questions differently, but psychological and medical answers have gained authority. Society has neatly divided the territory for debate into at least three isolated compartments—"subjective, value-loaded" religion, "objective, value-free" medicine, and psychotherapy as a third intermediary practice. Only a few theologians, little known and seldom referred to, have attempted to account for traditional doctrines of death's unnatural and evil nature. Psychology has promoted a naturalistic view of death as no more than biological arrest and at the most, an experience with psychological aspects. And medicine has reduced and restricted the questions of death to specific practical quandaries, from whether to pull the plug to who should get life-sustaining parts or treatment. As death became the property of physicians, therapists, hospitals, and clinics, it became progressively "de-valued" and "naturalized." Where, before, dying was a ritualized occasion with dramatic moral and spiritual considerations, now it is a diagnosis and course of treatment or a psychological description of stages.

Critical analysis of literature in psychology, medicine, and theology suggests that these images truncate and impoverish our understanding of the full nature of death as natural *and* unnatural, good *and* evil. Human mortality is a natural *and* a moral event, despite modern tendencies to forget or misunderstand the latter and reduce the former to "naturalistic" meanings. Contrary to Ramsey, the Christian tradition does not speak in a uniform voice. To argue that Judaism or Christianity simply asserts that death is an evil consequence of sin betrays the ambiguity of death in scripture and tradition. Nor, contrary to the Kübler-Ross discussion, is there only one psychological view. To say that psychology sees death as purely natural and theology as purely enemy, belies the subtleties embedded in both traditions.

Since Schleiermacher, theology has given increased prominence to the natural character of death. Partly as a result, people in general no longer have language to talk about the moral dimension. Forewarned by Freud, persons fear moralism and shy away from words like obligation, duty, sin, guilt, especially in relation to death. In many cases, restraint is appropriate. Pathology, not right and good action, results from perverse enforcement of these ideals. Theology wisely reconsiders its traditional doctrines of death and sin and whether they lead to overly fearful, detrimental attitudes.

Still, existential and theological reasoning prove death's essential dual nature. Although modern Christian thought emphasizes the "yes" of death's natural place in life more often than the "no" of moral judgment, both belong to the Christian answer. Based on my exploration of several reinterpretations of this tension, we can see important experiential realities that psychology overlooks and suggest fresh language to address the moral component.

Death is not entirely our enemy. This view ignores life's natural rhythms and intrinsic limitations. Decay, decline, and finitude itself are integral to life, essential ontological structures, Tillich says, not adventitious evils that descend upon us as external punishment. They belong to the nature of being, to creation, and thereby, to human nature. Humans are created mortal with a beginning and an end. Not only does modern science confirm this, Kass declares, but Aristotle, Maimonides, Thomas Aquinas, and others do as well. In Karl Rahner's words, death at least possesses a basically neutral essence as an event common to all, even if it is at the same time a decisive expression of sinful perdition and retribution.

And this death is also. We are more than an animated mass of cells. Less clearly understood, however, is the exact nature of this "more." For Lifton and Erikson, we are not just organic creatures, but actors and symbolizers in a transpersonal, intergenerational network of relationships. To delve deeper, in Kierkegaardian style, we are not only body and soul, but spirit. We struggle between finitude and freedom over finitude, creatureliness and transcendence. This understanding says to psychology and medicine "life is not only a 'chronological and developmental,' but also a moral, movement."[3] We cannot die a merely natural death, we are not merely biological creatures.

Even the Kübler-Ross scholars allude to moral conflicts of business unfinished, projects undone, promises broken, purposes thwarted, potentials unrealized. Disease, illness, and ultimately death remind us that our accomplishments are finite, and failure and guilt inevitable. Moral interdiction and guilt do not always indicate infantile, neurotic fixation as Freud assumed. Albeit ambiguous, there are non-infantile, non-neurotic, creative meanings of guilt. Therefore we ought not always attempt to relieve the patient of guilt at the expense of a rightly acquired sense of responsibility and the need for insight, perseverance, and reconciliation.

Moreover, death's unnaturalness includes not only the disappointment of human hopes but the loss of God's gracious purpose in creation. We are created with obligations to live in faith. We sense that we are not created to die and, as Tillich asserts ,that we deserve this dreaded ordeal. Thus, in contrast to Kübler-Ross's stoic view of death "as easily acceptable" and "as posing no real threat to life, to its meaning or to its integrity," in Gilkey's words, "death is more terrible than this,more annihilating to our finitude, our rationality, our will, and more destructive of the personal relations and the communal tasks that make life meaningful."[4] Death makes clear our unmet obligation to respond to God in loving obedience, as Ramsey would say, or the demand to turn toward God as center and ground of our being, as Tillich would say. No one can dispose of herself unambiguously. We all meet our demise under the shadow of a darkened conscience. Hence "death brings with it for all of us the negativity of guilt."[5] The end of life does not end life's moral ambiguity. Death only makes guilt more definite and permanent. In this sense, death is an ultimate negativity, despite its place as a positive part of life's natural evolution.

The problem of death, therefore, is not only the problem of finiteness, but of sin and tragedy, a problem beyond human remedy, whether through Kübler-Ross's stage of beatific acceptance, Lifton's modes of immortality, or Erikson's virtues of integrity and wisdom. These ideologies deny the reality of a "boundary situation" worse than death that threatens on another level than that of bodily existence[6] with moral and religious guilt, anxiety, and despair. The natural view, though accurate, does not exhaust death's meaning. In fact, unto itself, this view is inadequate insofar as it omits an important dimension of human experience and inaccurate when it degenerates into reductive naturalism, subject to the entrance of new moralisms. An adequate approach takes seriously both natural and moral components and responds to the problems raised by both. In this sense, the Kübler-Ross discussion is the least adequate. The model of mortality as the expiration of a biochemical or psychological organism must not exclude the model of death as the dying of a responsible self. These two models are integrally related as concentric circles, or in Tillich's metaphor, as multidimensional realms of life. Technical reason or psychological understanding alone cannot fully fathom the realities of death, sin, and guilt. We must have religious and moral meanings to understand and respond to both the naturalness of death's reality as part of creation and to our responsibility for moral worthiness or unworthiness in the face of its limitation.

I suggest a significant, if not simple, conclusion. In death and dying, we must preserve room for *both* forgiveness *and* moral vision, acceptance *and* moral demands, or, as Tillich says, "acceptance without suspending judgment."[7] These two factors share an important role in any viable construction of a modern perspective on death. Without a clear sense of moral demand, a clarity lacking in the initial psychological discussion, we fail to grasp the full meaning of forgiveness. Lacking moral certainty and aware that in risk-fraught choices no action nor all its consequences are entirely right or wrong, we need a sense of grace and unconditioned acceptance. As physicians and therapists attempt to decide whether to cut off artificial feeding to the hopelessly ill or whether to encourage a terminally ill patient to die at home, it matters that sins are forgiven, that the forces of evil and despair submit to God's ultimate will, and that the life, death, and resurrection of Christ transform the sting of death. When our actions fit into this context of life-giving trust, then, in H. Richard Niebuhr's words, "death no less than life appears to us an act of mercy, not of mercy to *us* only, but in the great vicariousness of responsive and responsible existence, as mercy to those in whom, with whom, and for whom we live."[8]

Development of trust and mistrust is an important life cycle issue, no less in the early attachment to the mother than in the final act of integrity before death. But while of importance, no amount of social and psychological reinterpretation of the past or hope for the future can radically change the ultimate context undergirding our actions and responses. Only the One whose redemptive power is greater than ours can effect such a *metanoia*. Then, and only then, is the context of death transformed into one of life.

The Moral Implications

Without a clear sense of moral demand, a clarity lacking in the initial psychological discussion, we fail to grasp the full meaning of forgiveness. We uncovered in the Kübler-Ross discussion a pervasive quasi-hedonistic attitude. The need to promote happiness initiated the original interdiction of death in the eighteenth century. This same factor subtly motivates recent attempts to accept death. One should live and die so as to secure personal fulfillment. The discussion defines fulfillment as gratifying subjective desires; dissipating frustrations, anxiety, and guilt; producing contentment and a passive peace. Individual wants dictate moral choice and define the good death. The role of physicians, therapists, and others is to free persons to obtain their wishes, with freedom defined as the absence of constraints. The actual content of decisions is immaterial and the nature of a person's reasons a matter of indifference. Theoretically, besides lack of personal or political power, such an "ethic" knows few limits to action and to personal proclivities in the pursuit of an optimal life.

These observations raise extremely important questions. How should we act in health and illness? Even more trying judgments arise in the face of death. How should we live knowing that we will die? Do we do that which is personally desirable, that which pleases and provides pleasure? Ought we live only for the moment, for the "now" and "what turns you on," as Kübler-Ross says? Or are particular actions or virtues required, perhaps in response to principles, goods, or communities beyond ourselves? These are difficult questions with no simple answers.

I suggest that we must consider the effects of our actions upon others, even when our future is too short to directly experience these effects. Moreover, we are liable to certain obligations and responsibilities, even in a state of declining health and vigor. In other words, we should not follow the dictates that flow from the drive for self-preservation and the pursuit of happiness without some regard for other persons, principles and aims.

Granted, in meeting our end, personal realization has a valid, even crucial place. Still the ethic of the Kübler-Ross discussion is not sufficient as a basis for determining norms for behavior. It constricts moral meaning by limiting its reference point to self and to biological and psychological necessities of survival and pleasure. Understanding dying as one deems most appropriate, so long as one does not infringe upon another's idiosyncratic rights, is less a moral principle than a tenet for sustaining psychological egoism and moral relativism.

Viewed from a more adequate psychological perspective, a complex network of relationships ties persons to persons and persons to the cycle of generations as further reference points transcending the self. While it is true, as existentialism attests, that everyone meets her death alone, the individual does not live and die entirely unto herself. We exist in binding relation to one another. Death, then, has significant moral implications that extend beyond the immediate self, beyond personal or psychological needs, to public commitments. The Kübler-Ross discussion reduces the idea of "public" to the plurality of individual consciences that make decisions in privatized contexts. By contrast, we can resolve the problems of death *only* when we consider them publicly, that is, in light of the cycle of generations and continuity in society. "Public" means the social and normative web in which we are embedded, upon which we depend for development, and to which we are accountable as we mature. We must guide decisions by a teleological concern, not only for ourselves but for our connectedness to this wider normative web. Terms like mutuality, integrity, wisdom, evolutionary responsibility, and continuity must enter into the definition of individual need satisfaction. Integrity before finitude requires a capacity to move beyond the immediate context and see universal horizons that border not only our own life but the whole of life. One should act so as to strengthen oneself and one's potential *even as* one strengthens that of the other. Evolutionary responsibility requires ability to balance personal needs and detachment from these in order to make fair judgments about concerns beyond oneself. Conflict, regret, guilt, and despair are inevitable. Rather than attempting to alleviate these, we must incorporate them into a balanced synthesis of negative and positive. Real as distinct from neurotic or static guilt signals rightful responsibility for separation, disintegration, and stasis in the person and her community.

From a theological perspective, the relationship between persons and God points a person beyond the self. Terms like love, justice, covenant, and community of persons enter into the definition of personal needs. For Tillich, the moral action in the face of death is that which participates in the realization of personhood in the fullness of Being-itself. Only actions aimed at the *telos* of God's reuniting love are "stronger than death." They overcome the separation inherent in death and create a new kind of "participation in which there is more than that which the individuals involved can bring to it."9

But I hesitate to give complete prominence to teleological images at the expense of reflection on principles and duties, that is, acts that are right regardless of the final good achieved. Love defined according to the principle of obedient fidelity to covenant suggests specific rules of practice which must guide consideration of such questions as whether to prolong dying or to hasten death. We must never prolong the agony of the irreversibly dying by useless means of treatment, never abandon care, and never choose death as a means or an end. In so doing, we love others as God has loved us and as persons for whom Christ died. We have a duty to nurture and protect bonds of covenantal love, to make a human presence felt, to accompany, care, and comfort others. Personal benefit remains an indirect result of right action and not a reason for justifying action. We act in faith to covenants regardless of consequence, positive or negative, for ourselves. We affirm such faithfulness-claims for their own sake, even unto death, not because the good done for others rebounds to ourselves or to the good of the whole, but because these principles are good in themselves, particularly in meeting the challenges of death. For death tests our resilience as care-givers and the community itself as a network of care.

It is less important to decide which approach, teleological or deontological, is right or wrong, than to recognize the differences and the usefulness and limitations of both. Whether we define love as responsive obedience to divine mandates or as purposive striving toward union with God, in some measure a mediating approach is optimal. We are best advised to attend to duties *and* benefits as two intransigent elements in moral discourse. We should seek harmony between the requirement to produce the greatest care and the requirement to follow the rule of practice that proves most caring. Ideally we should strive "to stay within the boundaries of permissible practice fixed by both together."[10] A good and right death entails concern for human values in relationship and requires responsiveness in genuine community. In other words, loving action in the face of death must be guided by (1) determination of what we should do case by case to achieve reuniting love, and (2) determination of what we should do according to rules of practice for the most generally caring action.

Behind these requirements, I perceive three even more essential directives that must inform response to critical illness and dying: the irreducible worth of human life, the importance of responsibility in relationships, and freedom as more than absence of constraints. We must never reduce the inherent worth of the person to some inhuman goal, such as the future of medical science, or to a quantification of potential for self-realization. We should never use persons as means to other ends. Freedom is the capacity to respect others and to be respected as an end, never as a means. For Ramsey, freedom means a conscience ordered according to the covenantal command of God. For Tillich, it means deliberation, decision, and responsibility for shaping human destiny in relation to the unity of being. In either case, freedom is not only release *from* restraints, but freedom *for* renewed commitment to covenantal love and participation in the community of being. Redemption frees us from concern for satisfying our own needs, without necessarily sacrificing them. It liberates us to see the larger picture and, as Tillich would say, takes the threat of non-being—death, guilt, and meaninglessness—into itself. We are thereby empowered to risk moral action and to care for others in a world where death is one among the many events fraught with inexplicable tragedy.

While rightfully wary of moralism, we must avoid moral sloppiness and resist the temptation of abstract principles that fail to address the hard facts. Yet no single response adequately answers the specific questions of how we should approach the fact of our own mortality. At the very least, death remains an unknown parameter to the moral life. At the most, from a religious perspective death holds the promise and hope of salvation. In the latter case, death's meaning and value rest upon moral relationships to others and spiritual relationship to God. But in the end mortality remains life's mystery. It undercuts false assurance that we know and control everything and that everything services our benefit. As technology alters life and as we struggle with the question of our existence and destiny, the search for clarity on death continues to invite illumination.

Footnotes to Concluding Remarks

/1/   Tracy, *Blessed Rage,* pp. 105–109; idem., *Analogical Imagination,* pp. 160–167.

/2/   Leon Kass, "Modern Science and Ethics: Time for Reexamination?" *University of Chicago Magazine* 76, no. 4 (Summer 1984), p. 29.

/3/   Vaux, *Reformed Tradition,* p. 68.

/4/   Gilkey, "Meditation on Death," p. 29.

/5/   Ibid.

/6/   Tillich, *Protestant Era,* p. 197.

/7/   Tillich, *Meaning of Health,* pp. 120–121.

/8/   Niebuhr, *Responsible Self,* p. 144; see also pp. 140–145.

/9/   Tillich, *New Being,* p. 173.

/10/   Ramsey, "Nature of Medical Ethics," p. 126.

SELECTED BIBLIOGRAPHY

Abram, Morris B. *Deciding to Forego Life-Sustaining Treatment: A Report on Ethical, Moral and Legal Issues in Treatment Decisions.* Washington, D.C.: Government Printing Office, 1983.

———. *Defining Death: A Report on the Medical, Legal and Ethical Issues in the Determination of Death.* Washington, D.C.: Government Printing Office, 1981.

Ariès, Philippe. "Death Inside Out." *Hastings Center Studies* 2, no. 2 (May 1974), 3–18.

———. *The Hour of Our Death.* Translated by Helen Weaver. New York: Alfred A. Knopf, 1981.

———. "The Reversal of Death: Changes in Attitudes toward Death in Western Societies." In *Death in America.* Edited by David E. Stannard. Philadelphia: University of Pennsylvania Press, 1975.

———. *Western Attitudes toward Death: From the Middle Ages to the Present.* Translated by Patricia M. Ranun. Baltimore: Johns Hopkins University Press, 1974.

Augustine. *City of God.* Translated by Henry Bettenson. London: Penguin, 1972.

———. *The Confessions of St. Augustine.* Translated by Rex Warner with an Introduction by Vernon J. Bourke. New York: The New American Library, 1963.

———. *Enchiridian, Or Manual to Laurentius Concerning Faith, Hope, and Charity.* Translated by Ernest Evans. London: Richard Clay, 1953.

———. *A Treatise on the Merits and Forgiveness of Sins and on Baptism of Infants in Three Books.* Addressed to Marcellinus, A.D. 412. In *The Nicene and Post-Nicene Fathers*, vol. 5. Edited by Philip Schaff. Grand Rapids: Eerdmans, 1971.

———. *The Trinity.* In *The Fathers of the Church*, vol. 45. Translated by Stephen McKenna. Washington, D.C.: Catholic University of America Press, 1963.

Backer, Barbara A., Natalie Hannon, and Noreen A. Russell. *Death and Dying: Individuals and Institutions.* New York: Wiley and Sons, 1982.

Bailey, Lloyd. "Death in Biblical Thought." In *Encyclopedia of Bioethics*, 4 vols. Edited by Warren Reich. New York: Free Press, 1973.

Bane, J. Donald, et al. *Death and Ministry: Pastoral Care of the Dying and the Bereaved.* New York: Seabury, 1975.

186 Death, Sin and the Moral Life

Becker, Ernest. *The Denial of Death*. New York: Free Press, 1973.

Blauner, Robert. "Death and Social Structure." *Psychiatry* 29 (1966), 378–394.

Branson, Roy, "Is Acceptance a Denial of Death?" *The Christian Century*, May 7, 1974, pp. 464–468.

Brown, Norman. *Life Against Death*. Middletown, Conn.: Wesleyan University Press, 1959.

Browning, Don S. *Generative Man: Psychoanalytic Perspectives*. New York: Dell, 1973.

———. *Pluralism and Personality: William James and Some Contemporary Cultures of Psychology*. Lewisburg, Pa.: Bucknell University Press, 1980.

———. "Psychology as Religioethical Thinking." *The Journal of Religion* 64, no. 2 (April 1984), 139–157.

———. *Religious Ethics and Pastoral Care: Protestant and Catholic Ethics and the Cure of Souls*. Philadelphia: Fortress Press, 1983.

———. *Religious Thought and the Modern Psychologies*. Philadelphia: Fortress Press, 1987.

———, ed., *Practical Theology*. San Francisco: Harper and Row, 1983.

Callahan, Daniel. "Biological Progress and the Limits of Human Health." In *Ethics and Health Policy*. Edited by Robert M. Veatch and Roy Branson. Cambridge, Mass.: Ballinger, 1976.

———. "The Emergence of Bioethics." In *Science, Ethics and Medicine*. Edited by H. Tristram Engelhardt, Jr. and Daniel Callahan. Hastings-on-Hudson, N.Y.: Institute of Society, Ethics and the Life Sciences, 1976.

———. "Health and Society: Some Ethical Imperatives." *Daedalus* 106, no. 1 (Winter 1977), 22–33.

———. "The WHO Definition of 'Health.'" *Hastings Center Studies* 1, no. 3 (1973), 77–88.

Calvin, John. *Commentaries on the Book of Genesis*. Vol. 1. Translated by John King. Grand Rapids: Eerdmans, 1948.

———. *Commentaries on the Epistles of Paul the Apostle to the Romans and to the Thessalonians*. Translated by Ross MacKenzie. Edited by David W. Torrance and Thomas F. Torrance. Grand Rapids: Eerdmans, 1960.

———. *Institutes of the Christian Faith*. Edited by John T. McNeill. Philadelphia: Westminster Press, 1977.

———. *Letters of John Calvin Compiled from the Original Manuscript and Edited with Historical Notes by Jules Bonnet*. Translated by David Constable, et al. 3 vols. Philadelphia: Presbyterian Board of Publication, 1958. Letters numbered LXXXXVI, CCXXXXIX, CCXL; vol. 1, pp. 331–335; vol. 2, pp. 217–223. Cited by William A. Clebsch and Charles R. Jackle. *Pastoral Care in Historical Perspective*. Englewood Cliffs, N.J.: Prentice-Hall, 1975.

Carey, John J. "Morality and Beyond: Tillich's Ethics in Life and Death." In *Tillich Studies:* 1975 Papers Prepared for the Second North American Consultation on Paul Tillich Studies. Tallahassee, Fla.: Florida State University, 1975.

Cassell, Eric J. "Dying in a Technological Society." *Hastings Center Studies* 2, no. 2 (May 1974), 31–36.

———. *The Healer's Art*. Philadelphia: J. B. Lippincott, 1976.

Choron, Jacque. *Death and Western Thought*. New York: Macmillan, 1963.

———. *Modern Man and Mortality*. New York: Macmillan, 1964. Churchill, Larry R. "The Amoral Character of Our Attitudes about Death: Some Implications." *Journal of Religion and Health* 176, no. 3 (1978), 169–176.

———. "The Human Experience of Dying: The Moral Primacy of Stories over Stages." *Soundings* 62 (Spring 1979), 24–37.

Cocks, Lovell H. F. "Death." In *A Handbook of Christian Theology: Definition Essays on Concepts and Movements in Contemporary Protestantism*. Edited by Marvin Halverson and Arthur A. Cohen. New York: Meridian Books, 1958.

Crouse, Moses C. "Reflections on Our Fascination with Death." *Religion in Life* 49 (Summer 1980), 136–156.

Dubos, René. *The Mirage of Health*. New York: Harper and Row, 1971.

Dumont, Richard. *The American View of Death: Acceptance or Denial?* Cambridge, Mass.: Schenkman Publishing, 1972.

Dyck, Arthur J. "An Alternative to the Ethic of Euthanasia." In *Ethics in Medicine: Historical Perspectives and Contemporary Concerns*. Edited by Stanley Joel Reiser, Arthur J. Dyck, and William J. Curran. Cambridge, Mass.: MIT Press, 1977.

Eissler, Kurt R. *The Psychiatrist and the Dying Patient*. New York: International Universities Press, 1955.

Engelhardt, H. Tristram, Jr. "Human Well-Being and Medicine: Some Basic Value-Judgments in the Biomedical Sciences." In *Science, Ethics and Medicine*. Edited by H. Tristram Engelhardt, Jr., and Daniel Callahan. Hastings-on-Hudson, N.Y.: Institute of Society, Ethics and the Life Sciences, 1976.

Erikson, Erik H. "Autobiographical Notes on the Identity Crisis." *Journal of American Academy of Arts and Sciences* 99, no. 4 (Fall 1970), 730–759.

———. *Childhood and Society*. 2nd edition. New York: Norton, 1963.

———. *Identity: Youth and Crisis*. New York: Norton, 1968.

———. *Insight and Responsibility*. New York: Norton, 1964.

———. *The Life Cycle Completed: A Review*. New York: Norton, 1982.

———. "Ontogeny of Ritualization." In *Psychoanalysis—A General Psychology: Essays in Honor of Heinz Hartman*. Edited by Rudolph M. Loewenstein, et al. New York: International University Press, 1966.

————. "On Protest and Affirmation." *Harvard Medical Alumni Bulletin* (Fall 1972), 30–32.

Farber, Leslie H., Robert Jay Lifton, et al. "Questions of Guilt." *Partisan Review* 39, no. 2 (Fall 1972), 514–530.

Feifel, Herman. "Attitudes Toward Death: A Psychological Perspective." In *Death: Current Perspectives*. Edited by Edwin S. Shneidman. Palo Alto, Calif.: Mayfield, 1976.

————. "Attitudes Toward Death in Some Normal and Mentally Ill Populations." In *The Meaning of Death*. Edited by Herman Feifel. New York: McGraw-Hill, 1959.

————. "Death in Contemporary America." In *New Meanings of Death*. Edited by Herman Feifel. New York: McGraw-Hill, 1977.

————. *The Meaning of Death*. New York: McGraw-Hill, 1959.

————. "The Problem of Death." In *Death: Interpretations*. Edited by H. M. Ruitenbeck. New York: Delta, 1969.

Foucault, Michel. *The Birth of the Clinic: An Archeology of Medical Perception*. Translated by A. M. Sheridan Smith. New York: Pantheon Books, 1973.

Fox, Renée C. *Essays in Medical Sociology: Journeys into the Field*. New York: John Wiley and Sons, 1979.

————. "The Medicalization and Demedicalization of American Society." *Daedalus* 106, no. 1 (Winter 1977), 9–22.

————, special ed. "The Social Meaning of Death." *The Annals of the American Academy of Political and Social Sciences*, vol. 446 (July 1980).

Frankena, William K. *Ethics*. Englewood Cliffs, N.J.: Prentice-Hall, 1973.

Freud, Sigmund. "Analysis Terminable and Interminable." In *Therapy and Technique*. Edited with an Introduction by Philip Rieff. New York: Mac-Millan, 1963.

————. *An Autobiographical Study*. Translated by James Strachey. New York: Norton, 1963.

————. *Beyond the Pleasure Principle*. Translated and edited by James Strachey with an Introduction by Gregory Zilboorg. New York: Norton, 1961.

————. *Civilization and Its Discontents*. Translated and edited by James Strachey. New York: Norton, 1961.

————. "The Economic Problem in Masochism." In *General Psychological Theory*. Edited with an Introduction by Philip Rieff. New York: Macmillan, 1963.

————. *The Ego and the Id*. Edited by James Strachey. Translated by Joan Riviere. New York: Norton, 1962.

————. *The Future of an Illusion*. Translated and edited by James Strachey. New York: Norton, 1961.

————. *Inhibitions, Symptoms and Anxiety*. Translated by Alix Strachey. Revised and newly edited by James Strachey. New York: Norton, 1959.

————. *The Interpretation of Dreams*. Translated and edited by James Strachey. New York: Basic Books, 1965.

————. *New Introductory Lectures on Psychoanalysis*. New York: Norton, 1933.

————. *The Origins of Psychoanalysis*. Translated by Eric Mosbacher and James Strachey with an Introduction by Ernest Kris. New York: Basic Books, 1954.

————. *An Outline of Psychoanalysis*. Translated and edited by James Strachey. New York: Norton, 1969.

————. "Reflections upon War and Death." In *Character and Culture*. Edited with an Introduction by Philip Rieff. New York: Macmillan, 1963.

————. "The Theme of the Three Caskets." In *Character and Culture*. Edited with an Introduction by Philip Rieff. New York: Macmillan, 1963.

Fulton, Robert, ed. *Death and Identity*. New York: Wiley and Sons, 1965.

Fulton, Robert L. and Gilbert Geis. "Death and Social Values." In *Death and Identity*. Edited by Robert L. Fulton. New York: Wiley and Sons, 1965.

Galdston, Iago. *Social and Historical Foundations of Modern Medicine*. New York: Brunner/Mazel Publishers, 1981.

Gatch, Milton McC. *Death: Meaning and Mortality in Christian Thought and Contemporary Culture*. New York: Seabury, 1969.

Gaylin, Willard. Foreword to *Moral Problems in Medicine*. Edited by Samuel Gorovitz. Englewood Cliffs, N.J.: Prentice Hall, 1976.

————. "Medical Ethics: The Issues at Stake." In *The Teaching of Medical Ethics*. Edited by Robert M. Veatch, Willard Gaylin, and Councilman Morgan. Hastings-on-Hudson, N.Y.: Institute of Society, Ethics and the Life Sciences, 1973.

Gilkey, Langdon. "Meditation on Death and Its Relation to Life." Instituto Di Studi Filosofici. Roma: N.p., 1981.

Gorer, Goeffrey. *Death, Grief, and Mourning*. Garden City, N.Y.: Doubleday, 1965.

Greshake, Gisbert. "Towards a Theology of Dying." In *The Experience of Dying*. Edited by Norbert Greinacher and Alois Müller. New York: Herder and Herder, 1974.

Gruman, Gerald J. "Ethics of Death and Dying: Historical Perspective." *Omega: Journal of Death and Dying* 9, no. 3 (1979), 203–237.

————. "Euthanasia and Sustaining Life:Historical Perspectives." In *Encyclopedia of Bioethics*. Edited by Warren Reich. 4 vols. New York: Free Press, 1978.

————. "An Historical Introduction to Ideas about Voluntary Euthanasia." *Omega* 4, no. 2 (Summer 1973), 87–138.

Gustafson, James M. "Theology Confronts Technology and the Life Sciences." *Commonweal* 105 (June 1978), 386–392.

———. *Ethics from a Theocentric Perspective*. Vol. 2: *Ethics and Theology*. Chicago: University of Chicago Press, 1984.

———. *Protestant and Roman Catholic Ethics: Prospects for Rapprochement*. Chicago: University of Chicago Press, 1978.

———. *Theology and Christian Ethics*. Philadelphia: United Church Press, 1974.

Gutmann, David L. "Dying to Power: Death and the Search for Self-Esteem." In *New Meanings of Death*. Edited by Herman Feifel. New York: McGraw-Hill, 1977.

Hick, John. *Death and Eternal Life*. San Francisco: Harper and Row, 1976.

Hoffman, Frederick J. *The Mortal No: Death and the Modern Imagination*. Princeton: Princeton University Press, 1963.

———. "Mortality and Modern Literature." In *The Meaning of Death*. Edited by Herman Feifel. New York: McGraw-Hill, 1959.

Howard, Alan, and Robert Scott. "Cultural Values and Attitudes toward Death." *Journal of Existentialism* 6 (Winter 1965), 161–174.

Illich, Ivan. *Medical Nemesis: The Expropriation of Health*. New York: Bantam, 1977.

Jonas, Hans. *The Imperative of Responsibility: In Search of an Ethics for the Technological Age*. Translated by Hans Jonas with the collaboration of David Herr. Chicago: University of Chicago Press, 1984.

———. "The Philosophy of Technology." *Hastings Center Studies* 9 (February 1979), 34–43.

Jung, Carl G. "The Soul and Death." In *The Meaning of Death*. Edited by Herman Feifel. New York: McGraw-Hill, 1959.

———. "The Stages of Life." In *The Structure and Dynamics of the Psyche*. New York: Pantheon Books, 1960.

Kalish, Richard A. "Attitudes Toward Death." In *Encyclopedia of Bioethics*. Edited by Warren Reich. 4 vols. New York: Free Press, 1978.

Kass, Leon R. "Averting One's Eyes or Facing the Music?—On Dignity in Death." *Hastings Center Studies* 2, no. 2 (May 1974), 67–80.

———. "Biology and Human Affairs: Whether to Wither and Why?" Presented at a Woodward Court Lecture, The University of Chicago, October 1979.

———. "Man's Right to Die." *The Pharos of Alpha Omega Alpha* 35 (April 1972), 73–77.

———. "Regarding the End of Medicine and the Pursuit of Health." *The Public Interest* 40 (Summer 1975), 11–42.

———. *Toward a More Natural Science: Biology and Human Affairs*. New York: Free Press, 1985.

Kastenbaum, Robert. "Death and Bereavement in Later Life." In *Death and Bereavement*. Edited by Austin H. Kutscher. Springfield, Ill.: Charles C. Thomas, 1969.

————. "Death and Development through the Lifespan." In *New Meanings of Death*. Edited by Herman Feifel. New York: McGraw-Hill, 1977.

————. *Death, Society, and Human Experience*. St. Louis: C. V. Mosby Co., 1977.

Kastenbaum, Robert, and Ruth Aisenberg. *The Psychology of Death*. New York: Springer Publishing, 1976.

Kierkegaard, Søren. *The Concept of Dread*. Translated by Walter Lowrie. Princeton, N.J.: Princeton University Press, 1941.

————. *Concluding Unscientific Postscript*. Translated by David F. Swenson. Completed with an Introduction and Notes by Walter Lowrie. Princeton, N.J.: Princeton University Press, 1941.

————. "The Decisiveness of Death (At the Side of a Grave)." In *Thoughts on Crucial Situations in Human Life, Three Discourses of Imagined Occasions*. Translated by David F. Swenson. Minneapolis: Augsburg Publishing, 1941.

————. *Journals and Papers*. Edited by Howard and Edna Hong. Bloomington, Ind.: Indiana University Press, 1967.

————. *The Sickness Unto Death*. Translated by Walter Lowrie. Princeton, N.J.: Princeton University Press, 1941.

King, Lester S. "Some Basic Explanations of Disease: An Historian's Viewpoint." In *Concepts of Health and Disease: Interdisciplinary Perspectives*. Edited by Arthur L. Caplan, H. Tristram Englehardt, Jr., and James J. McCartney. Reading, Mass.: Addison-Wesley, 1981.

Knowles, John. "The Responsibility of the Individual." *Daedalus* 106, no. 1 (Winter 1977), 57–80.

Kübler-Ross, Elisabeth. *On Death and Dying*. New York: Macmillan, 1969.

————. "On Death and Dying." In *The Phenomenon of Death: Faces of Mortality*. Edited by Edith Wyschogrod. New York: Harper and Row, 1973.

————. *Death: The Final Stage of Growth*. Englewood Cliffs, N.J.: Prentice Hall, 1975.

————. "Dying as a Human-Psychological Event." In *The Experience of Dying*. Edited by Norbert Greinacher and Alois Müller. New York: Herder and Herder, 1974.

————. "The Dying as Teachers." In *Moral Problems in Medicine*. Edited by Samuel Gorovitz. Englewood Cliffs, N.J.: Prentice Hall, 1976.

————. "The Dying Patient's Point of View." In *The Dying Patient*. Edited by Orville G. Brim, Howard E. Freeman, Sol Levine, and Norman A Scotch. New York: Russell Sage Foundation, 1970.

————. *Living with Death and Dying*. New York: Macmillan, 1981.

————. *Questions and Answers on Death and Dying*. New York: Macmillan, 1974.

Landau, Richard, and James M. Gustafson. "Death is Not the Enemy."

Journal of the American Medical Association 252 (November 2, 1984), 2458.

Lieb, Irwin C. "The Image of Man in Medicine." *Journal of Medicine and Philosophy* 1 (June 1976), 162–176.

Lifton, Robert Jay. *The Broken Connection: On Death and the Continuity of Life*. New York: Simon and Schuster, 1979.

———. "On Death and Death Symbolism: The Hiroshima Disaster." In *The Phenomenon of Death: Faces of Mortality*. Edited by Edith Wyschogrod. New York: Harper and Row, 1973.

———. *Home from the War: Vietnam Veterans: Neither Victims nor Executioners*. New York: Simon and Schuster, 1973.

———. *The Life of the Self: Toward a New Psychology*. New York: Basic Books, 1976.

———. "Psychological Effects of the Atomic Bomb in Hiroshima: The Theme of Death." In *Death and Identity*. Edited by Robert Fulton. New York: Wiley and Sons, 1965.

———, and Eric Olson. *Living and Dying*. New York: Praeger Publishers, 1974.

———, Shuichi Kato, and Michael R. Reich. *Six Lives Six Deaths: Portraits from Modern Japan*. New Haven: Yale University Press, 1979.

Lindemann, Eric. "Symptomatology and Management of Acute Grief." In *Death and Identity*. Edited by Robert Fulton. New York: Wiley and Sons, 1965.

Mack, Arien, ed. *Death in American Experience*. New York: Schocken Books, 1973.

McNeill, William H. *Plagues and Peoples*. Garden City, N.Y.: Anchor Books, 1977.

Maguire, Daniel C. "Death and the Moral Domain." *St Luke's Journal of Theology* 20 (June 1977), 197–216.

———. "The New Look at Death." In *Science and Mortality: New Directions in Bioethics*. Edited by Doris Teichler-Zallen and Colleen D. Clements. Lexington, Mass.: Lexington Books, 1982.

Marty, Martin E., and Kenneth L. Vaux. *Health/Medicine and the Faith Traditions: An Inquiry into Religion and Medicine*. Philadelphia: Fortress Press, 1982.

Mechanic, David. "Health and Illness in Technological Societies." *Hastings Center Studies* 1, no. 3 (1973), 7–18.

Morison, Robert S. "Rights and Responsibilities: Redressing the Uneasy Balance." *Hastings Center Report*, 4, no. 2 (April 1974), 1–4.

Niebuhr, Reinhold. *The Nature and Destiny of Man: A Christian Interpretation*. 2 vols. New York: Charles Scribner's Sons, 1941–1943, 1964.

———. "A View of Life from the Sidelines." *Christian Century*, December 19–26, 1984, pp. 1195–1198.

Parsons, Talcott. "Death in the Western World." In *Encyclopedia of Bioethics*. Edited by Warren Reich. 4 vols. New York: Free Press, 1978.

———. "Definitions of Health and Illness in the Light of American Values and Social Structure." In *Patients, Physicians and Illness*. Edited by E. Jaco. Glencoe, Ill.: Free Press, 1958.

———, and Victor M. Lidz. "Death in American Society." In *Essays in Self-Destruction*. Edited by Edwin S. Shneidman. New York: Science House, 1967.

———, Renée C. Fox, and Victor M. Lidz. "The 'Gift of Life' and Its Reciprocation." *Social Research* 34 (Autumn 1972), 367–415.

Pellegrino, Edmund D. *Humanism and the Physician*. Knoxville, Tenn.: University of Tennessee Press, 1979.

———, and David C. Thomasma. *A Philosophical Basis of Medical Practice: Toward a Philosophy and Ethic of the Healing Professions*. New York: Oxford University Press, 1981.

Rahner, Karl. *On the Theology of Death*. New York: Herder and Herder, 1961.

Ramsey, Paul. *Basic Christian Ethics*. Chicago: University of Chicago Press, 1950.

———. "Conceptual Foundations for an Ethics of Medical Care: A Response." In *Ethics and Health Policy*. Edited by Robert M. Veatch and Roy Branson. Cambridge, Mass.: Ballinger Publishing, 1976.

———. "Death's Duel." A sermon delivered in University Chapel, Pennsylvania State University, University Park, Pa., January 8, 1961.

———. "Death's Pedagogy: The Assault on the Last Taboo." In *Death, Dying and Euthanasia*. Edited by Dennis J. Horan and David Mall. Washington, D.C.: University Publications of America, 1977.

———. *Deeds and Rules in Christian Ethics*. New York: Charles Scribner's Sons, 1967.

———. *Ethics at the Edges of Life: Medical and Legal Intersections*. New Haven: Yale University Press, 1978.

———. "Faith Effective through In-Principled Love." *Christianity and Crisis* 20 (1961), 76–78.

———. "Incommensurability and Indeterminacy in Moral Choice." In *Doing Evil to Achieve Good*. Edited by Richard A. McCormick and Paul Ramsey. Chicago: Loyola University Press, 1978.

———. "The Indignity of 'Death with Dignity.'" *Hastings Center Studies* 2, no. 2 (May 1974), 47–62.

———. "Kant's Moral Philosophy or a Religious Ethics?" In *Knowledge, Value and Belief*. Edited by H. Tristram Engelhardt, Jr., and Daniel Callahan. Hastings-on-Hudson, N.Y.: Institute of Society, Ethics and the Life Sciences, 1977.

———. "The Nature of Medical Ethics." In *The Teaching of Medical Ethics*. Edited by Robert M. Veatch, Willard Gaylin, and Councilman Morgan.

Hastings-on-Hudson, N.Y.: Institute of Society, Ethics and the Life Sciences, 1973.

———. *Nine Modern Moralists*. Englewood Cliffs, N.J.: Prentice-Hall, 1962.

———. *The Patient as Person*. New Haven: Yale University Press, 1970.

———. "Prolonged Dying: Not Medically Indicated." *Hastings Center Report* 6 (February 1976), 14–17.

Rawls, John. "Two Concepts of Rules," *Philosophical Review* 64 (1955), 3–32.

Reiser, Stanley Joel. *Medicine and the Reign of Technology*. Cambridge: Cambridge University Press, 1976.

———. "Therapeutic Choice and Moral Doubt in a Technological Age." *Daedalus* 106, no. 1 (Winter 1977), 47–56.

———, Arthur J. Dyck, and William J. Curran, eds. *Ethics in Medicine: Historical Perspectives and Contemporary Concerns*. Cambridge, Mass.: MIT Press, 1977.

Ricoeur, Paul. *Freud and Philosophy: An Essay on Interpretation*. Translated by Denis Savage. New Haven: Yale University Press, 1970.

Rieff, Philip. *Freud: The Mind of the Moralist*. New York: Viking, 1959.

———. *The Triumph of the Therapeutic: Uses of Faith after Freud*. New York: Harper and Row, 1968.

Schleiermacher, Friedrich. *The Christian Faith*. Edited by H. R. Mackintosh and J. S. Steward with an Introduction by Richard R. Niebuhr. 2 vols. New York: Harper and Row, 1963.

———. *On Religion: Speeches to its Cultured Despisers*. Translated by John Oman with an Introduction by Rudolf Otto. New York: Harper and Row, 1958.

———. *Soliquies*. Translated by Horace Leland Friess. Chicago: Open Court Publishing, 1957.

Shneidman, Edwin S. *Deaths of Man*. New York: Quadrangle/The New York Times Book Co., 1973.

———. "The Enemy." *Psychology Today*, August 1970, pp. 37–66.

———. "Orientations Towards Death." *International Journal of Psychiatry* 2, no. 2 (1966), 167–190.

———, ed. *Death: Current Perspectives*. Palo Alto, Calif.: Mayfield, 1976.

Siegler, Miriam, and Humphry Osmond. "The 'Sick Role' Revisited." *Hastings Center Studies* 1, no. 3 (1973), 40–58.

Smart, Ninian. "Death in the Judaeo-Christian Tradition." In *Man's Concern with Death*. Edited by Arnold Toynbee. London: Hodder and Stoughton, 1968.

———. "Some Inadequacies of Recent Christian Thought about Death." In *Man's Concern with Death*. Edited by Arnold Toynbee. London: Hodder and Stoughton, 1968.

Sontag, Susan. *Illness as Metaphor.* New York: Farrar, Straus, and Giroux, 1977.

Stannard, David E., ed. *Death in America.* Philadelphia: Univeristy of Pennsylvania Press, 1975.

Starr, Paul. *The Social Transformation of American Medicine.* New York: Basic Books, 1982.

Steinfels, Peter, and Robert M. Veatch. *Death Inside Out.* New York: Harper and Row, 1974.

Tarlov, Alvin R. "Shattuck Lecture—The Increasing Supply of Physicians, and Changing Structure of the Health Services System, and the Future Practice of Medicine." *New England Journal of Medicine* 308, no. 20 (May 19, 1983), 1235–1244.

Thielicke, Helmut. *Death and Life.* Translated by E. H. Schroeder. Philadelphia: Fortress, 1970.

Thomas, Lewis. "On the Science and Technology of Medicine." *Daedalus* 106, no. 1 (Winter 1977), 35–46.

Tillich, Paul. "Autobiographical Reflections." In *The Theology of Paul Tillich.* Edited by Charles W. Kegley. New York: Pilgrim, 1982.

———. *The Eternal Now.* New York: Charles Scribner's Sons, 1956.

———. *The Courage to Be.* New Haven: Yale University Press, 1952.

———. *The Meaning of Health: Essays in Existentialism, Psychoanalysis, and Religion.* Edited by Perry LeFevre. Chicago: Exploration Press, 1984.

———. *Morality and Beyond.* New York: Harper and Row, 1963.

———. *The New Being.* New York: Charles Scribner's Sons, 1955.

———. *The Protestant Era.* Translated by James Luther Adams. Chicago: University of Chicago Press, 1959.

———. "Reply to Interpretation and Criticism." In *The Theology of Paul Tillich.* Edited by Charles W. Kegley. New York: Pilgrim, 1982.

———. *The Shaking of the Foundations.* New York: Charles Scribner's Sons, 1948.

———. *Systematic Theology.* 3 vols. Chicago: University of Chicago Press, 1951–1963.

———. *Theology of Culture.* Edited by Robert C. Kimball. London: Oxford University Press, 1959.

Vaux, Kenneth L. *Health and Medicine in the Reformed Tradition: Promise, Providence, and Care.* New York: Crossroads, 1984.

———. *Will to Live/Will to Die.* Minneapolis: Augsburg, 1979.

Veatch, Robert M. "The Clergyman as the Dying Patient's Agent." In *Death and Ministry: Pastoral Care of the Dying and the Bereaved.* Edited by Donald J. Bane. New York: Seabury, 1975.

———. *Death, Dying, and the Biological Revolution: Our Last Quest for Responsibility.* New Haven: Yale University Press, 1976.

————. "The Medical Model: Its Nature and Problems." *Hastings Center Studies*, no. 3 (1973), 59–76.

————, ed. *Life Span: Values and Life-Extending Technologies*. New York: Harper and Row, 1980.

————, Willard Gaylin, and Councilman Morgan. *Teaching of Medical Ethics*. Hastings-on-Hudson, N.Y.: Institute of Society, Ethics and the Life Sciences, 1973.

Weisman, Avery D. "Discussion of Orientations toward Death." *International Journal of Psychiatry* 2 (1966), 196–197.

————. *On Dying and Denying: A Psychiatric Study of Terminality*. New York: Behavior Publications, 1972.

————. "The Psychiatrist and the Inexorable." In *New Meanings of Death*. Edited by Herman Feifel. New York: McGraw-Hill, 1977.

————. *The Realization of Death: A Guide for the Psychological Autopsy*. New York: Jason Aronson, 1974.

————, and Thomas P. Hackett. "Predilection to Death: Death and Dying as a Psychiatric Problem." *Psychosomatic Medicine* 23, no. 3 (1961), 232–256.

————, and Robert Kastenbaum. *The Psychological Autopsy: A Study of the Terminal Phases of Life*. New York: Behavioral Publications, 1968.

————, and J. William Worden. "Psychosocial Analysis of Cancer Deaths." In *Death, Dying, Transcending*. Edited by Richard A. Kalish. Farmingdale, N.Y.: Baywood Publishing, 1977.